Digital learning content

A guide

Clive Shepherd

onlignment

© Copyright 2012 Clive Shepherd

All rights reserved. No part of this publication may be reproduced or transmitted in any form or by any means, electronic or mechanical, including photocopy, recording or any other information storage and retrieval system, without prior permission in writing or from the publisher.

Clive Shepherd has asserted his right under the Copyright, Designs and Patents Act 1988 to be identified as the author of this work.

First published in 2012.

ISBN: 978-1-4710-2920-2

http://www.onlignment.com

Digital learning content
A designer's guide

Contents

Making the most of this guide	5
Coming to terms with content	9
Building on sound foundations	21
Determining roles and processes	29
Working with subject experts	43
Starting with some universal principles	49
Exploiting the power of interactivity	57
Working with the basic media elements	69
Distributing your content	87
Assembling your toolkit	95
Creating learning podcasts	103
Creating learning slideshows	113
Creating learning screencasts	125
Creating learning scenarios	135
Creating learning videos	151
Creating learning tutorials	165
Creating quizzes	181
Creating reference information	203
What does exemplary digital learning content look like?	217

onlignment

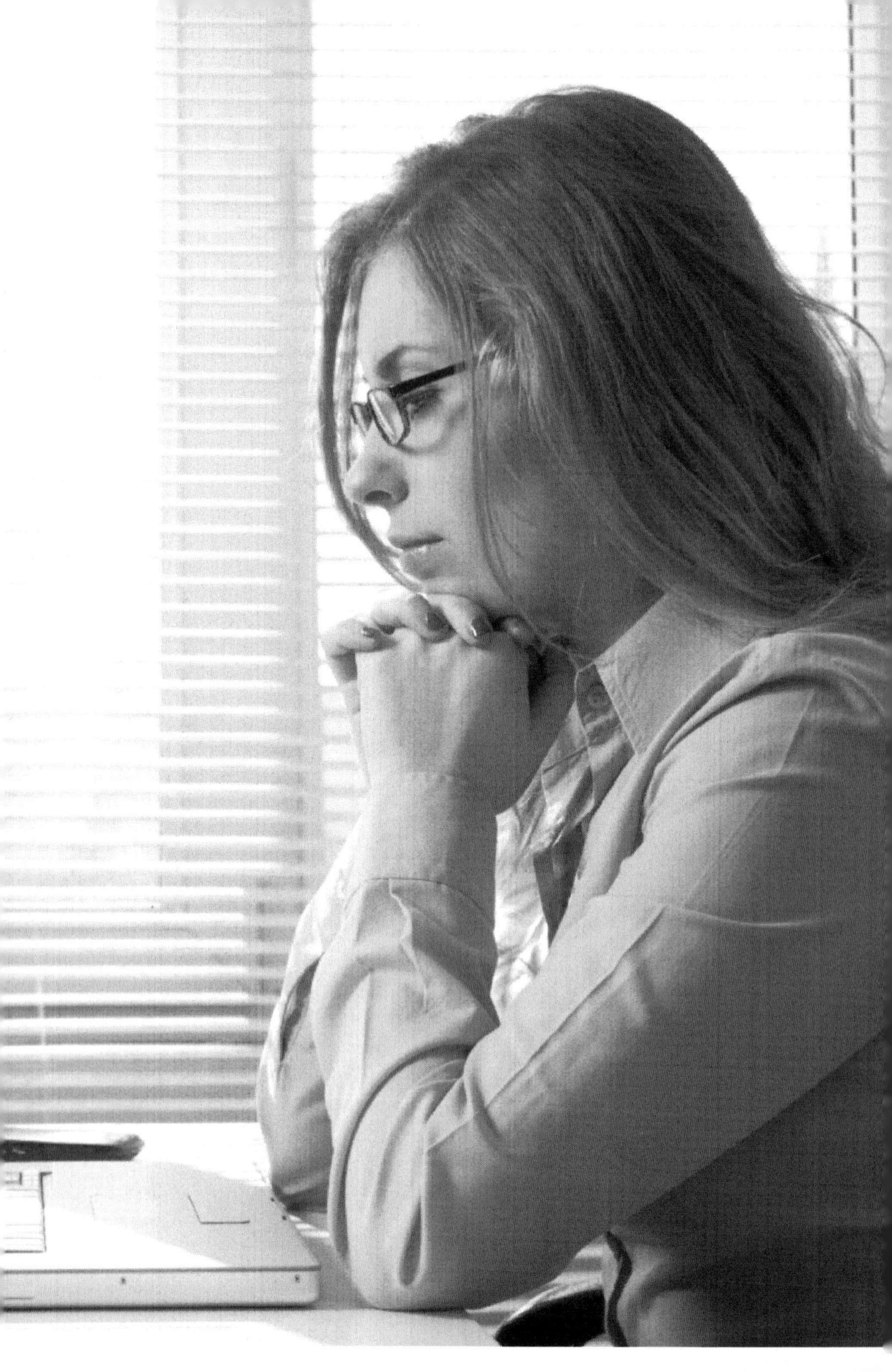

Making the most of this guide

Making the most of this guide

This guide is for anyone with an interest in helping others to learn.

You may be a teacher, trainer, lecturer or coach. You may be a subject expert with knowledge you want to share or an experienced practitioner who wants to pass on their tips. You may already be a creator of learning content, looking to update their skills. Whatever your interest, this guide will help you to design learning materials that really make a difference.

No-one is pretending that packaged content is all that anyone needs if they are to acquire new knowledge or develop new skills. Clearly there is also much to be gained from interaction with teachers, experts and peers, as well as opportunities to practise.

But content, in all its forms, is capable of playing a very big part in anyone's development. It can be made available in manageable chunks when and where a learner chooses. It can be revisited as often as is necessary. It leaves the learner to decide what it is they access and at what pace, depending on their interest and ability.

Historically, the primary carrier of learning content has been the printed page, a format that has served us well for many hundreds of years. In fact books can be said to have revolutionised education, providing knowledge to the masses without the need for a professional mediator.

From the early twentieth century, advances in technology made it possible to record sound and pictures in a variety of formats, including film, tape and disc. Now learning content extended beyond the printed word.

The 1990s heralded the start of the digital multimedia revolution, as analogue formats were swiftly superceded by CDs and DVDs. Now with a common digital language, we saw a coming together of traditional media and computing, providing users with unprecedented flexibility in how, where and when they accessed content, as well as greater opportunities for interactivity.

However, it is the internet that has prompted the greatest leap forward in learning content. The ability for learners to download audio, video and textual materials to their laptops, iPods, smart phones and e-book readers has meant that most content now has no recognisable physical form. It is simply transferred from one digital storage device to another as and when required. However much we may regret their passing, books, CDs and DVDs are in inevitable and terminal decline.

Most learning content we will never 'own' at all. We will simply visit it as and when we need it. You don't collect web pages, YouTube videos or e-learning materials – they sit patiently in the 'cloud' ready for you to access whenever you see fit.

Making the most of this guide

True, to get to this content, we need to be online – to have an internet connection – but being online brings some great benefits. It allows us to access the very latest information, not just from our PCs but from wherever we are in the world, on our smart phones and tablets. We can hunt down content using powerful search engines. The content that we find takes up no room on our devices. It is easy to maintain, because there is only ever one copy to update. We can append the content with comments and share it with our friends. And our progress can be tracked, so others can measure what learning we have achieved and assist us when we need help. In fact the potential for digital, online learning content is practically limitless.

That's why it is so important for today's learning professionals (and all those enthusiastic amateurs out there) to sharpen up their content creation skills and make sure they are part of the revolution and not just passive observers.

This guide will provide you with a sound foundation and get you started on your learning journey. Hopefully it will also prove to be a valuable source of reference. But in the end it is down to you to put all this into practice, to have a go and then to share your efforts with learners and with colleagues.

Unless you are truly exceptional you will make lots of mistakes and not all your content will be as effective – or as popular – as you would like. But stick with it, because content creation is a craft skill that takes a while to develop. The rewards, when you get it right, will more than make up for any disappointments along the way.

This guide is not intended to be read from beginning to end in a linear fashion, although it works that way too. Each chapter is independent and makes no assumptions about what else you may already have read.

Generally speaking, the first nine chapters introduce the key concepts, principles and processes. The next eight provide practical guides to particular forms of learning content. We finish with a look at some standards that you can use to measure your progress.

Time to get started.

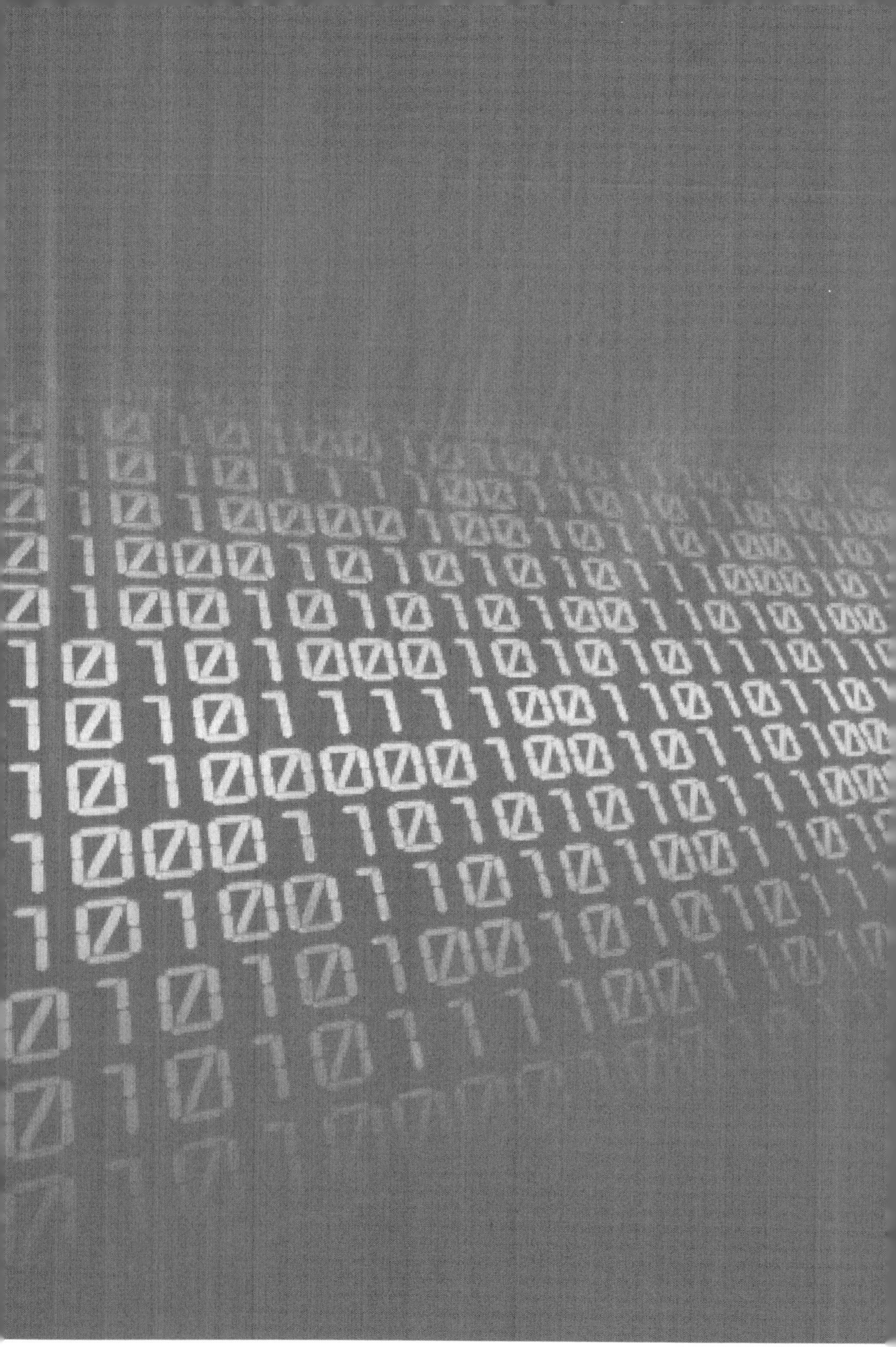

1

Coming to terms with content

1
Coming to terms with content

Content plays a big role in our lives. We consume vast quantities of content every day in emails, web pages, newspapers, magazines, TV and radio programmes. Content informs us, entertains us and persuades us. It provides a basis for many of our discussions with family, friends and colleagues.

According to the Concise Oxford Dictionary content is: "The substance or material dealt with in a speech, work of art, etc. as distinct from its form or style; what is contained in something, such as a book."

That's not a bad start. This is a book about content and, as such, we're clearly focused on 'material', in particular material that's designed to support learning. But in our case we very definitely *are* interested in the form that this material takes, in the nature of the container for our content. We want to know what is different when the material is digital.

We'll be defining digital content quite broadly, as material stored on a network server, local drive or some form of removable storage, which is accessed through a browser, media player or some other application, whether that's on a personal computer, tablet, mobile device or any other piece of computing equipment, however disguised. A long definition perhaps, but then digital content comes in many shapes and sizes, as we shall see.

In particular, our interest is in content which is designed to support learning and/or performance. There is a difference. Learning is a more or less permanent rewiring of the synapses, manifested as knowledge, skill or a shift in attitude. Performance, on the other hand, doesn't always depend on learning – it can be supported by information provided at the point of need.

Digital learning content can be used in a number of ways:

- as the basis for self-paced learning;
- as reference materials, accessed by employees on demand;
- as classroom aids, for use by teachers and trainers with a group.

Interestingly, content is not always an input to a learning activity; it can also be the result. Many learning assignments require individuals or groups to create their own content in the form of documents, postings to forums or blogs, wiki pages, presentations, podcasts or videos. This content can then, in turn, form an input to the learning of others. In this way, every participant in the learning process can be seen as a creator as well as a consumer of (typically digital) learning content.

Digital learning content comes in many forms

Learning can be achieved in many different ways and content can play a number of different roles in this process. Here's a sampling of some of the more common forms of digital learning content:

Interactive tutorials have a long history going back some thirty years, but still represent the most common type of digital learning material, particularly for corporate training. Historically labelled as CBT (computer-based training), this content has typically been employed on a stand-alone basis, but can just as easily be integrated into a blended solution.

Interactive tutorials are typically delivered in web-native formats (HTML, JavaScript, Java, Flash) through a web browser, but if designed for usage offline (such as on CD-ROM), could also be delivered as Windows, Macintosh or mobile applications.

Games and simulations represent the most interactive and potentially engaging types of digital learning content, but can be complex and expensive to develop. Like interactive tutorials, most learning games and simulations are now designed for delivery online over the internet or an intranet, although they could also be delivered offline as self-contained applications.

E-assessments provide a convenient way of testing knowledge and some skills. They are relatively easy to develop from a technical perspective but must be carefully designed to ensure reliability and validity. E-assessments are typically delivered online, so they can be graded and scored centrally. They can be deployed independently, but can also be integrated into interactive tutorials. Similar software can be used to develop questionnaires, such as evaluation forms.

Streaming media allow audio and video to be accessed easily online, without the need for users to first download the media files on to their local computers. Given reasonable bandwidth, streamed media commences playback quickly and at an acceptable quality. Streaming requires specialist server software and a fair amount of bandwidth so should probably only be employed with the full co-operation of the IT department.

Sites such as YouTube allow you to watch videos without having to download them first to your own computer

DIGITAL LEARNING CONTENT

Digital content comes in many forms and can be delivered to a wide variety of devices

Simple web pages provide an ideal way to communicate information online, particularly when this can successfully be presented using text and still graphics. It used to be that some technical knowledge was necessary to create web pages, but modern online content management systems have made the process accessible to all. Web pages provide an ideal way to view information that can be succinctly presented. On the other hand, where a substantial amount of reading is required, users will typically prefer to work with printed materials.

Word, Excel and PowerPoint documents (or their counterparts from sources other than Microsoft) can be easily distributed online for learners to download. Assuming the learner has a copy of the relevant application, they will also be able to edit the documents.

PDF files provide an excellent way for distributing Word, Excel and other documents in a non-editable format and without the need for the learner to have a copy of the application that was used to create the original document. Although PDF files can be viewed on-screen, many users will still want to print out extracts to read more comfortably away from their computer.

Presentations developed in PowerPoint or similar programs can be exported to web-friendly formats such as HTML and Flash for easy viewing online. A number of applications also allow presenters to record a narration to accompany their slides, which enhances their ability to be used on a stand-alone basis. Narrated slide shows can also be exported as movies.

Podcasts are essentially downloadable audio files which can be transferred from a computer to a portable media player such as an Apple iPod, for listening to offline, while on the move. Vodcasts are the video equivalent.

Screencasts are recordings of the steps needed to carry out a task using a software application, sometimes with explanatory labels and/or a voiceover. Screencasts can be exported as Flash movies or as videos, for distribution online.

Four strategies for learning content

Those who design learning interventions and performance support materials have big choices to make, not only in terms of the social context in which the learning or support will occur (will the learning be self-directed, one-to-one or in a group?) and the medium (will the learning take place face-to-face, online or offline?), but

12   www.onlignment.com

Coming to terms with content

also in terms of the underlying learning strategy. We're going to be taking a look at the potential applications for four key learning strategies, in particular the role that digital learning content can play.

Exposition is the delivery of information from teacher or subject expert to learner. The process is essentially one-way, although it may include some modest Q&A or discussion. The strategy is top-down and teacher-centred because it is the person designing and/or delivering who determines what information is to be delivered and how (and sometimes also where and when).

Exposition can take place in the context of an event, such as a lecture, a seminar or a presentation, face-to-face or online, but it can also take the form of content, using text, images, animation, audio and video. Historically this content was delivered using offline media, such as books, tapes, CDs and DVDs, although now it is as likely to be consumed online or downloaded for delivery on portable platforms such as iPods and e-book readers.

For exposition to work as a strategy, the student must be a relatively independent learner, with a good awareness of what they do and do not know about the subject in question. That way they will be able to determine what is most relevant and therefore most important to focus on and process further, whereas the dependent or novice learner could easily be overwhelmed by the sheer volume of undifferentiated information.

Because of the risk of cognitive overload, it is common for teachers, trainers and learning designers to opt for more interactive strategies such as instruction or guided discovery (which we'll come to in a minute). This is fine where the target audience really needs support and structure to help them learn, but a major irritation to those who can cope by themselves (particularly senior professionals, such as hospital consultants, lawyers, accountants, executives, academics, etc.).

Because of the absence of interaction, exposition requires less design than, say, highly-participative face-to-face workshops and self-paced tutorials. However, careful

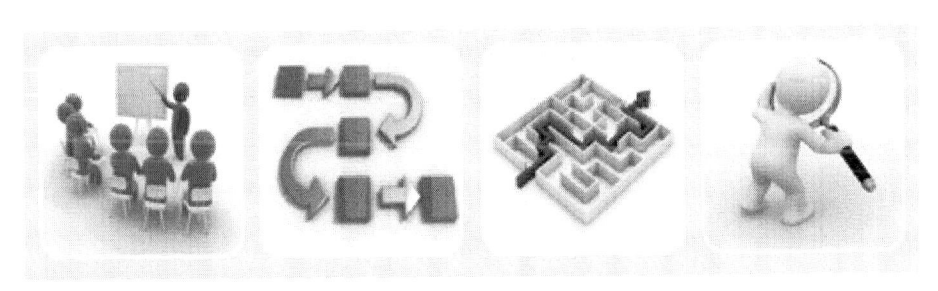

Four learning strategies: exposition, instruction, guided discovery and exploration

www.onlignment.com

DIGITAL LEARNING CONTENT

planning is still going to be a great help to the reader, listener or viewer:

- making clear what is the most important information and what is just nice to know;
- using story-telling and anecdotes to bring abstract concepts to life;
- making the most appropriate use of media elements – text, images, animation, audio and video;
- paring down the volume of content to reduce wasted time and minimise the risk of overload;
- modularising the content so it can be easily random-accessed and reviewed.

In summary, choose exposition as a strategy when you need to control what information is delivered and to whom, and when you feel confident that the target audience will happily be able to work with this information without a great deal of support. If you judge the situation right, then you'll save an awful lot of money by not having to run workshops or create interactive online materials.

Instruction, the second strategy, is still a teacher/trainer-centred approach, but is much more carefully crafted to ensure that the learning outcomes are actually achieved, regardless of the learner's ability. In this sense it is process rather than content driven. This process depends on the explicit and up-front definition of learning objectives and then the careful selection of appropriate activities and resources that will enable those

Instruction can take place live, in a virtual classroom or using self-paced materials

objectives to be achieved. The process of 'instructional design' is teacher/trainer centred because it focuses on learning objectives rather than learner goals. On the other hand, the fact that instruction is typically an interactive rather than a passive learner experience, means that the process can be adaptive to some degree to the individual differences of particular learners.

Instruction can be a live experience, whether in the workplace ('on-job training') or in a physical or virtual classroom; it can also be self-paced, through interactive materials delivered online or using offline media (workbooks, CDs, etc.). While learning at work occurs in many different ways, it would be fair to say that, for most workplace trainers and e-learning designers, formal instruction is what they do. Hopefully they will be doing it well, and that means the following:

- being clear about outcomes;
- concentrating on meeting a small number of key learning objectives

thoroughly, rather than a large number only superficially;

- following an instructional process which is appropriate for the objectives in question;
- engaging the learner;
- helping the learner to make new connections with prior knowledge;
- presenting new material clearly and at an appropriate level, making use of demonstrations, stories, examples, visual aids and other tools to aid comprehension;
- providing activities that allow new knowledge and understanding to be reinforced and consolidated;
- allowing for plentiful opportunities for new skills to be practised, with the aid of timely and constructive feedback;
- being responsive to the needs of individual learners;
- providing support until all objectives are achieved.

Perhaps strangely, one of the key skills for instructional designers is to recognise when instruction is and is *not* an appropriate strategy. You're likely to be safe going the instructional route when your target population consists of less confident learners, particularly those who are novices in the field in question, who need or want to be led step-by-step through the learning process, knowing they are capably supported. When these conditions are not met, instruction may still work, but you run the risk of 'over-teaching' and even patronising your population. Best to reserve your efforts for those who need them most.

Guided discovery, the third strategy, has many similarities with instruction in that it is very much a structured and facilitated process, but follows a very different sequence of events.

While instruction moves from theory to practice, from the general to the specific, guided discovery starts with the specific and moves to the general. It is an inductive process – it leads the learner towards insights and generalisations, rather than providing them on a plate. Because this process is much less certain and predictable, guided discovery rarely has specific learning objectives – every learner will take out of the process something unique and personal. What they take out will depend not only on the insights they gain from the particular learning experience, but also to a great deal on their prior knowledge and previous life experience.

Learning by discovery is engaging and memorable, but the outcomes are uncertain

DIGITAL LEARNING CONTENT

Guided discovery can take many forms – experiments in a laboratory, simulations, scenarios, case studies or teambuilding activities. In each case, the learner is presented, alone or in a group, with a task to accomplish. Having undertaken the task, the learner is encouraged to reflect on the experience – what went well, what less well; how could the successes be repeated and the failures avoided? The conclusions can be taken forward to further exercises and then hopefully applied to real-world tasks.

Content can play many parts in discovery learning:

- it can be used to set the scene and communicate the task, perhaps in the form of a case study;
- it can lead the learner interactively through the task, such as with a scenario or simulation;
- it can provide support to learners who are experiencing difficulties with the task (sometimes described as the goal-fail-fix process – you set the learner a goal, you allow them to fail, you fix the problem).

Less confident, dependent learners should be comfortable with guided discovery, as long as the process is carefully structured and facilitated, and does not leave them floundering.

What is more important is that the learner should have enough knowledge and experience of the subject matter or situations underlying the learning activity that they can make a reasonable attempt at completing the task – you can't build on prior knowledge if you don't have any.

Guided discovery works best when the topic is less black and white, when you require more than a superficial commitment to a set of ideas. When poorly designed and facilitated, discovery learning will seem pointless, perhaps even manipulative; well managed and the result could be much deeper learning. As Carl Rogers once warned us, "Nothing that can be taught is worth learning."

Exploration, the fourth strategy, is by far the most learner-centred and the only strategy that concentrates on 'pull' rather than 'push' (more on this in a minute). It also represents the closing of the circle, because as with exposition, the first strategy we looked at, the learning design is both simple and relatively unstructured, in stark contrast to instruction and guided discovery.

With the exploration strategy, you are making resources available for the learner to pull down when and where they want

Coming to terms with content

	Exposition	**Instruction**	**Guided discovery**	**Exploration**
Examples	Lectures, presentations, policy documents, all types of required reading / viewing / listening	Group instruction, on-job training, self-study materials	Simulations, scenarios, games, discussion, case studies, projects, action learning, coaching	Reading lists, links, online search, 'unconferences', social networking, social bookmarking, blogs;
Role of the content designer / trainer	Subject expert	Instructor	Facilitator	Curator
Nature of the learning experience	Learning material is delivered to the learner	From the general to the specific / theory to practice; questioning and practical exercises are used to check for learning at each stage	From the specific to the general; practical exercises and real-world experiences provide a basis for reflection and for the formulation of general principles	The learner uses their own initiative to satisfy their particular needs for information and understanding, making use of available resources
Outcomes	Communication of the material according to an established curriculum; no guarantee of the extent to which the material is retained	Knowledge and skills transfer, with relatively predictable results based on specific objectives	Development of insights and deeper levels of understanding; outcomes will vary from learner to learner	Learners access whatever expertise it is they need; outcomes are entirely unpredictable
Nature of the interaction	Minimal – perhaps just Q&A	Structured exercises, Q&A	Structured exercises	Ad-hoc, peer-to-peer
Who's in control?	The teacher/trainer – this is a push process	The teacher/trainer – this is a push process	The teacher/trainer – this is a push process	The learner – this is a pull process
Suitable for what type of learner	Independent learners and those with more experience of the subject	Anyone, but particularly more dependent learners and relative novices	Anyone, as long as they are well supported and personal risk is minimised	Independent learners and those with more experience of the subject
Suitable for what type of learning	Familiarisation with a body of knowledge	All types of knowledge and skill, particularly those that really do have to be acquired	Understanding of principles and processes; attitude shifting; refinement of skills	Just-in-time information; knowledge updates; exploration beyond the curriculum; creating new knowledge

www.onlignment.com

With the exploration strategy, each learner determines their own learning process, taking advantage of resources provided not only by teachers and trainers but also by peers.

What they take out of this process is entirely individual and largely unpredictable. As such, exploration may seem a relatively informal strategy, but no less useful for that. In fact it's probably the way that a great deal of learning takes place.

With exposition, instruction and even guided discovery, learning activities and resources are 'pushed' at the learner by the teacher/trainer. With the exploration strategy, activities and resources are 'pulled' by the learner according to need.

Exploration may play a small part in a formal course, perhaps a list of books or links which learners can choose to dip into if they wish; but it could just as easily constitute the central plank in the provision of, say, just-in-time performance support in the workplace.

The role of the teacher/trainer is clearly very different from that in the three previous strategies. With exploration, the emphasis shifts 'from courses to resources', so what is needed is no longer a lecturer, instructor or a facilitator, more a curator.

What's important here is to smooth the way for learners to find resources and to locate like-minded peers; that means providing repositories, search engines and all manner of social media tools.

Anyone working in l&d should have at least a basic level of competence in the design and development of content, even if they don't become a specialist

Exploration is not a universal strategy by any means. Novices and dependent learners will struggle with so little structure and direction. Important top-down initiatives cannot rely on such woolly and inconsistent outcomes.

But there's no doubt that the trend is towards more learner-centred approaches: more pull less push, more just-in-time than just-in-case, more flexibility and less structure. The key, as ever, is not in following the fashion, but knowing when the time is right to use each of these strategies appropriately.

Who creates digital learning content?

Probably just about every l&d professional should have at least a basic level of competence in the design and development of digital learning content, at least those forms of content most relevant to the subject area or population for which they are responsible.

In some ways this can be thought of as a natural evolution from their traditional responsibility for the production of the visual aids and handouts which support most classroom events. The pressures for this to happen are becoming increasingly strong:

- the need, with reduced budgets, to do as much as before or more, but for less money;
- the demand for quicker ways to address learning needs;
- a shift in emphasis away from courses to resources;
- the desire for more flexible, learner-centred approaches;
- the need to cut back on expensive travel costs while at the same time reaching out to learners who are geographically dispersed or on the move.

What this is not saying is that every l&d professional needs to be able to create interactive self-study courses which completely replace their face-to-face predecessors. While some teachers and trainers will have the aptitudes and interests which will help them to excel in this area, in most cases this will remain a job for specialists.

It is much, much harder to create a set of fully self-contained instructional materials than it is to develop the components – the explanations, the examples, the demonstrations, the practice exercises and the assessments – yet the latter are often more versatile and perform a more useful function.

Web 2.0 tools such as social networks, blogs and wikis, not to mention ever more powerful and easy-to-use computing devices, are making it ever simpler for consumers to become publishers, for learners to become teachers. It would be ironic if those in the traditional roles of publishers and teachers were not empowered to play their full role in such a revolution.

2
Building on sound foundations

2

Building on sound foundations

Pausing for thought

"More haste, less speed," used to be the saying, and whoever came up with that knew what they were talking about. If you are to avoid your rapid e-learning becoming vapid e-forgetting, you're going to have to take advantage of that unique human ability – to contemplate, to reflect.

Chew over the options a little. Clarify what you're trying to achieve. Consider how best to communicate with your audience. Ten minutes later you may have more scribbles on a piece of paper than you do characters on the screen, but you'll be much better placed to do a good job.

Establishing direction

The first stage in just about any activity – and the design of learning materials is no exception – is to establish what it is you are trying to achieve. So start off by being absolutely clear about the goal you're aiming for with your learning content. Here are some examples:

- To ensure call centre staff feel confident using a new call handling system.
- To support engineers in the field who will be responsible for maintaining a new range of products.
- To provide new hires with an overview of the organisation they will be joining, its history, structure, business activities and corporate values.

If you don't know where you're going, you're likely to end up somewhere else

- To ensure every employee knows exactly what to do in the event of a fire.
- To update software engineers on new thinking in software design.
- To ensure all employees understand and are committed to a new corporate strategy.
- To ensure sales assistants are fully familiar with the features and benefits of a new product range.

Bear in mind that digital learning content may only play a part in achieving your goal; there may well be other elements required to form a complete solution. For that reason, and because it will help you enormously later as you get down to the detailed design of your content, it pays at this stage to spell out with some precision what you want to achieve with every piece of content that you produce. These are your objectives. How you format them will depend to some extent on the strategies you are following:

- If your materials are instructional, then you should define exactly what you want your target population to be able to do once they've completed your materials. Express these objectives in the form of specific behaviours that you will be able to reliably and validly assess within the content itself.

- If you wish your materials to have an emotional impact, perhaps in order to influence attitudes or register the importance of a particular idea, then try and articulate what reaction you intend to achieve.

- If the purpose of your materials is to provide information on-demand, then you clearly have to define what content needs to be covered and at what level of detail.

Although it depends a lot on how complex the topic is and how thoroughly you need the material to be learned, try to keep the number of objectives for a single module down to a manageable level.

If your goal represents where you'd like to end up, your audience forms your starting point

Be realistic about what you can achieve with your materials, in terms of both breadth and depth. Don't forget that you can always break your content up into a number of shorter modules or supplement what you produce with other materials and activities, such as practice on-the-job, quick reference guides, one-to-one coaching or the use of discussion forums.

Knowing your audience

If you're a subject matter expert, then it can be really hard to empathise with learners who are completely new to your subject. You'll be tempted to try and pass over everything you know, because to you it's all interesting and all important. If you're passing on knowledge to other experts, you'll have no difficulty, but novices will swiftly become overwhelmed. Take some time to think about the people who will be using your materials. What prior knowledge are they likely to have of the subject? How interested are they likely to be? How much structure and hand-holding are they going to require?

Newbies require a lot of care, but so do those who are accessing your content under sufferance, perhaps because they've been forced to use it and simply don't get why it's relevant to them. If this is not an issue you're in luck, because you can get straight on with providing the information. But if interest is low, then you're wasting your time until you've engaged them in the topic and secured their attention. If possible, make sure you're on the right track by checking your ideas out early on

DIGITAL LEARNING CONTENT

with one or two people who are typical of your target audience – they'll soon tell you if you're making the wrong assumptions.

When you've gathered all your material, review it piece by piece to make sure that it all directly contributes to the objectives that you set previously. Be ruthless in removing anything that won't directly help learners achieve these objectives. Be equally careful to make sure that you're providing enough support in terms of explanations, visual aids, examples and practical exercises to ensure novices and less independent learners get the structure and support they require. More of this later.

Three tiers in the content pyramid

Many of your design decisions will be constrained by such mundane issues as time and money, or the subject expertise, design and technical skills you have available to you. It's very easy to get frustrated when you haven't got all the resources you'd like, but remember that all design and development takes place within constraints and that these constraints can help to concentrate your thoughts. Whether or not you stand any chance of achieving your goals with the resources available depends as much as anything on where your project sits within the pyramid of learning interventions (my gratitude goes here to Nick Shackleton-Jones for sharing this model - see opposite):

Formal responses: The top tier consists of digital learning content that delivers something special, something that can't be achieved easily other ways. This tier is reserved for projects with complex and/or high impact objectives, sensible lead times and appropriately generous budgets. These projects require the care and attention of professionals, typically working as teams of specialists.

You would expect e-learning content at this higher level to include at least some of the following:

- a degree of intelligence or personalisation;
- challenging scenarios using rich media;
- simulations with a high degree of functional realism;
- elements of game play;
- 3D models of interesting objects that can be manipulated and explored;
- virtual worlds with high physical realism.

At very least, you should expect high-end content to be professionally crafted to be clear, engaging and memorable, whether or not it employs leading-edge techniques.

Because of its cost, high end content is almost always going to be a top-down learning intervention, created at the initiative of an organisation's management.

Rapid responses: The second tier consists of 'good enough' digital content, designed to communicate simple information or provide basic knowledge without fuss. The format may be a simple interactive tutorial, a short video, a podcast, a screencast, a PowerPoint or a PDF. This content may be designed and developed in-house, by subject experts or generalist trainers, or

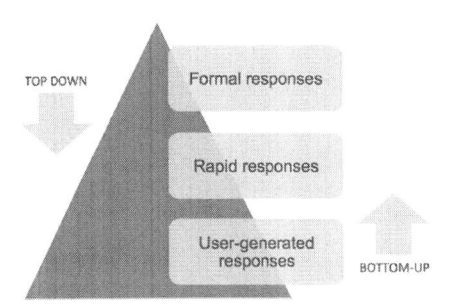

Three tiers in the content pyramid – thanks to Nick Shackleton-Jones

outside by a new breed of rapid developers. The turnaround time could be anything from a few hours to a few weeks, and the cost is likely to be less than 20% of formal content, perhaps much less.

Rapid development of this sort could result from a top-down management initiative, but it could also be created from the bottom-up, on the initiative of subject experts who are empowered with the tools, the time, the skills and the authority.

User-generated responses: However hard you try and however much money you throw at it, you'll never be able to satisfy every learning need from the top down – there are too many things that need to be learned and they change far too rapidly. In the absence of a formal course or resource people have always relied on informal help from their colleagues, typically face-to-face, but now we have so many more ways of getting assistance when we need it, wherever we are.

Content created and shared using social learning technologies such as wikis, forums, blogs and the like, is an entirely bottom-up initiative. It occurs because managers are not the only ones with an interest in learning and performance improvement – it is to every individual's advantage that they have the knowledge and skills necessary to carry out their current jobs effectively, to take advantage of opportunities for advancement and to remain competitive in the jobs marketplace.

High end, rapid and user-generated content are not in competition with each other, any more than Hollywood movies are competing with corporate videos or with YouTube movies shot with a mobile phone or webcam. They all serve different purposes and, as a result, adopt different production values. Professional designers should not feel threatened by this proliferation of content created by enthusiastic amateurs – the more experience people have with creating content for themselves, the more they will appreciate the skills the professionals bring to bear.

Striking the right balance with learning content

It can be hard knowing where to direct your efforts as you set out designing your learning content. There are at least three key factors all competing for your attention and it's typically very difficult to concentrate on them all.

The first major consideration is *the subject matter itself*. How relevant is this to the target population? How timely is the

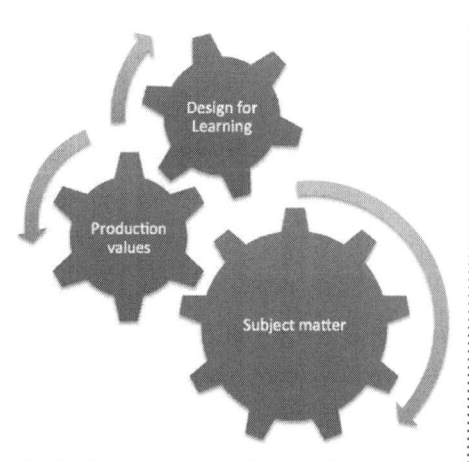

It is hard sometimes to strike the right balance between three inter-connected design goals

information provided in the content? Is it accurate, clear, concise? If you are commissioning the content, or you are a subject expert capable of determining what is or what is not accurate, then this consideration is going to be paramount. And, of course, you would be right. After all, it doesn't matter how well the content is designed and developed; if it's saying the wrong things to the wrong people at the wrong time, then it's a complete waste of effort. It may even be doing more harm than good.

The second consideration is *the level at which to set the production values*. How professionally should the content be presented? How novel and eye-catching should it be? How rich should be the media mix? Production values are tricky, because it's hard to be sure what they add in terms of learning outcomes.

There's probably a minimum expectation from the learner's perspective when it comes to the professionalism of the media they consume, but this is highly variable depending on the level you are working at in the content pyramid we discussed previously. Just as a consumer is happy to move freely between Hollywood blockbusters, TV game show and home movies, judging each on its own merits in the context of its competitors and predecessors, so the employee will happily digest the product of corporate communications, their local training specialist and the person who sits next to them, without ever comparing these like-for-like.

Assuming minimum expectations are met in terms of production values, it's doubtful whether going any further yields any benefits at all. It's likely that employees cannot be wowed by *any* production feature (video, animation, effects) of any learning or communications content because they've seen it all before, executed far more extravagantly and expensively by the mass media. After all, they don't go to work to be entertained; they want work-based communications media to help them in what they do – work.

Nevertheless, the dynamics of the customer-supplier relationship, whether that supplier sits within the organisation or outside, mean that rational thinking of this kind rarely enters the frame. That's because production values are one of the only ways in which content developers can distinguish themselves from their competitors – "Look at my content, it looks great. Spend your money with me and bathe in the reflected glory, perhaps even win an award."

The final consideration is *the design for learning*: What learning strategy should be employed? How can interactivity be used to support this strategy? How can the subject matter best be communicated using examples, stories, cases and demos? Now, it's very hard to argue that this shouldn't be a focus of attention, second only to the subject matter itself. Once you've established what you need to teach, your learning design is the major factor in whether you'll pull this off, certainly of much greater importance than the production values.

Yet the stakeholder that has most to gain from the learning design – the learner – does not have a major voice in the decision-making. It's sometimes said that selling training is like selling dog food – you sell to the owner of the dog, not the dog itself, and you sell training to the manager, not the learner. Nevertheless dogs and learners cannot be ignored, because if they don't like what they've been asked to consume, they'll certainly let you know!

It's a sad situation that, many years after the software industry discovered user-centred design, it is still rare for any learner to be consulted at any stage in the design and development process. As a result, learning design is often relegated to an afterthought, as attention focuses on the subject matter and how the content is looking.

Perhaps this might explain why, however self-satisfied the subject experts (and their lawyers) might be with how faithfully they've conveyed every item of information that could possibly be conveyed, and how smug your average developer might look as they show off their Flash animations and green-screen avatars, their consumers are quietly confiding in each other that this stuff simply doesn't work.

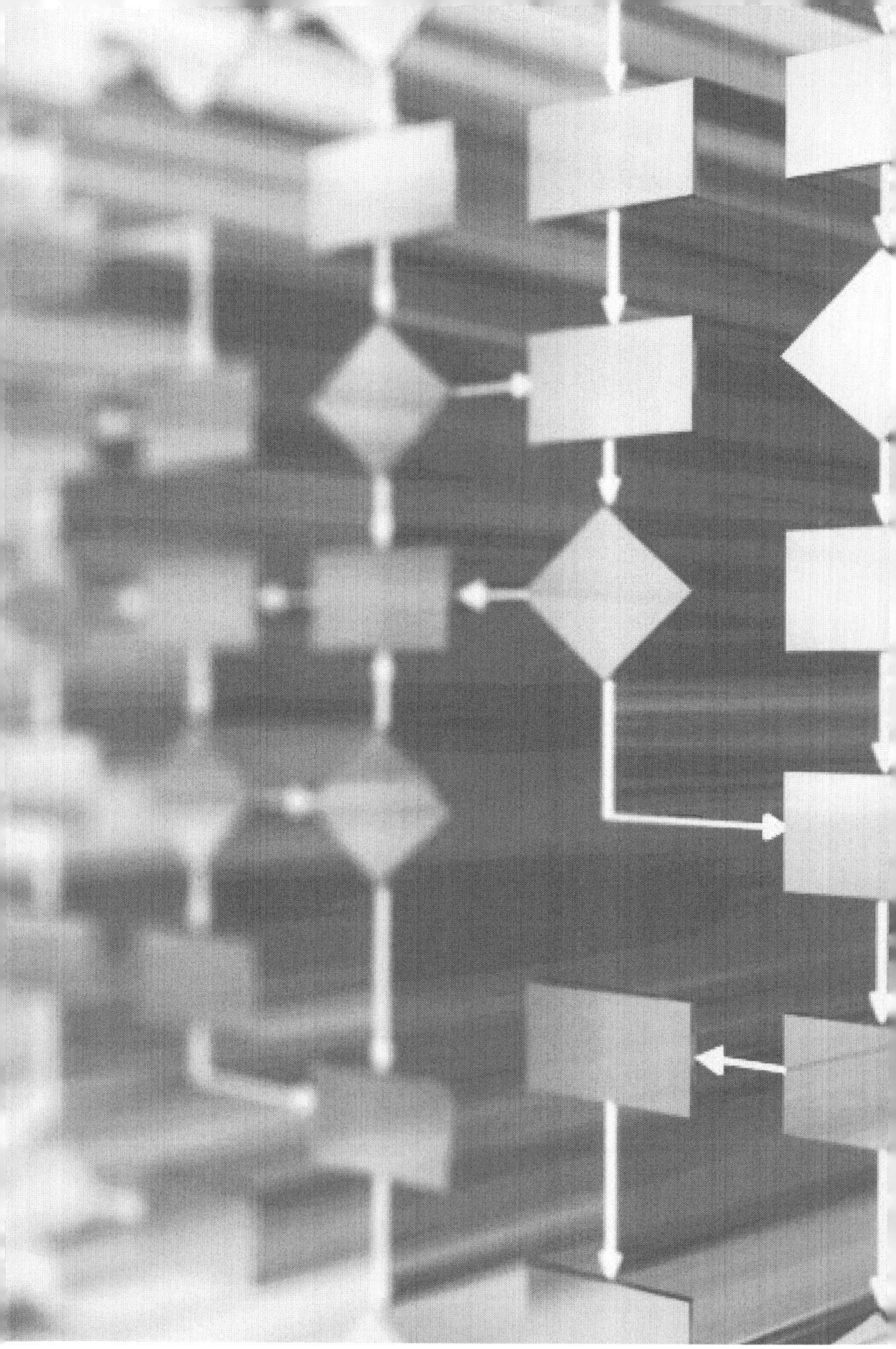

3
Determining roles and processes

3

Determining roles and processes

Resourcing digital learning content

There are four ways to obtain the content that you require:

1. Develop it in-house, whether on your own or as part of a team.
2. Have the content developed for you by an external contractor.
3. Purchase it off-the-shelf.
4. Use some combination of the above. For example, you might buy content off-the-shelf and then customise or supplement it in-house, or selectively subcontract certain elements of the development, while finishing the rest yourself.

A number of factors will influence your decision:

- **Cost:** You may or may not have the budget to use contractors or purchase off-the-shelf. On the other hand you should be well aware that in-house development does cost money, perhaps more than any of the alternatives, when your indirect costs such as salaries are taken into account. Buying off-the-shelf should be your cheapest option, because the cost of development will be borne by many customers, not just you.

- **Availability:** Another consideration is how soon the content will be available for use. Many learning requirements are time-critical, and you will not always have enough time to develop the content you want from scratch. As a rule, off-the-shelf content will be your quickest option.

- **Suitability:** The third factor to consider is the suitability of the content to your specific requirement. When you purchase off-the-shelf you will undoubtedly have to compromise in this respect, although you may be able to customise the materials or supplement them with your own.

- **Quality:** The final consideration is whether the content will be fit for purpose. Will it be easy-to-use? Will it conform to the required technical standards? Will it bring about the required level of learning?

If you decide to work with an external contractor, particularly where you want them to carry out the whole job, you'll need to check out the following:

- Their track record – nothing beats speaking to previous customers to check this out.

- Their understanding of the sort of work you do – some contractors may specialise in your sector or have worked for you in the past.

- Financial stability – bear in mind that many contractors are small and poorly-funded cottage industries.

Determining roles and processes

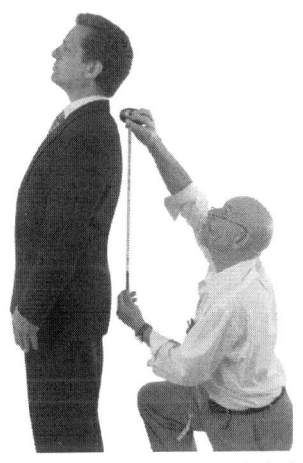

A tailor-made solution may offer you the highest quality but it comes at a preimium price and takes time to develop

- The quality of their project management – meeting time and budget constraints are as important as creative and technical wizardry.

- Do they have all of the key skills in-house or will they have to subcontract? If they're simply subcontracting every aspect of the development, you may consider doing this yourself and cutting out the middle man.

- How responsive will they be to your needs? Some contractors may be a little too precious about their own viewpoints. Others work to rigid processes or use specific tools that may not sit well with your requirements.

- Is the price fair, allowing for reasonable contingencies and profit? Remember that screwing down a contractor to a measly budget or an overly back-ended payment schedule may backfire if they end up going bust on you.

It is worth considering whether you really do need to hire an external contractor to carry out all the development work. If you have good project management and learning design skills, you might decide just to bring in specialist creative and technical skills when you need them.

Similar care is needed when choosing a supplier of off-the-shelf content:

- How well matched is the content to your needs?
- Is the material up-to-date?
- Will it be kept adequately up-to-date in the future?
- Can the materials be customised to better meet your requirements? Can you do this yourself or is this a service you have to pay for?

www.onlignment.com

DIGITAL LEARNING CONTENT

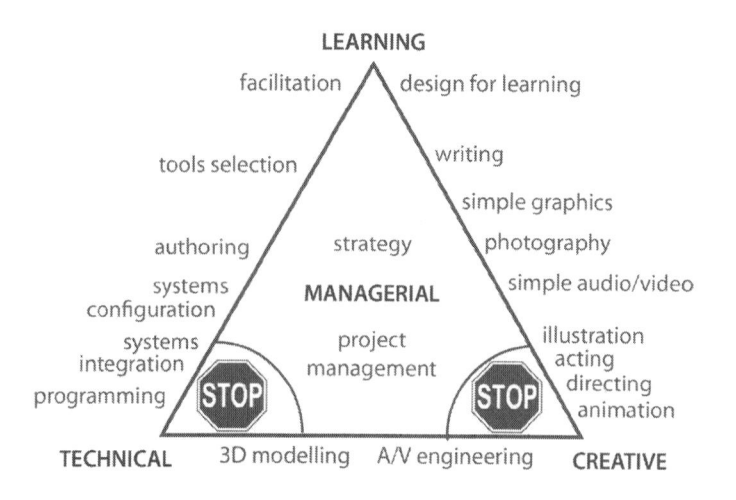

```
                    LEARNING
           facilitation  /\  design for learning
                        /  \
          tools selection   writing
                    /        \ simple graphics
           authoring  strategy  photography
           systems    MANAGERIAL  simple audio/video
         configuration
          systems     project    illustration
         integration  management  acting
         programming [STOP]  [STOP] directing
                                    animation
         TECHNICAL  3D modelling  A/V engineering  CREATIVE
```

- Are the materials sufficiently modular? If they are, you will find it much easier to insert your own custom modules.
- How effective are the materials in delivering the required level of learning?
- How easy are the materials to use?
- Is the content compatible with your technical standards? Will it work with the hardware and software used by your target audience? Will it communicate scores and progress data with your learning management system? Will it be accessible by those with visual, auditory or other impairments?
- Does the provider offer any support to learners?
- What levels of customer service can you expect?
- Are the pricing structures sufficiently flexible for your needs? In particular, you do not want to be paying for content that never gets used.

Roles in design and development

Content design and development can involve a wide range of roles, some of which are always needed, some only rarely. Sometimes a single individual can perform a number of different roles; at other times, a whole team of people may be needed to carry out a single role. These roles include:

- Project management
- Providing subject matter expertise
- Designing for learning (sometimes called instructional design)
- Writing the textual and spoken content
- Creating, sourcing or editing media assets such as photos, diagrams, illustrations, animations, 3D models, audio and video, etc.
- Using 'authoring tools' to build the content
- Software engineering, where functionality is required that goes

Determining roles and processes

beyond the capabilities of available authoring tools

- Testing

In a big team, these roles will be specialised. In other cases, you may be asked to undertake many, perhaps even all the tasks. It is worth considering the e-learning skills triangle (see diagram opposite).

This diagram shows how three distinct professional disciplines – the technical, the creative and the educational – need to interact in the development of learning content. Pulling all these together in the middle is the role of project management. Your background may be in any of these disciplines, but whatever the case you're going to find it hard to cover all the bases.

Let's assume that you're primarily a learning professional, sitting proudly at the top of the triangle (those of you who have experienced creatively and technically-led projects may regard this as optimistic). You're probably quite happy to undertake modestly technical roles, such as using an authoring tool, but you'd be all at sea if you were asked to configure a learning management system, create a 3D model, edit a complex video or write some code in Flash ActionScript.

Similarly you may be comfortable with routine creative tasks – some writing, taking photos, creating simple diagrams, using a basic camcorder perhaps – but you'd hopefully stop short of illustrating, animating, directing an acted scene in a video or composing music. It's not that

you may not be capable of doing some of these – after all many of us have technical and creative hobbies which have led us to develop near professional levels of prowess – it's just that you cannot reasonably be expected to have these skills. In fact, as a learning professional, you could be wasting enormous amounts of time trying to excel in every aspect of content development, when you would be much wiser to call in professionals.

The extreme corners of the triangle will typically require full-time professional expertise, even if only for very short periods. Professional specialists can typically carry out their tasks many times faster than an enthusiastic amateur and to a much higher level of proficiency. What's more, there are plenty of them around, certainly more than the Renaissance men and women who can master all disciplines.

A formal process for design and development

In the traditional, formal process of content design and development, work progresses through a number of logical stages. While there are various models that describe this process, most contain the following elements in some shape or form:

Analysis

It's difficult to make a start on design or development until the requirement has been analysed. This analysis may already have been conducted as part of the design of a much wider learning intervention. If not, it's useful to clarify the following:

DIGITAL LEARNING CONTENT

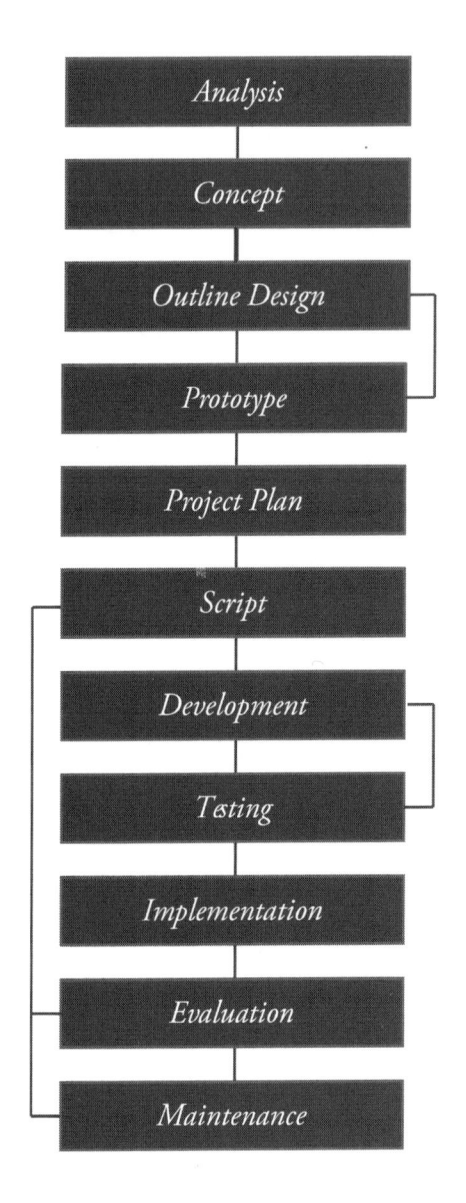

```
Analysis
   ↓
Concept
   ↓
Outline Design
   ↓
Prototype
   ↓
Project Plan
   ↓
Script
   ↓
Development
   ↓
Testing
   ↓
Implementation
   ↓
Evaluation
   ↓
Maintenance
```

A formal process for design and development

- *The learning outcome(s) to which the content is expected to contribute.* Are you looking to impart knowledge (facts, concepts, processes, etc.), develop skills (cognitive, motor or interpersonal) or shift attitudes. It's worth being quite specific about this, because the learning outcomes will direct your design and form the basis of any assessment that you might build into your content.

- *The characteristics of the target audience.* In particular you'll want to know what prior knowledge they have of the subject matter (because novices need much more in the way of structure and support) and how interested they are in the topic (because if they're not interested, you'll have to find a way of engaging them).

- *Any practical opportunities and constraints,* including the hardware and software your learners will be using, the bandwidth available, how long you have before the content needs to be published, the budget available to you and the tools you will be expected to use.

For more information, see chapter 2, *Building on sound foundations.*

Concept

Having clarified the requirement, the next task is to come up with ideas for the design of the materials. This is a genuinely creative process that is worth taking some time over. Generate as many ideas as you can, then weed out those that obviously don't meet the requirement. If you can, involve key stakeholders, including typical learners, subject experts and technical or creative

Determining roles and processes

specialists. When you're happy that you've got one or more workable ideas, you'll want to check these out with your client or sponsor, assuming you have one, before you go any further.

Outline design

At this stage you return to analytical mode. Your task is to specify in some detail how the materials will be structured and how they should look:

- The modular structure
- The sequencing of modules
- The way the learning objectives for each module are to be accomplished, including the use of interaction
- The media elements (text, graphics, animation, audio, video, etc.) required in each module
- The hardware and software required to deliver the content

This design will usually be documented and circulated for approval by all interested parties, including:

- The client/sponsor
- Subject matter experts
- Those responsible for the technical implementation
- Those responsible for creating media

Prototype

It is not unusual with large development projects to prototype one or more of the modules, to iron out any design, usability or technical issues before full-

Larger-scale development efforts will require you to produce a project plan

scale development begins, and to make the design ideas more visible to stakeholders who find a design document hard to comprehend. The creation of a prototype is a project in its own right that involves all members of the team.

Project plan

Much larger development efforts may require a project plan. This should specify:

- The tasks to be accomplished, by whom and when
- The dependencies between tasks, i.e. the order in which they need to be completed
- Milestones along the route
- Risks and how they can be avoided
- How progress will be monitored

Content development projects are not unique, but hard experience suggests that a limited number of elements will generate the majority of difficulties when it comes to project management:

www.onlignment.com

DIGITAL LEARNING CONTENT

```
Giving Cats Medicine: Psyching Yourself for the Job        M1L2S4 (module 1, lesson 2, screen 4)

                                                    Narration:
         How do you feel about giving your cat medicine?
                                                    Prior to attempting to administer
                                                    a pill to a cat, it is important to
   ☐ I am looking forward to placing a pill down my cat's throat.
                                                    achieve the correct frame of mind.
   ☐ I'd rather have a root canal.                  In order to do this, you must face
                                                    your true feelings about the
   ☐ I plan to hire a cat consultant to do it three times a day.
                                                    experience. Select all the items
   ☐ My cat has very long claws. How do you think I feel?
                                                    that express your feelings.

If user clicks 1, go to screen 5.                   Notes:
If user clicks 2 or 4, go to screen 6.              Female narrator projecting a
If user clicks 3, go to screen 7.                   soothing voice.
```

A sample storyboard courtesy of Connie Malamed - www.theelearningcoach.com

- Changes in requirements
- Limited availability of subject experts
- Longer than expected approval processes
- Over-optimism in estimating the time required to overcome technical obstacles

Script

The script is a document that specifies in detail what the materials will contain. It should include:

- Textual content
- Questions and feedback
- Any narrated content or dialogue
- Requirements for graphics, animation, video material, etc.
- Instructions with regard to branching (if the content needs to respond conditionally to user input)
- Specifications for any special programming code that must be developed

Instead of a script, you may develop a storyboard. This goes further than a script in that it also includes a simple visual representation of each page, screen or scene. Although this will make it much easier for media specialists and other stakeholders to understand how the content is intended to look, it will also add significantly to the work involved.

Whether this is necessary will depend on the type of content, the criticality or novelty of the visual components and who is going to be involved in realising the contents of the storyboard.

The script or storyboard should be checked carefully by all parties as before. Ideally, any subject matter issues will be completely resolved at this stage.

One way to carry out user testing is to record all of the user's interactions with the content, as well as an on-going audio narration and webcam picture. In this case the tesing software being used is Techsnith's Morae.

Development

The development phase is when the various elements are created and assembled in accordance with the script. Depending on the nature of the materials, this could involve a number of specialists:

- Graphic designers / animators / illustrators / photographers
- Audio and video specialists
- Programmers (if the materials require functionality that cannot be obtained using your authoring tools)
- Authors, i.e. those responsible for assembling all the ingredients using your chosen authoring tools

Testing

Before release, your materials need to be tested in two distinct ways:

- To remove any bugs and other technical problems (the alpha test)
- To ensure that the materials are clear and easy to use (the beta test)

Testing is likely to be an iterative process, as problems are ironed out and the materials submitted for retesting.

Implementation

Once testing has been completed, the content can be published and made available to the target population.

Evaluation

By this stage, many project teams have disbanded and don't ever want to see or hear about the content again, but it's naive to believe that you can get every piece of content right first time. There's still work to be done, checking that the materials work as intended, fulfill learner expectations and satisfy the original requirement.

Maintenance

Requirements change and materials do not update themselves. Someone needs to take responsibility for ensuring the content is kept up-to-date and remains compatible

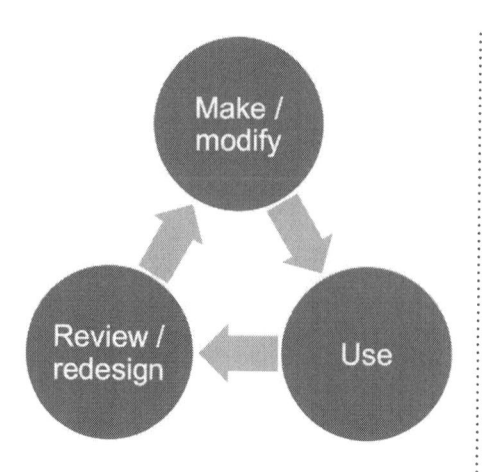

An alternative, iterative development model

with developments in the hardware and software used by learners. So often this stage is overlooked and otherwise excellent material is discarded prematurely.

Challenges to the formal process

The process described above represents the classic approach to large-scale development efforts. It is carefully structured to reduce risk and assure quality, but is also expensive, time-consuming and inflexible.

Although the process can be made to work iteratively and creatively, it all too often ends up resembling a waterfall – just as water can descend but not ascend, you can proceed through the formal process but you cannot easily go back. The formal process depends on the assumption that every stage can be executed on a 'right first time' basis, yet experience tells us that:

- you can rarely gather all the information you need at the analysis phase
- good ideas take time to germinate and could occur at any stage in the project; they can originate from any member of the team or any other stakeholder
- clients change their mind (there's a surprise)
- the need for the content changes
- new hardware or software becomes available mid-way through the project
- learners fail to behave as predicted (another surprise!)

Classroom courses are rarely developed using a formal development process. What usually happens is that the first time a course is run, very little goes according to plan and major tweaks are required. The next time will go a little better, but the design will still require some attention. Years later and the course is probably still being revised, as new ideas occur to the facilitator and participants suggest improvements. What we have is a process of continuous improvement.

Clearly, such a flexible, iterative model cannot be applied to all content development projects, just as it would be hard to see it working for the production of Hollywood movies or the building of skyscrapers. While agile design may be possible in these cases, iterative development would be unrealistically expensive and sometimes completely impractical. Having said that, a great deal of content development does lend itself to more flexible processes, particularly with the tools now available. Which brings us to rapid development.

Rapid development

There may well be times when you need to develop materials in days rather than months, sometimes to meet a relatively short-term need. In this case, and given the following conditions, a rapid development model may suffice:

- The majority of the work is being conducted by a single person, perhaps a subject-matter expert, perhaps a learning professional
- The materials are being created using simple, template-driven authoring tools
- The content is being produced in small chunks
- Not too many stakeholders need to approve the content
- Any graphical content can be sourced quickly and simply using digital cameras, clip art, and simple graphical tools, such as those found in PowerPoint
- Any audio or video content can be recorded easily using a hand-held device or directly to a computer
- There's little or no need for specialist technical or creative expertise

The priority in rapid development is to get content that is 'good enough' out and in the hands of learners in the shortest possible time. The idea is that whatever is the current release is essentially just

According to a survey by the eLearning Guild in 2005, 72% of all training challenges are time critical. It's unlikely to have got any easier since then.

work-in-progress (like the classroom course discussed earlier) and always open to improvement based on feedback from learners. Functionality is kept to a minimum and only added when it is clearly going to be of benefit. Production values are kept at the level required to satisfy reasonable user expectations, but no higher. The aim is not to win awards but to get the job done.

This is not Hollywood, this is YouTube.

Working with reusable learning objects

Historically, e-learning courses, while they were usually structured into modules, were 'hard-wired' so that the modules could not easily be dissembled. The average learning time for these courses often ran into many hours.

An increasing number of designers believe that digital learning content is better organised as small, reusable 'learning

www.onlignment.com

DIGITAL LEARNING CONTENT

objects', capable of being used in a number of contexts. Learning objects ...

- *are small* – typically 2-20 minutes (although never shorter than they need to be to do the job; games, simulations and scenarios may well need to be longer to be effective)
- *are self-contained* – they make as few assumptions as possible about objects the learner will have already seen
- *are reusable* – they are capable of being re-used in different contexts, including completely different courses
- *can be combined* – learning objects can be grouped into larger collections of content, including traditional course structures
- *are described by metadata* – every learning object is appended with descriptive information which allows it to be catalogued by learning management systems and found by search engines
- *communicate with management systems* – learning objects can talk to a learning management system to get information about the learner and to record information about their performance

It would be fair to say that most designers' experience of working with learning objects has been disappointing. While the duration of most learning content has reduced substantially over the past ten years, this has been more a response to the expectations and preferences of learners, than a concerted effort to adhere to a new modular architecture.

Learning objects are the building blocks of learning content

The problem is that reusability depends on higher levels of co-operation and forward planning than has traditionally been needed in learning and development. For reusability to be a reality, designers need to think beyond their own immediate priorities, to put in the effort in the short term in order to generate benefits for the organisation as a whole further down the line.

Designers also need a platform, such as a learning content management system (LCMS), that makes it easy to share learning objects and media assets (images, animations and so on).

All this is easier said than done. Perhaps only the most disciplined of organisations will be able to successfully manage an architecture requiring such top-down control. The more anarchic, bottom-up processes employed by sites such as YouTube, Flickr and SlideShare, in which users determine the objects they will share and how, tag content according to their own informal taxonomies, and sort out the wheat from the chaff through a process of star ratings and commenting, could ultimately prove to be a more viable form of content management for many organisations.

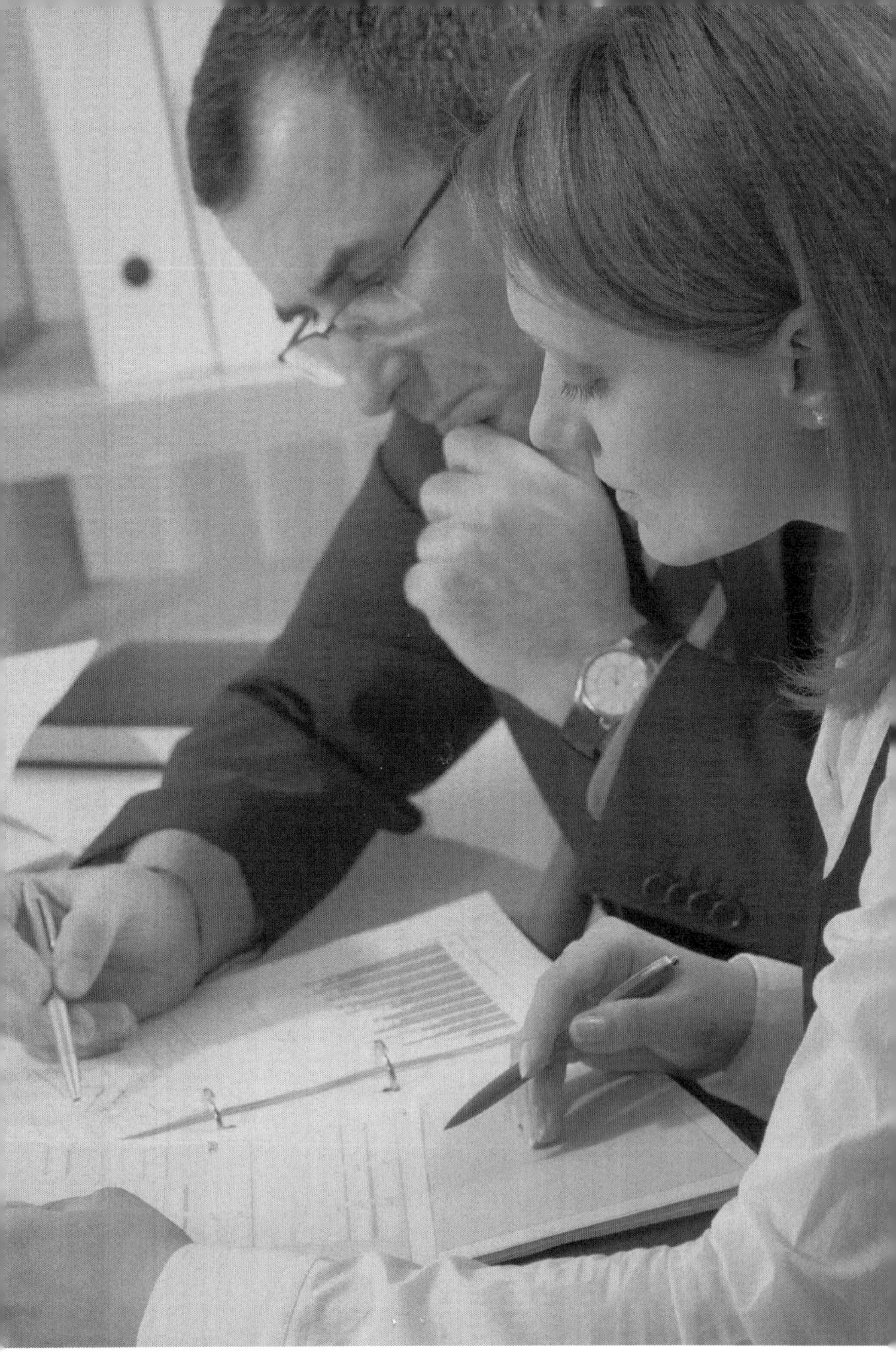

4

Working with subject experts

4
Working with subject experts

The theory is straightforward enough. You're the content design expert. You want to create some learning content but, in order to do this, you need to clarify the goals for this content and, as a result, what it needs to cover. You seek out someone who's an expert who can help you with this. You meet with this expert and they provide you with all the information you need and no more. They leave you to work out how - if at all - you use all this. At key stages in the process of design, the expert casts a helpful eye over your work just to make sure you've got it all straight. They even throw in ideas for ways in which you could get some of the information across, for you to use if you see fit. You get the content designed and developed on schedule and learners find it helpful. Both you and the expert are happy to take a share of the credit.

OK, things may not always go so smoothly. Perhaps they never do. But they certainly *can* if you take the time to establish the right relationship with your subject matter expert (SME) and then make sure you ask the right questions. It would be no exaggeration to suggest that getting this right could make or break your project.

So, why are SMEs such a problem?

The first problem is that there is no such thing as an SME. At least, no-one has that as their job title. Generally speaking, SMEs

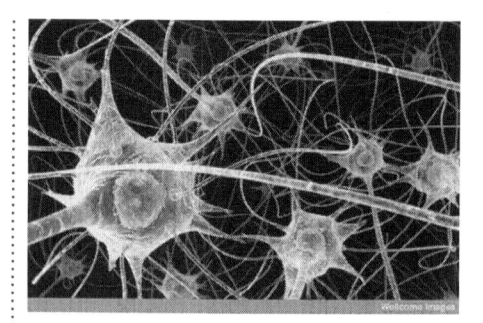

Experts have elaborate mental schema which help them to solve problems and make decisions

are co-opted on to your project because they are the ones who know how things are done. They also have a day job and that will undoubtedly be their first priority.

An even greater problem is that SMEs are experts. Sure they are supposed to be, but this provides you with a major obstacle to overcome. In their 2007 book *Made to Stick*, Chip and Dan Heath describe the 'curse of knowledge', the difficulty that experts have in empathising with novices and with the difficulties that novices face. They find it hard to conceive that people exist with less enthusiasm for their subject than they do, and less appetite to lap up every last morsel of information.

Over time, experts (and this includes you, because just about everybody has become expert at something, even if just playing Angry Birds) build elaborate schema in their brains that connect together the various facts, concepts, rules and principles that underlie their field of interest. They

Working with subject experts

may not be aware of it, but by virtue of millions of synaptic connections, they have a fully functioning, working model to guide them in dealing with all the problems and decisions they have to deal with on a daily basis. They are rarely overloaded by new information. In fact they are always thirsty for more.

Novices, on the other hand, do not have the benefit of all this understanding built up over years of experience. When confronted with a completely new subject, they struggle to relate this to what they already know. They are not sure what's important, what's superfluous and what's plain wrong. They are easily overwhelmed by new information. What they want is the absolutely essential information explained to them as quickly and simply as possible, and then a chance to put this into practice straight away. In this respect, SMEs are not always a lot of help.

Building a relationship with your SME

As with any important stakeholder, your first job is to establish a good working relationship with your SME. A good way to start is to read up all you can about the subject in question, particularly any materials already created by the SME. You're unlikely to remember it all, but at least you will have an overall picture of the subject in question, be aware of some of the terminology, and have an idea of the important issues. Don't expect the SME to have spent as much time beefing up on their knowledge of learning design, although they will certainly have ideas of their own to bring to the table, however ill-informed.

Right from the start it pays to be absolutely clear what you expect from the SME and what they can expect from you. They are the expert on the subject matter. You are the expert on adult learning. Your job is to construct a solution that will meet a performance need in the organisation. You cannot do this without the benefit of their experience and wisdom. Be 100% clear that your task is not to replicate the SME's wisdom in every member of your target audience, just to make sure these people can do their jobs. It takes years, if not decades, to build true expertise. You may only have 30 minutes.

Perhaps the biggest barrier to you getting the project ready on schedule is the time it takes to get SME approval of your designs and scripts. This work is almost always underestimated, leading to all sorts of delays and disruptions. It's best to spell out quite clearly when you will require SME time and for how long. Show the SME a typical design document or script so they know what to expect. Explain that approvals, while perhaps not completely binding, will be regarded as permission to proceed with the next stage of the project. Changes can still be made, but only with a corresponding risk to the schedule and budget.

Don't bore your SME with learning jargon. They will find this every bit as inpenetratable and uninteresting as you (and your target population) may well find

DIGITAL LEARNING CONTENT

Your first job is to establish a good working relationship with your SME

their subject expertise. But using plain English isn't the same as acting dumb. You have a duty as a professional to make clear how it is that adults learn best. Surprisingly, this isn't common sense. If it was, why are so many learning experiences no more than a knowledge dump? Explain how hard it is to engage the learner, to get them to focus enough on an idea to hold it in long-term memory and then be able to retrieve this learning when it really matters – doing the job. Transmitting information is the easy bit – your job of making it stick is really hard.

Asking the right questions

There are plenty of ways to get the information you need. The worst way is to get the SME to produce a PowerPoint deck. What you will get is far too much information, expressed almost entirely in bullet points. The SME will be aware that this isn't the finished article, but expects that somehow you will weave your magic by adding a load of pictures and other decorations, and sticking a quiz on the end. But you're not going to do that, are you?

Every slide, no every bullet, that you remove from the SME's slide deck will involve intense negotiations. The SME will be in mourning for ages afterwards, if indeed they ever recover. Better to avoid this process altogether.

One way to research the topic is to sit in on an existing class, perhaps one for which the SME is the instructor. Talk to participants to see what they found useful and what they found confusing. Extract the important learning points, but even more importantly, note down all the instructor's war stories, examples, anecdotes and jokes. All too often, the reason why learning content is so dull is because it is so matter of fact – it has no personality. The stories are a lot more than entertainment. They provide context and relevance. They allow learners to see patterns and make connections, which is what learning is really all about.

Chances are you'll also need to interview the SME. Documents and slide decks are OK up to a point but they are a long way from where you want to be. Your focus is on the performance. What do you want the learner to be able to do? What activities can you devise that will allow them to practise doing this? What knowledge does the learner need in order to engage in this activity? Credit is due here to Cathy Moore who spells out the questions to ask as part of the process she calls Action Mapping.

If your SME has only ever experienced knowledge dumps then you may have difficulty communicating what it is that you are aiming to achieve. The best way to overcome this barrier is to show the SME the best example you can find of performance-focused learning content. If you can't find anything, perhaps you need to create some demo material yourself.

Unless you are really lucky (or skilful), the SME will still want to include more material than you believe is really appropriate. This is the point to make the distinction between courses and resources. The aim of the course is to engage the learner's interest in the topic and help them to develop sufficient confidence to move forward independently. That is not the end of the story. Learning will continue back on the job and learners will inevitably have many questions of detail, which is where the resources come in, available online, on-demand. Resources are not an optional extra; they are step 2 in the plan. All the information that the SME recommends will be included; it's just that most of it will be at step 2.

Finally, don't forget to thank the SME for all their hard work. Even better, credit them within the materials. They will appreciate it.

What when you are the SME?

It is not that unusual for the content designer also to be the subject expert. After all, many teachers and trainers started their careers by practising what they now preach. If not, then they certainly will have picked up a lot of expert knowledge over years of teaching. Being your own SME has one major benefit and one big drawback.

The benefit is that you have no-one to create a relationship with (assuming you're feeling OK about yourself) and no-one to question. You can get straight on with the job of design.

The problem is that even teachers (some might say especially) suffer from the curse of knowledge. This means you have to display more than a little self-awareness and exercise a great deal of self-control.

A few years back, an informal community of instructional designers set about developing a guide for those people who were asked to get involved in design but for whom design was certainly not their principle activity (SMEs for example). The project was called *The 30-minute masters*, on the basis that 30 minutes was all the time a non-specialist would want to spend learning about design. By the time all the ideas were gathered and the curriculum finalised the project had to be renamed *The 60-minute masters*. So, even design experts find it hard knowing when to stop.

Perhaps it would be better if we left subject experts out of the equation altogether. As Jane Bozarth commented in her post *Nuts and Bolts: Working With Subject Matter Experts*: "The better choice isn't always the most experienced worker, but the most recently competent one: that newer person who remembers what it was like not to know how to do a task, who remembers having to learn and what that entailed."

5
Starting with some universal principles

5
Starting with some universal principles

Structure into modules

Digital learning materials work best when they are constructed on a modular basis. This has a number of significant advantages:

- The learner can more easily access the content that they want and ignore material that is less relevant for them. Some more advanced learning management systems may even be able to selectively filter out those modules which are not appropriate to a learner's role or current level of competency.

- Assuming the modules are kept small, the learner is less likely to be overloaded by an excess of material. Remember that if the learner wants more, they can always open another module. There is no golden rule for how long a module should be, but a reasonable guideline would be just long enough to achieve a single task but no longer. With some performance support materials, that might mean 1-2 minutes; if the user is being asked to engage in a complex case study or simulation, an hour or longer may be required.

- It will be easier for the learner to access the materials in a number of short sessions. When large volumes of material are hard-wired together in one large piece, then it becomes much harder for the user to find their place if they return to the materials at some future date.

If you design in a modular way then you will benefit as well as the learner

- The material is easier to maintain and to re-use. Let's say you wanted to develop a second version of a course, but with a customised case study that is specific to a particular audience. It's much easier to replace the module containing the case than to get inside a much larger chunk of material and replace a particular section (assuming you have the right to do this and the appropriate tool!).

- You can use the right medium for each module. Rather than trying to force fit all aspects of a solution into a particular format that suits a single authoring tool, why not use the most appropriate tool for each job – a video, a quiz, a game, a screencast, a PDF? It is usually much easier to develop these components than to integrate them within a single module.

- You can re-order the modules according to the job in hand. One sequence may not suit all audiences: for example, novices may benefit from a gentle step-by-step introduction building up to practice exercises; a more experienced learner may want to throw themselves into the practice exercises and then fill in any gaps in their knowledge depending on how they get on.

Hook the learner in

Now this one depends a bit on whether your materials are instructional or whether they're more a source for reference. In the case of the former, you cannot just assume you have the learner's full attention and yet, without this, you're pretty much wasting your time.

Try your best, as early as you can, to hook your learners in emotionally. If you do, you'll have an audience that's attentive, excited and curious. But if you don't, you risk them just going through the motions, doing as little as they can get away with, and getting distracted by other things. When you are emotionally engaged with a topic – you understand it's importance, you care about it – then you're much more likely to remember the key messages. Some might say it's impossible otherwise.

Hooking the learner in is a prerequisite to any learning taking place

So how do you accomplish this? First off, you can make clear just how much the learner can benefit from what you've got to say – in other words, what's in it for them. You might also make them aware of the risks – what might just happen if they don't take any notice. You might find a little humour helps or maybe a touch of drama. Whatever you do, keep it relevant and don't overdo it – just make sure you hook those learners in … emotionally.

Present your idea clearly and simply

Sometimes it can actually be a disadvantage to be a subject matter expert – a phenomenon that is sometimes called the 'curse of knowledge'. It's what leads you to believe that others have the same knowledge and interests as you, and are just as fascinated by all the theory and the detail.

Way back in 1657, French mathematician Blaise Pascal explained how he "had made this letter longer, because I have not had the time to make it shorter."

And according to actress and writer Louise Brooks, "Writing is 1 per cent inspiration, and 99 per cent elimination." Unfortunately it does takes longer to create content that is simple and concise, but it's definitely worth the effort.

When it comes to words it pays to keep it simple. That doesn't mean dumbing down or using an imprecise phrase when an accurate or more specific one is required; it just means choosing the simple, everyday option wherever possible. Use 'because' rather than 'as a consequence of' and 'help' rather than 'facilitate'.

Illuminate your material with imagery

According to the research, the most powerful influences on people's behaviour are strong, simple images – which is not surprising when you consider that up to 90% of the brain's sensory input comes from visual sources. By adding a visual element to your learning materials, you will be making a more powerful and memorable statement, and that's certainly going to help you achieve your objectives.

And remember that imagery – whether that's photos, diagrams, charts, illustrations, animations, screen captures or video – can often communicate what words simply cannot. Why describe 'the new office that we will all be moving to later this year' in words, when you can show an illustration? Why list the 'sales territories in the Indian sub-continent,' when you can show a map?

These days you don't have to be an artist or a video director to create great looking visuals for your learning materials. Use a digital camera or camcorder to take your own photographs and movies. Or see what's available elsewhere on sites such as Google Images, Flickr and YouTube. Products like Excel are great for generating charts and there are plenty of tools to help you demonstrate software.

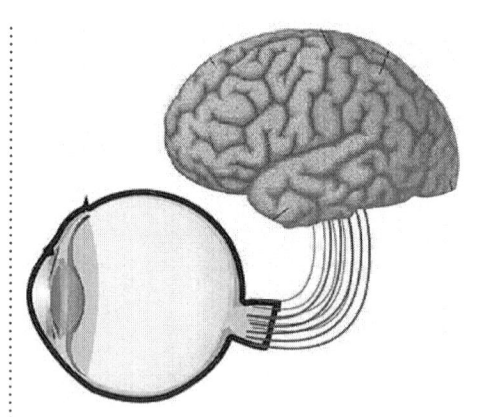

Vision is the predominant sense for acquiring perceptual information.

Do make use of all these new resources out there, but be careful to obtain the owner's permission before using copyrighted material.

And be careful to avoid imagery that does not aid learning. Images that are there simply to decorate the page or to fill an empty space are just noise as far as your audience is concerned. Rest assured that it's OK not to have images on every screen.

Use audio where appropriate

You should consider using narration to accompany and describe images. This frees up space on the screen that would otherwise be taken up by text and makes it easier for the user to digest the information. On the other hand, avoid using narration that simply recites the text on the screen – rather than helping, this actually serves as a barrier to comprehension. And don't use audio if your materials are going to be used purely for reference, as this slows down access.

If audio is going to work for you as an option, you have to be able to tick a number of boxes. First of all, you need the facility to record audio. Now this isn't as difficult as it sounds, because a microphone connected to your computer is all you require. Having said that, quality is important, and you may find you can get better results using a sound studio and even a professional voiceover artist.

Then, the software that you're using to create your materials and your organisation's network both need to support audio. That might mean you checking with IT (brace yourself!).

Lastly, your learners need audio playback facilities on their computers, whether that's through speakers or headphones. And remember that for some users bandwidth is still limited, so it's important not to use audio for the sake of it. Limit your use of sound to those situations where it provides real added value.

Put the idea into context using demonstrations, examples, cases and stories

Learners, particularly if they're at work, want ideas that are relevant to their current problems, not abstractions. Use plenty of relevant examples and your idea is much more likely to be understood and remembered.

Remember that learning occurs as synapses connect with each other in the brain. This means that new learning can only take place as a connection to prior learning. In other words, if you cannot position what you are teaching in a context to which the learner can relate, no learning will happen at all.

Use demonstrations to bring procedures to life, taking care to explain what decisions have to be made at each step. Start by showing how the procedure should be followed in a straightforward situation, but back this up with demonstrations of more difficult or complex scenarios, including how to recover from common mistakes.

And don't underestimate the power of stories. In any classroom course or presentation, you would feel short-changed if the speaker did not tell a myriad of stories to put their ideas into context. Why should learning materials be any different? Stories are easily remembered and passed

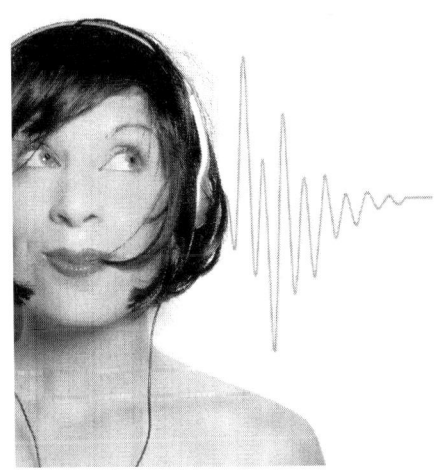

If you are to make use of audio, your learners must have access to audio playback facilities and your network must be able to support the bandwidth required.

DIGITAL LEARNING CONTENT

on from person to person. They are so important to our existence as social animals that the brain has a special place – episodic memory – to store them.

Encourage the learner to work with the idea

Use cases, problems, exercises, scenarios, simulations or whatever it takes to provide the learner with the opportunity to test out the new material and, where relevant, to build skill. The more realistic you can make these activities the better.

Unless you're developing materials that are intended purely for reference, you'll achieve far better results if you engage your learners with meaningful, challenging interactions. These interactions can be used to build on the learner's prior knowledge and help them on the path to new learning; they can provide opportunities for practice; they can also be used to assess progress. Without meaningful and challenging interaction, your materials could easily be ignored or forgotten.

Interaction helps maintain the learner's attention and aids retention of the content. Meaningful interactions are those that ask the learner to work with your material in a context that is comparable to their real-work situation. Questions that simply check for recall of information that has only just been presented are not meaningful.

Interactions that are not challenging will insult the intelligence of your learners. On the other hand, interactions that are too

Close with a call to action – a bridge to the next step

challenging will leave them baffled and deflated.

Be aware that there are limitations to what you can test validly using a quiz, particularly when your objective is for competent performance rather than knowledge acquisition. The reliability of your assessment may also be questionable if you test the learner right after you have taught new material, because many of the learner's answers will come from short-term memory. On the other hand, we know managers often want to see some record of achievement – however reliable – and that may well go for some learners too.

Bridge to the next step

You'll want to end with a call to action. It's very unlikely that your materials will be an end in themselves, so point your learners towards the next step. Consider how the learner will be able to provide feedback

Starting with some universal principles

on your materials or ask any questions they may have. Provide a mechanism for discussion of the content, using whatever medium you have available. And provide links to any supplementary materials, related web sites, email addresses, and so on.

Check your content for quality, usability and accessibility

By this stage you probably just want to get your materials up on the server and out there meeting a need. However, some checks really do need doing.

Check that your materials really are fit for purpose, for example:

- They are accurate and up-to-date.
- They are free of spelling and grammatical errors.
- They are free of racist, sexist and other discriminatory content.
- They are free of software bugs and broken links.
- They work without error on the hardware and software for which they have been designed.

Check that your materials conform to the rules of good usability, for example:

- It is always clear what the learner is expected to do next.
- Only the necessary controls are provided

and these are easy to use.

- Overviews and summaries are provided for each content block.
- Longer pieces of textual content are separated into sections accompanied by clear and meaningful headings.
- The material is sequenced logically.
- The number of menu levels is kept to an absolute minimum.
- Text is easily readable / visuals clearly visible / sound clearly audible!

Lastly, check that your materials are accessible by those who suffer from common disabilities, for example:

- Web pages are formatted such that the visually impaired can access them using screen readers.
- Colours are used in such a way that they do not disadvantage the colour-blind.
- Text is re-sizeable.
- Audio and video files are accompanied by transcripts.
- Interactions can be accomplished using the keyboard as well as a mouse.

Make sure you're not the only one who checks your materials, because you may well be blind to many of the problems which others will pick up. And don't be afraid of feedback, because that's the way you keep your materials fresh, relevant and useful.

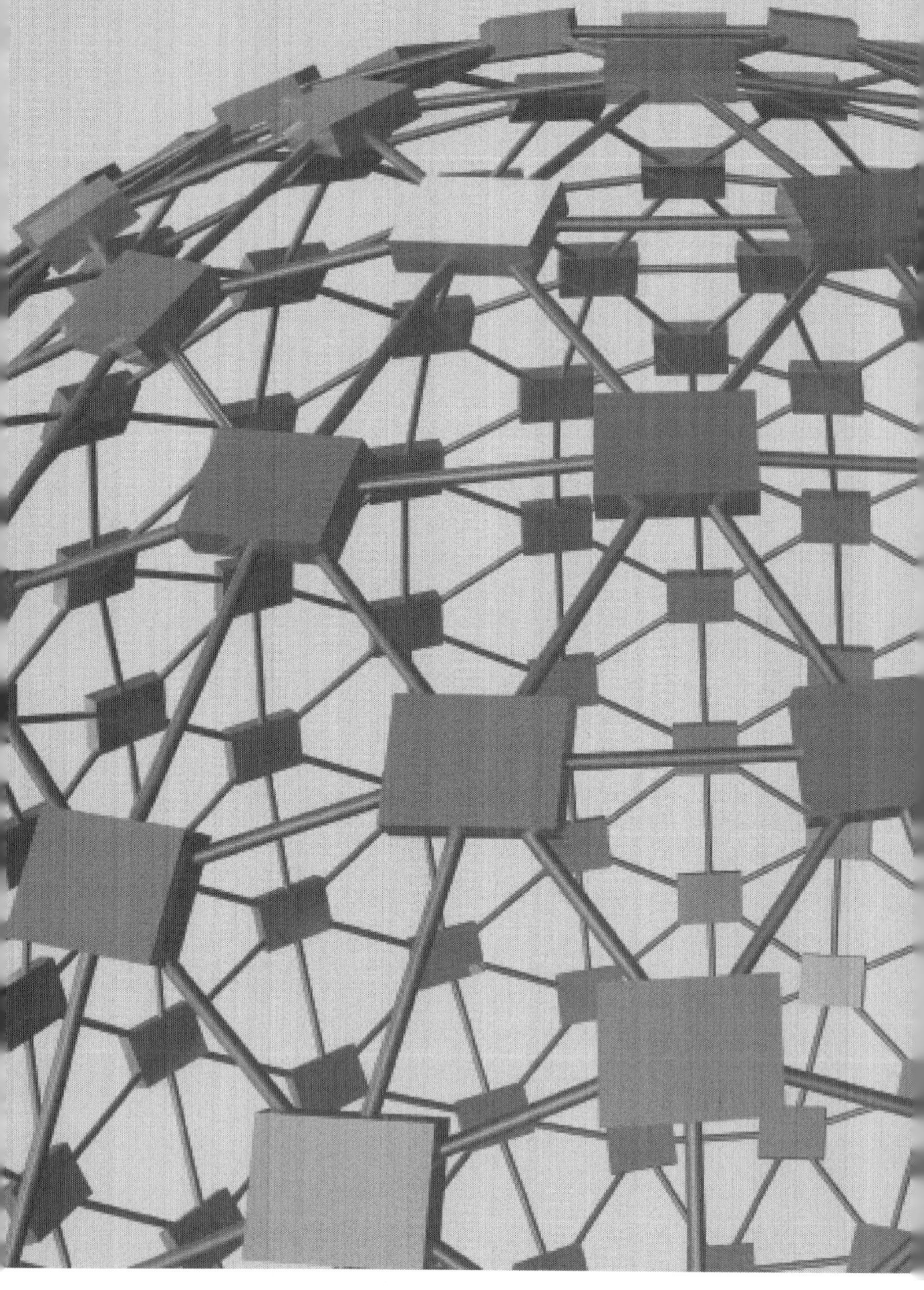

6

Exploiting the power of interactivity

6

Exploiting the power of interactivity

Interaction is key to the online experience. With traditional offline media – print, TV, radio, tapes, CDs – we were never anything but passive consumers.

Online we are active participants able to hunt down information, learn new skills, transact as buyers and sellers, form relationships, network with our peers and much more – all activities that we once had to carry out face-to-face or using much more primitive media such as the mail or telephone.

There are some very good reasons why we need to interact online:

1. **To navigate**, e.g. to follow links on the World Wide Web, to select from menus in an online application, or to move between pages in an e-learning module.
2. **To configure**, to set up the parameters of a particular decision or action, e.g. setting audio volume, or determining how often we wish to receive email updates.
3. **To explore,** to move around a space such as a map or 3D world, to scroll a document or search within an audio-visual resource.
4. **To converse** with others, whether synchronously (live) or asynchronously (at our own pace), using text, audio or video.
5. **To provide information**, such as when we complete a survey or form.
6. **To answer questions**, in order to demonstrate learning.

There are essentially four mechanisms for interacting with digital learning content (or any other online software for that matter):

- **selecting** – picking from the options provided
- **supplying** – coming up with our own responses
- **organising** – matching and sequencing the options provided
- **exploring** – finding what we want within a space or body of content

Let's take these in turn, starting with the most common, selecting.

Selecting

There are many forms that selections can take, some extremely commonplace, some more rarely deployed ...

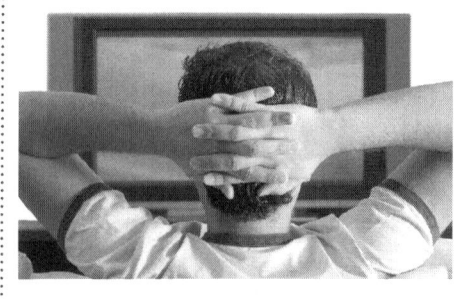

Online we are anything but passive consumers of content

Exploiting the power of interactivity

> Which of these tools could Erik use to help retail staff fully understand and relate to the complaint handling procedure?
>
> You can select more than one option.
>
> A table listing the steps to follow when a complaint occurs
>
> A walkthrough the procedure using stills and text or audio
>
> A case history of a complaint that was poorly handled and with negative consequences
>
> A video demonstration showing a fairly straightforward complaint being dealt with
>
> Video demonstrations showing more difficult or unusual situations being handled
>
> This could be a useful first step in conveying the correct procedure. Because of the format, learners could easily step back and forwards through the procedure.
>
> click here when you're done

This scenario challenges the user to make a critical judgement. Every option is accompanied by a tailored response.

Multiple-choice questions (MCQs)

In this familiar format, the user is presented with a question stem and picks an answer from the options provided. Typically the stem is presented textually, but could just as easily use images, audio or video as required. The options from which the user selects are also usually textual, but could also be pictorial. Some examples:

- Santa Cruz is the capital of La Palma. True or false?
- Which of the following countries is a member of the European Community?
- Tick those items on the list which best represent how you feel about working with customers?
- Click on the picture of the person you would select for the position.

The simplest questions ask the user to make a binary choice – yes or no, true or false. More typically, MCQs provide a wider range of alternatives, typically between 3 to 6, from which the user chooses one option.

A variant is the multiple response question, where the user can choose more than one option from the list.

MCQs can be used both as polls, for which the objective is simply to gauge the user's opinion, or as elements within learning materials and assessments.

www.onlignment.com

When the objective is to check knowledge, then well-constructed MCQs certainly can be valuable, although they can only assess *recognition* (of a fact, an instance of a concept, a cause or effect, a place or position, etc.) rather than the user's ability to *recall* the same.

Generally speaking, recognition will always be easier than recall. If the user needs to be able to recall something specifically to carry out a task effectively, then an MCQ (or any other interaction involving selection) will not test this adequately.

MCQs can also be used to challenge the user to make critical judgments, to think through a problem for themselves:

- What would you do if you were .... ?
- What do you think was the cause of ... ?
- How could ... have been avoided?
- How would you remedy ... ?

Ideally, in these circumstances, the user should be provided with a response that is specifically tailored to their particular choice.

This could take the form of some immediate feedback, but could also result in the scenario being taken to another stage with further decisions for the user to take.

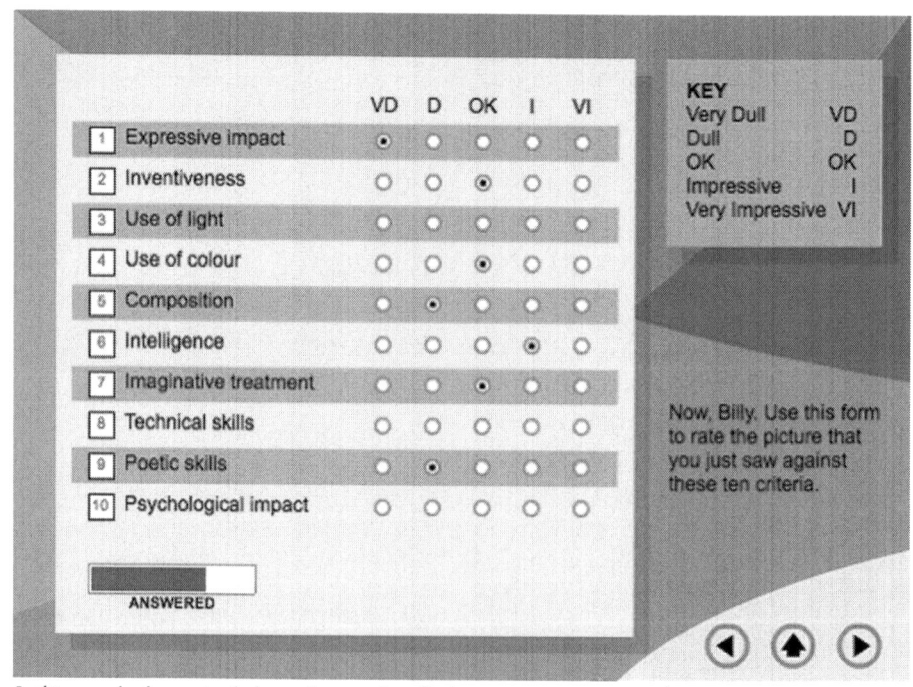

In this example, the user is asked to make a number of judgements against a rating scale

These so-called branching scenarios may sound complex, but in fact they are just MCQs sequenced conditionally according to the decisions that the user takes.

Pictorial selections

In this case the user is asked to select one or more parts of a picture, for example:

- Identify the tibula in this diagram of a skeleton.
- Where on this map of Europe is Estonia?
- Identify the safety risks in this photograph.

As you would expect, these interactions are extremely useful for assessing any knowledge that has a spatial element.

Event-based selections

Another interesting variant is to ask the user to stop an audio track, video or animation when they spot something occurring, for example:

- Press the stop button when you hear jargon used unnecessarily.
- Click on the pause button whenever you spot a good example of non-directive questioning.

This format, while more technically complex to implement, could play a valuable role in checking whether users can recognise particular behaviours or circumstances.

It could also be implemented with a group in a virtual classroom, perhaps by asking participants to click the 'raise hand' button, or something similar, when they spot something occurring in a piece of audio or video.

Rating scales

Here the user is presented with a series of statements and is asked to rate each one against a pre-defined scale. This scale may be expressed numerically (1-5, 1-10, etc.) or using labels (strongly disagree, disagree, etc.).

Hyperlinks

We all know what these do. A hyperlink, whether textual or pictorial, navigates the user to a different resource or a different part of the same resource. Links can be displayed separately (typically at the end of a resource) or embedded within textual content.

Menus

Menus provide a more structured means for navigation and for accessing the various features available within a resource.

Menus can be activated as simple lists (rather like multiple-choice questions), as scrolling lists, as rows or columns of buttons, as drop-down menus, as tabs, or as hierarchical trees. Menu selections can also be made by voice recognition.

All sorts of devices can be used for making selections, including keys, a mouse, a touch screen, or the user's own voice.

Whatever the device, the user is restricted to choosing from predetermined options, a constraint that is lifted when we take a look at the next category, 'supplying'.

DIGITAL LEARNING CONTENT

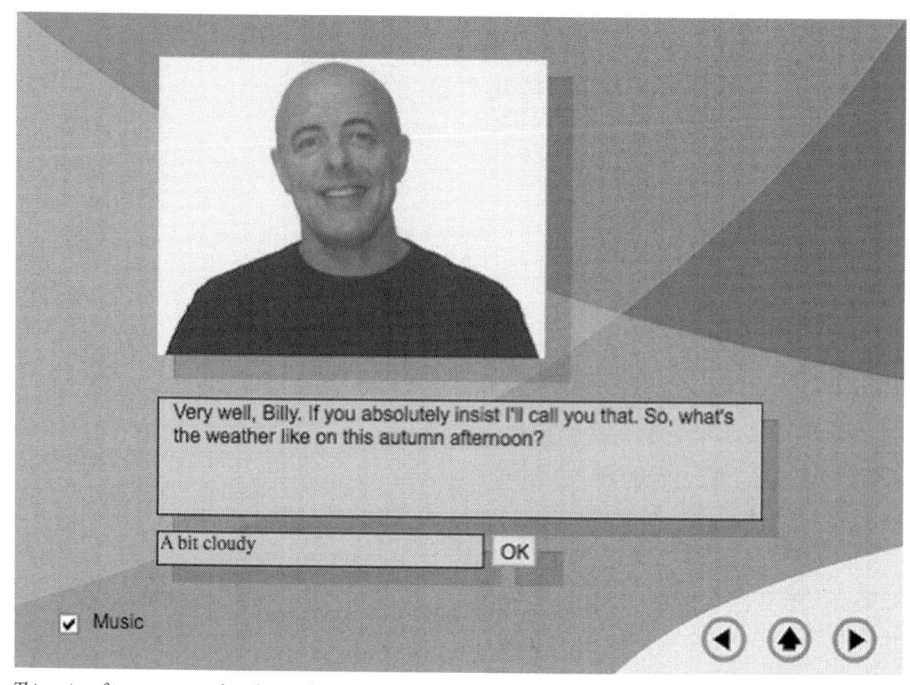

This series of interactions is based entirely on user textual responses. The program employs data previously entered by the user as well as information that is available to the system such as the date and time to give the impression of an intelligent conversation.

Supplying

While convenient and easy to work with, selections are limited by the fact that the user can only work with the options provided and he or she is therefore not able to express a preference which has not been predicted in advance.

And when selections are used as a basis for assessing knowledge, the user is faced not with recalling an answer from memory (think *University Challenge*) but with the much simpler one of recognising the right answer from a list (think *Who Wants to be a Millionaire?*).

There are many ways in which users might be asked to interact by supplying a response of their own making:

Textual responses

The user may be required to type a short string of characters into an input field (perhaps to enter their name onto a form or make a search query) or a longer response into a much larger text box (as with a chat program, a free-text field in a feedback form, or when responding to an essay-type question). In the case of the former, the program can more easily interpret the response, point out or correct possible errors ("Did you mean .... ?") and act accordingly. With free text, it is much harder for a computer to make sense accurately of what the user is trying to say, so typically this type of response has to be interpreted manually, in other words by a human.

In a self-directed learning context, textual responses are used much less frequently than they might be (and certainly much less than they were in the hey-day of instructional design, back in the 1980s).

This is probably because text responses are more tricky to set up and use than, say, multiple choice questions, but also because authoring tools no longer typically provide the functionality needed to successfully parse (make sense of) anything but the most basic text responses.

However, as long as textual response questions are phrased in such a way as to encourage no more than a one or two word response, they can be used successfully to test for recall, for example:

- What is the name of the current French President?
- Which software company created the Android operating system for mobile phones?

You can constrain the user's answer even more by using a 'fill-in-the-blanks' format. You may even provide a hint by showing how many letters you require and/or the first letter of the word:

- The name of the current French President is _____ _____.
- The company that created the Android operating system for mobile phones is G_____.

If your authoring tool will manage it, you can ask for multiple free text responses:

- List the applications that make up the Microsoft Office suite.

If you're lucky enough to have the right tool, you may be able to specify a range of possible right answers, perhaps some with common mis-spellings; you may also be able to look for keywords within the user's response, provide feedback for common mistaken responses, check for or ignore whether the answer is in upper or lower case, and so on.

The real joy of using typed responses in a self-paced lesson is that it provides the feel of a conversation between the author and user. As mentioned before, this technique was used widely at one time but is much less prevalent today. Perhaps we just need some new exemplars of this approach to provide inspiration.

Spoken responses

An alternative is to ask the user for a spoken response, which requires, of course, that they have access to a microphone and that their computer has sound capability. The most common application for this is during some form of live online session using instant messaging or web conferencing software. Clearly this type of interaction will normally depend on there being another human at the other end – voice recognition is improving, but as a

DIGITAL LEARNING CONTENT

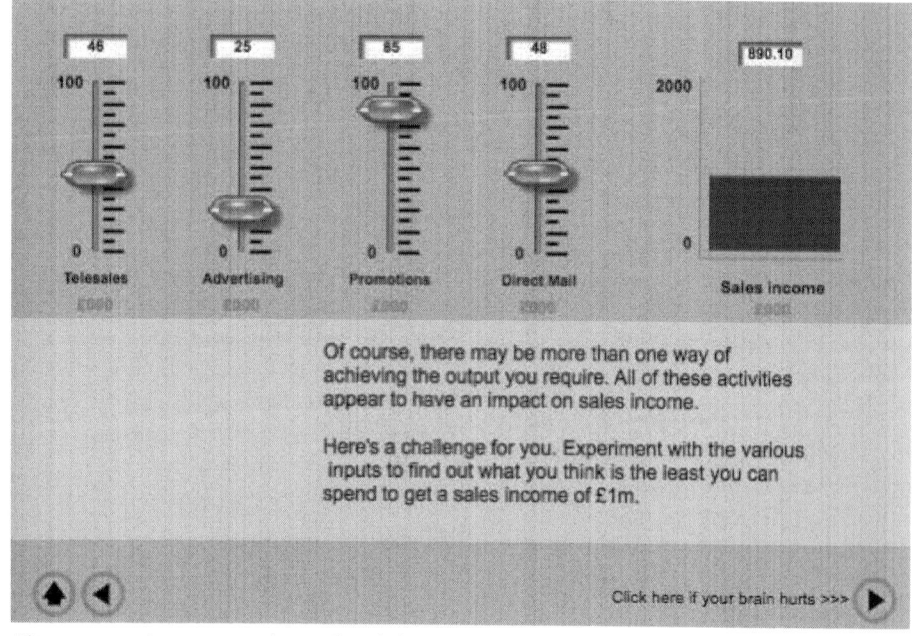

This interaction obtains numerical input through the use of sliders.

form of interaction is usually limited to simple selections from a list, not free form responses.

Another option, within a self-directed lesson, is to have the user record a response to a question, usually within the context of a scenario. The user can then listen back to their recorded response to reflect on their performance, a technique that would work well in the training of call centre operators.

Numeric responses

Simple numeric responses can be simply implemented using single-line text form fields as described earlier:

- In what year was the Great Fire of London?
- How many players are there in a Rugby League team?
- What percentage of the UK population dies from heart disease?

If your software allows, you can provide feedback based on how close the user gets to the right answer.

Other ways of obtaining a numeric value are by using sliders or rotary controls:

- Move the slider to set manufacturing volumes for your product range.
- Move the knob to set the required volume.

Exploiting the power of interactivity

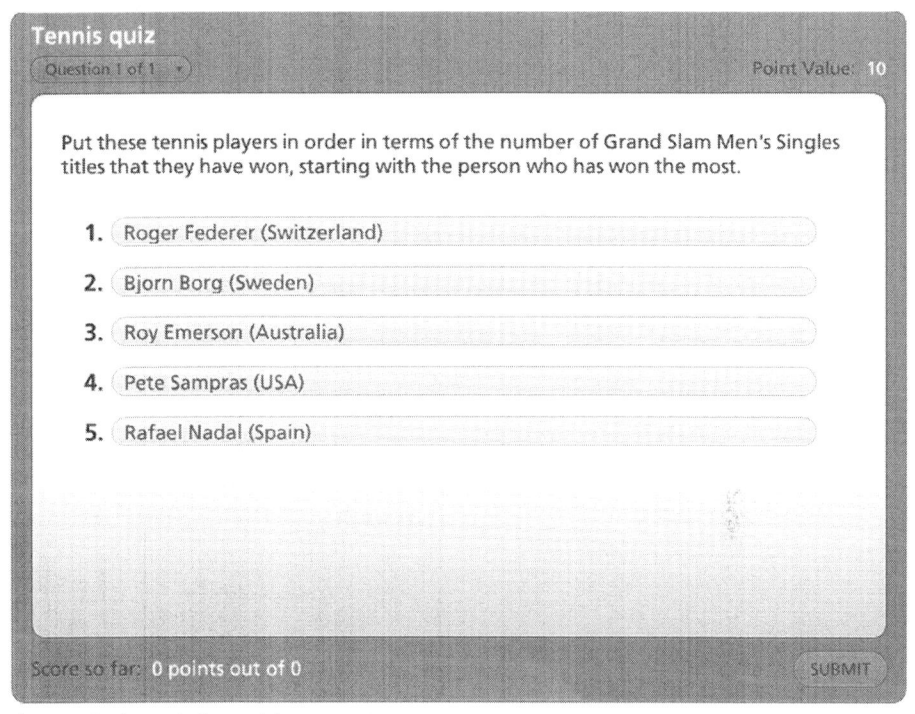

> **Tennis quiz**
> Question 1 of 1 ▾   Point Value: 10
>
> Put these tennis players in order in terms of the number of Grand Slam Men's Singles titles that they have won, starting with the person who has won the most.
>
> 1. Roger Federer (Switzerland)
> 2. Bjorn Borg (Sweden)
> 3. Roy Emerson (Australia)
> 4. Pete Sampras (USA)
> 5. Rafael Nadal (Spain)
>
> Score so far: 0 points out of 0   SUBMIT

An example of a simple drag and drop sequencing question

Pictorial responses

Another way of allowing users to interact in a free-form manner is by sketching, perhaps on an electronic whiteboard in a web conferencing system or in a graphics program.

And when you allow users to size or adjust the position of a window or icon you are also allowing a free response.

In summary, while selecting is convenient, supplying is expressive and checks for recall (or the user's ability to copy and paste!).

Organising

Organising is not so prevalent as a mode of interaction but you'll definitely need to use it from time to time, particularly in online learning materials and assessments.

Matching

Matching interactions require the user to identify related pairs in two sets of items. Typically one of the sets is made up of concepts and the other of attributes which characterise those concepts, for example:

- Match these animals with their natural habitats.

DIGITAL LEARNING CONTENT

- Match these regions with their primary economic outputs.
- Match these books with their authors.

Matching can be accomplished with drag and drop interfaces or by selecting items from a drop-down list. Most e-learning authoring tools provide one or both of these options. Note that the lists don't have to have an equal number of options.

There are two ways in which these interactions can work: you can have the user make all the matches and then submit their answer as a whole, or you can deal with each match as a separate answer, rejecting the mis-matches and providing feedback. The former is better suited to a mastery test; the latter to learning by having a go.

Sequencing

In this case, the user places a number of items in sequence, whether that's their logical order (ordering) or their order of importance (ranking), for example:

- Place these steps in their correct order.
- Place these events in time sequence.
- Place these risks in order of seriousness.
- Rank these authoring tools in order of preference.

These interactions can be accomplished with drag and drop interfaces or by selecting numbers from a drop-down list. Another possibility is that the user selects an item and then uses up and down arrows to re-position that item in the list. Most

Zooming and rotating a 3D model on an iPhone is an example of an exploring interaction

e-learning authoring tools will support at least one of these.

Exploring

The fourth category – exploring – is somewhat different, in that it is much more user-centered. The purpose of the interaction is not to gather information that the program can process, but rather to provide the user with an opportunity to search within a space or body of content. The following examples should make this clear:

- Scrolling a document or menu, using scroll bars, a mouse wheel or a touch gesture.
- Navigating within an audio-visual resource, such as an animation, video or audio file. This could include rewinding, fast forwarding or viewing in slow motion, typically accomplished with a transport bar.
- Zooming or panning a large image such as a map or, on a mobile device, the contents of a document.

- Stepping back and forwards through a slide show.

- Rotating a 3D image, such as a model of a piece of equipment.

- Moving an avatar in a 3D world using keys or game controllers.

All of these interactions put the user very firmly in control – they determine what he or she can see and how. And if we put all this in an adult learning context, you can soon see how exploring is going to be more engaging and more immersive than any number of multiple-choice questions and navigation buttons.

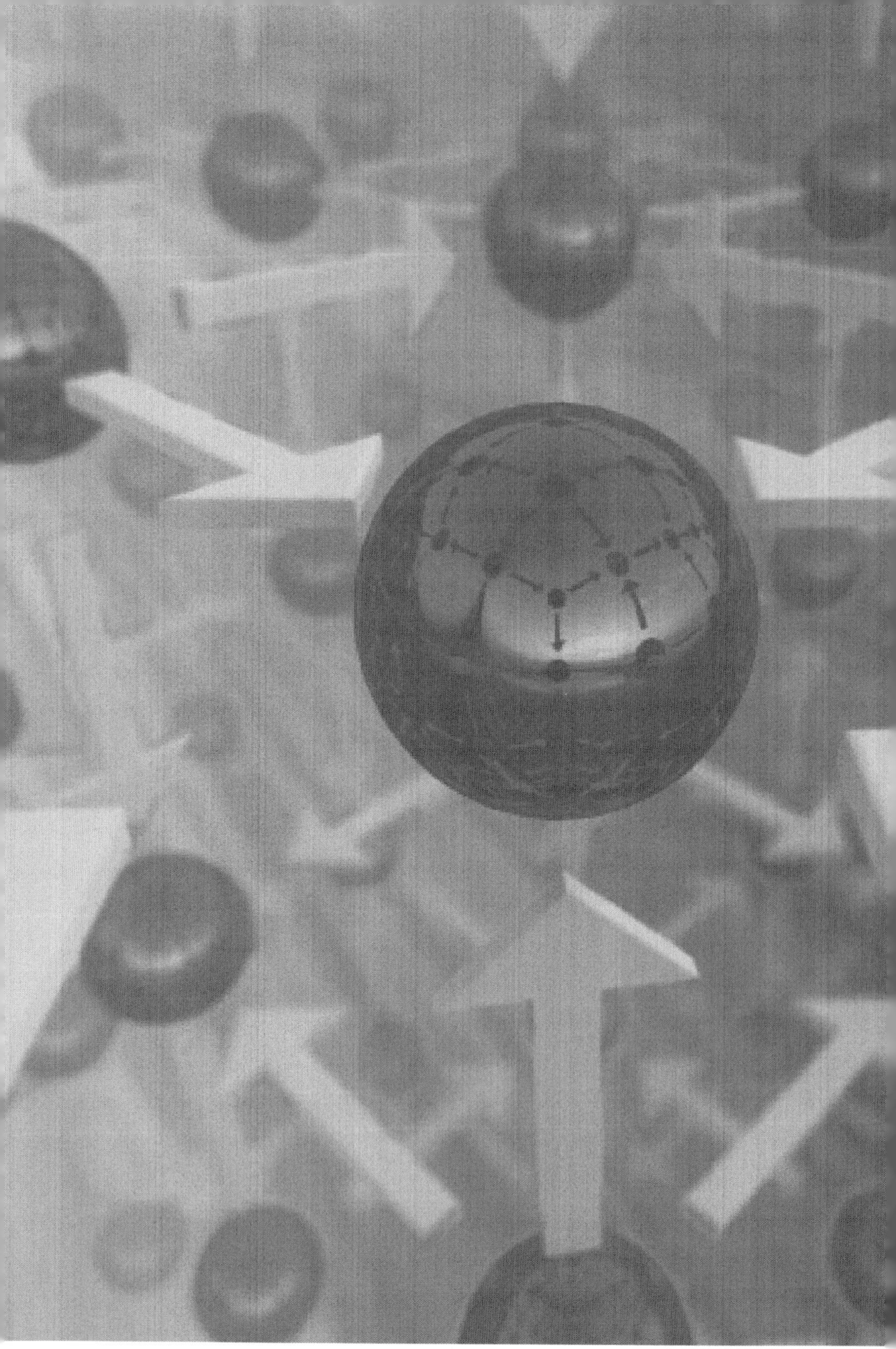

7
Working with the basic media elements

7

Working with the basic media elements

All content, regardless of its format, makes use of the same key media elements: text, audio, images, animation and video. As a content designer, you need to know when to use each of these elements, how to do so effectively within the particular constraints associated with working digitally and online, and how best to combine these media elements to achieve your learning objectives. Let's take them in turn:

Text

We start our tour with the medium we all take for granted – simple text. What is it good for? In which situations does it struggle? How is it best presented online?

What text is good for

Text is by far the most flexible and pervasive of all the media elements. When carefully composed, it is capable of conveying precise meaning.

In most circumstances (where it not integrated into a video or animation), text can be absorbed at the reader's own pace, which reduces stress for the learner and makes it much easier for those who want to skim content or hunt down a particular piece of information.

When text is not so suitable

Text is not as expressive as speech, because it does not convey tone of voice. For this reason, text messages can be easily misinterpreted.

Without considerable skill on the part of the author, text is not great at describing the physical appearance of an object or person (use photos or illustrations instead), actual events (use video), layouts (use diagrams or screen grabs in the case of software), or complex processes (use diagrams or animations). Text is also not ideal for describing sounds (so use audio instead!).

Optimising text for online delivery

Text is harder to read from a screen than it is from paper, partly because the resolution of the screen is so much lower (less dots per character) and also because, unless the reader is using an e-book device such as the Kindle, the light is projected rather than reflected. With scrolling and paging, it is also much easier for the reader to lose their orientation within an online document.

With these points in mind, best practice suggests that you:

- Limit your word count to half of what it would be in print.
- Use clear, descriptive headings to separate sections.
- Keep sentences short.
- Cover only a single point in each paragraph.
- Use bulleted or numbered lists rather than present a series of related items as ordinary prose.

Be aware that, for the visually impaired, text can be read aloud by screen readers. To help these readers work at their best, text should be formatted and displayed in accordance with the latest accessibility guidelines. In most cases these issues will be dealt with by the person designing the website or authoring tool rather than the author.

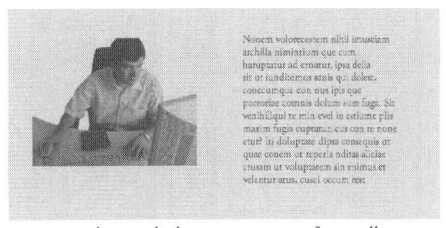

Text provides an ideal accompaniment for a still image

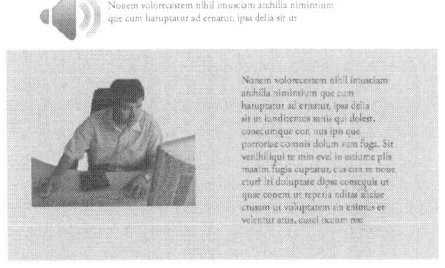

Combining text with other elements

As a verbal element, text combines well with visual elements but clashes badly with a second verbal element such as speech. So, text plus still images works well, whereas text plus speech causes all sorts of confusion and overload for the user. The brain cannot process two verbal inputs simultaneously, so the user has to block out one element (usually the speech because this is conveyed much more slowly than text) in order to concentrate on the other.

... but if speech is added as well, then the combination of two verbal sources is confusing for the user.

How text is represented online

Text is represented digitally as individual ASCII characters of one byte each. For this reason, text is by far the most bandwidth-friendly element.

Portions of a piece of text can be emboldened, italicised or underlined. As a general rule, underlining should be avoided as it implies that the text is a hyperlink. Bold and italicised text should be used sparingly.

Text can also be formatted in terms of point size, colour, font, spacing, column width and alignment, although these aspects of typography are now more normally handled through what is called a 'cascading style sheet' (CSS), set up by a web designer, leaving the author to worry about the content.

Typography has an important impact on legibility and usability and so determines much more than the style. The following general pointers will help:

- Constrain column width to 5" (12cm) to reduce the eye strain involved in tracking back to the start of each new line.
- Left align paragraphs in most circumstances.
- Limit the use of text that is all capitals.
- Present body text at 10 or 12 point.

DIGITAL LEARNING CONTENT

- Maintain a high contrast between text and background. In most cases, black on white is fine.
- Use fonts that are optimised for the screen.

Audio

We continue our tour with audio. What contribution can it make? Where is it less effective? How is it best delivered online?

What audio is good for

To rather state the obvious, audio is useful when we want to know what something sounds like – a human voice, a piece of music, a fire alarm, a bird song. In these situations, textual descriptions will always be second best.

More commonly, we use sound as an alternative verbal channel to text. In fact, it's a very rich alternative because it conveys tone of voice as well as the words.

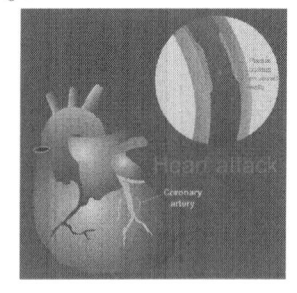

Audio takes up no space on the screen, allowing the user to maintain visual focus on the graphical content.

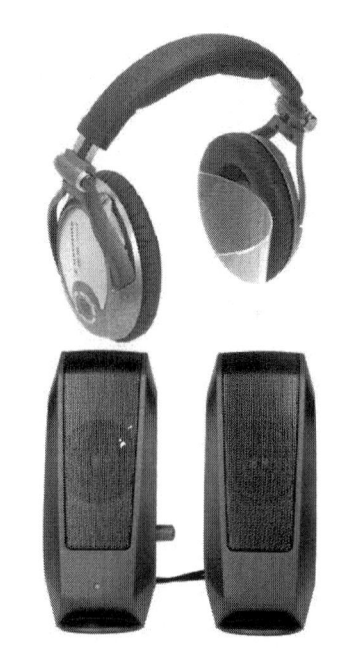

Audio requires much more in terms of technical paraphernalia.

In an online context, audio is useful because it takes up no space on the screen. When you're presenting a sequence of images, an animation, a software demonstration or a movie, the verbal content of your message can be delivered in sound without taking attention away from the visual elements.

Music is rarely a major ingredient in digital learning content, but as you are undoubtedly aware, it does have enormous power to influence the listener's mood. Although gratuitous use of music is likely to be an annoying distraction, there may be opportunities when it makes a real difference.

When audio is not so suitable

Unlike text, audio is not self-paced. Although the user may have the facility to rewind and fast forward recorded audio, they cannot control the speed at which the sound is delivered; and with a live audio stream, even this capability is lost. Delivery of the spoken word is much slower than the speed at which a person can read, which might, in some circumstances, frustrate a user from achieving their goal as quickly as they would like.

Audio also requires more in terms of technical paraphernalia. The listener needs an audio-enabled device (with a PC that means a sound card) and either speakers or headphones. In an open office environment, there is the additional risk of causing disturbance to those working nearby if headphones aren't used and at an appropriate volume.

It goes without saying that sound will be inadequate when the subject matter is highly visual or is better understood with visual aids. In these situations audio can be combined with, or replaced entirely by photos, illustrations, video, diagrams, screen grabs or animations. Audio-only media, such as podcasts, will clearly struggle when a visual element is required to convey meaning.

Optimising audio for online delivery

If your audio is pre-recorded and intended for the user to download (that's when they wait while the file is saved in full to their computer, but can then play it repeatedly offline), then it pays to keep the duration of the audio short and therefore minimise the file size. A good example is with podcasts – it's better to distribute your programme in three 5MB sections rather than one of 15MB. This constraint does not apply when the audio is streamed directly from the server; in this case the audio plays almost immediately but is not stored on the user's computer.

Interviews and discussions make much more engaging listening than monologues.

Generally speaking, it pays to limit the user's exposure to a single voice. However interesting the speaker and however expressive the voice, any listener will begin to tune out after 10 minutes or so. On radio, you will rarely hear a single voice continuously for more than a minute or two. For this reason, interviews, discussions, question and answer sessions and drama work much better than monologues.

In *The Media Equation*, Stanford University researchers Byron Reeves and Clifford Nass reported on the impact that audio quality had on a user's overall impression of their media experience. Their conclusion was that audio quality does matter a great deal, an argument for taking care

DIGITAL LEARNING CONTENT

It pays to use a quality microphone, ideally with a pop shield fitted, as above. The speaker should be 4-5" away from the microphone.

when recording and editing, and then sampling at the best rate possible given the bandwidth constraints.

When recording it pays to use a quality microphone, ideally fitted with a pop shield, which reduce the explosive peaks that occur when speakers say the letter 'p'. Ideally the room will be free of reflections (so there are few natural reverberations or echoes) and the speaker should be a comfortable distance (say four or five inches) from the microhphone. The recording level should be high enough to avoid background hiss, while avoiding the high peaks that cause 'clipping'.

When editing, bad takes and gaps can be removed and the overall volume level equalised using a process called 'compression'.

If you are recording a narration to accompany a video, a screencast, a slide show or an e-tutorial, it pays to employ a professional voiceover artist. While this may appear to be extravagant, the cost rarely exceeds a few hundred dollars

and can make a big difference to the professionalism of the end result. Generally speaking, tightly-scripted speech is better delivered by the pros, who are skilled at making the words sound natural. If you can get away without a script the effect will be much more relaxed and personal, and you will not need a professional voice.

Audio can be captured on a portable recording device (a digital recorder, a phone or camera) or directly into a computer. In the case of the latter, it pays to work with dedicated audio software if you can, as this will provide you with much more flexibility when it comes to editing. Although professional audio editors are expensive, free software such as Audacity is good enough for most purposes. On the other hand, many authoring tools allow you to record directly into the tool and, with a little care, the results can be more than adequate.

To accommodate those users who have a hearing impairment, you need to provide a transcript of any important audio components within recorded media.

Combining audio with other elements

As a verbal element, speech combines well with visuals but clashes badly with a second verbal element such as text. So, audio over a sequence of images works well, whereas if the words are also replicated on the screen as text, the user stands to be confused and frustrated. The brain cannot process two verbal inputs simultaneously, so the most likely consequence is that the user will

Working with the basic media elements

reach for the volume control to block out the slower of the two verbal sources, the speech. Of course, if the audio consists primarily of music or sound effects, this will not clash with the text and can work well.

How audio is represented online

Digital audio is represented as a stream of 'samples'. The quality of these samples is determined by the frequency with which these samples are taken (the more often the better) and the resolution of the samples (the more bits used to describe each sample the better). As an example, CD audio is sampled 44,100 times per second (44.1KHz) with a 16 bit resolution. Typically, much lower sample qualities are used online in order to reduce the strain on bandwidth (the speed with which data can be transmitted across the network). Similarly, most music is recorded as two-channels of samples (stereo), whereas a single channel (mono) is acceptable in many circumstances and certainly when the content is simple speech.

Even when the audio is encoded in mono and at a lower sample quality, it will still be far too bulky to download or stream without extensive compression. The most common compression formats are:

- MP3
- AAC (Apple's alternative to MP3)
- WMA (Windows Media Audio)

Most audio editing software will be able to export in a wide variety of compression formats.

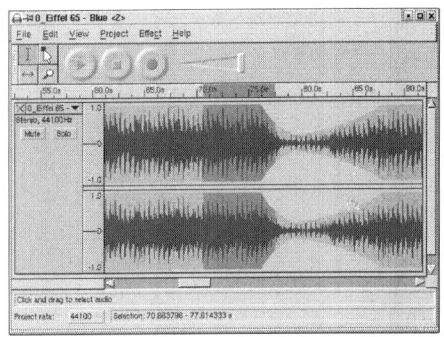

Dedicated audio software, such as Audacity, will provide you with the greatest flexibility when it comes to editing.

Images

Third stop on our tour is the still image. What contribution can these make? Where are they less effective? How are they best delivered online?

What images are good for

Perhaps the best way to answer this question is to imagine how difficult it would be to convey the following information without the aid of images:

- The new office that we will all be moving to later this year.
- Sales territories in the Indian sub-continent.
- Welcome to our new head of HR.
- The process to follow when troubleshooting a machine breakdown.
- Our fall fashion collection.
- The process of condensation.
- The workings of the internal combustion engine.

www.onlignment.com

DIGITAL LEARNING CONTENT

- Comparative sales figures over the past five years.
- The cypress tree.
- The structure of the Internet backbone.

Images come in a variety of forms and these all have their particular place:

- Photographs are capable of accurately depicting real-life people, objects, places and events.
- Illustrations, including clip-art and cartoons, will not capture people, objects, places and events as faithfully as photos, but can depict what is impossible or impractical to photograph. In their relative simplicity, they may also communicate more clearly than photos.
- Diagrams show cause and effect and the relationships between the parts of something and the whole. They include timelines, organograms, maps and flow charts.
- Charts provide a rapidly-accessible, visual representation of numerical data, highlighting trends and proportions.
- Screen shots faithfully capture the elements of a software interface.

Charts, illustrations, diagrams and photographs make it possible to describe relationships, trends, structures, likenesses and much more in ways that words can not.

Working with the basic media elements

When images are not so suitable

As a general rule, images struggle to convey precise meaning without verbal support from either speech or text; and it goes without saying that they have little practical function when there is no strong visual aspect to the content.

Still images will be second best to animation or video when communicating movement or representing live action.

When used for purely decorative purposes, images use up valuable bandwidth and screen space without adding anything to the communication process. In fact, gratuitous images are likely to be harmful to learning, distracting attention away from more meaningful elements.

Optimising images for online delivery

When displayed online, images need to be large enough to be clear but not so large as to require excessive scrolling.

The screen is not the ideal setting for highly detailed images because of the limited resolution of most screens, typically less than 100 dots per inch. Compare this with print, where resolutions start at 300 dpi and can be very much higher. As a general rule, highly detailed images are better made available for download and viewing with a dedicated graphics application or delivered as hard copy.

Copyright laws apply as much online as in any other medium. If you use copyrighted images in your online communications without permission, then you are taking a risk.

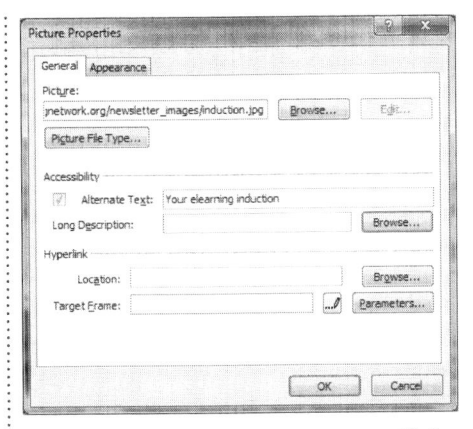

Any web editor or content management system will allow you to enter alternate text which can be read aloud to visually-impaired users by screen reader software.

Accessibility guidelines dictate that, when you use images online, you provide each image with an alternative textual description. This allows those users with a visual impairment to gain some benefit from your images, because screen readers can convert your textual descriptions into synthesised speech.

Combining images with other elements

Images combine well with audio or text. With audio, you have the advantage that the eye can concentrate on the image, while the verbal content is communicated aurally; with text, on the other hand, the eye has to switch back and forth.

Images do not combine well with a second visual source such as live video. If you want the user to focus on the image, then it's best to close any video down, at least temporarily.

www.onlignment.com

DIGITAL LEARNING CONTENT

How images are represented online

Online images can be held in one of a number of compressed, bit-mapped formats. With bit-mapping, the images are stored digitally as a data structure describing a rectangular grid of pixels. Each pixel in this grid is represented by a colour or greyscale value.

Bit-mapped images can be contrasted with vector graphics, which describe the image as a series of geometric functions (lines, curves, etc.). Vector graphics have the advantage of being more scalable, retaining their quality however large they are displayed. Most images other than photographs are created and edited in vector format, but must be exported as a compressed bit-map for use online. Because this removes the ability for high-quality scaling, it makes sense to export the images at the maximum size at which they will be displayed online. If you leave it to the browser to do the scaling, be prepared to lose quality.

When delivering images online, you have three choices of bit-mapped image formats:

- **JPEG** (Joint Photographics Experts Group) – pronounced 'jaypeg' and sometimes shortened to just JPG. This format is 'lossy' in that the more you compress the image and thus reduce file size, the greater you will lose clarity and detail. JPEG graphics can render in full colour and are ideally suited to the display of photographs.

- **GIF** (Graphics Interchange Format) is 'lossless' in that the compression process

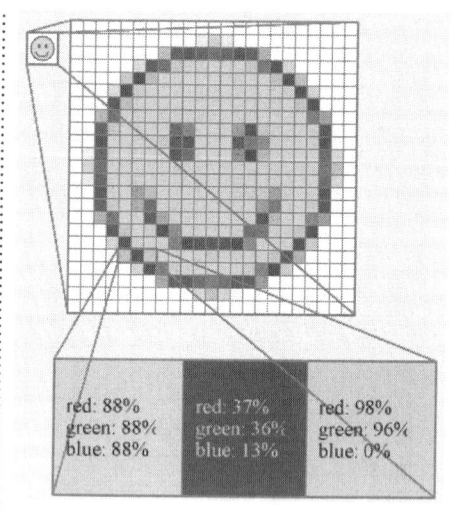

This enlarged bit-map shows how the image is stored as a rectangular grid of pixels, each with a specific colour, defined as a combination of red, green and blue.

does not involve sacrificing quality. GIF graphics are limited to 256 colours, which is fine for computer graphics with hard edges and block colours, but not so good for photos. GIFs can also have a transparent background, which is useful if you want to display your images in anything other than a simple rectangular arrangement.

- **PNG** (Portable Network Graphics) – pronounced 'ping' – is another 'lossless' format but is not restricted in colour rendition, making it a superior format to GIF. PNGs are ideal for computer-generated graphics such as buttons, logos, diagrams and maps, but are less suited to photographs, where the resulting file size is likely to be excessive. Be a little careful, because not all applications or firewalls support PNG.

Animation

And so, we move on to animation. What contribution can it make? In which situations is it less effective? How is animation best delivered online?

What animation is good for

Animation is to diagrams and illustrations what video is to photographs. The added ingredient in each case is motion, and motion can be useful: it is eye-catching; it can represent in simplified form the events that we experience in real-life; it can also help in explaining how elements interact with each other.

Online animations come in a variety of forms:

- Transitions provide a bridge from one state to another, usually just for decorative purposes.

- Animated diagrams are particularly useful when explaining how things work and what the stages are in a process.

- Animated cartoons function primarily as entertainment.

- Interactive games and simulations have the potential to engage users in motivating challenges, free of risk.

- Screencasts explain how tasks are completed in software packages.

- 3D environments go beyond the 2D to provide a more immersive experience, whether for gaming, for simulation or both.

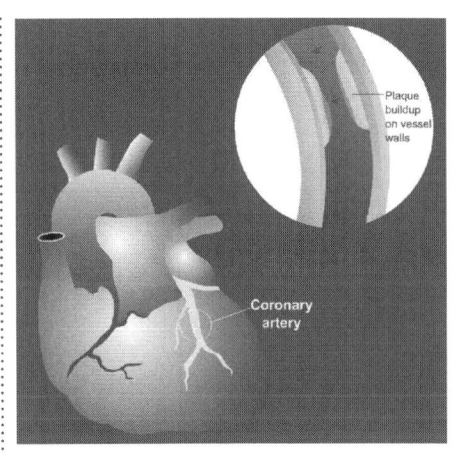

Animated diagrams are useful for explaining how things work, in this case a heart attack.

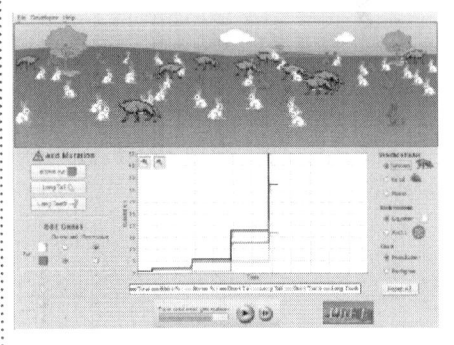

Interactive simulations allow users to explore cause and effect relationships, as in this simulation of natural selection, created by the University of Colorado at Boulder.

When animation is not so suitable

Animations, like images, struggle to convey precise meaning without verbal support from either speech or text; and they clearly have little practical function when there is no strong visual aspect to the content.

When used purely as an attention grabbler,

DIGITAL LEARNING CONTENT

animations can be annoyingly distracting. Users have been known to cover up a repetitive animation with their hand so they can concentrate on a task elsewhere on the screen.

Optimising animations for online delivery

As a general rule, animation should be used only very modestly for decoration or show. If a user is engaging with an online experience primarily for their own amusement or entertainment then fine, but more often than not the user is goal-orientated and does not want any distractions that get in the way of achieving that goal.

A good example is the way in which elaborate animations are sometimes used to provide a gateway into a web site – more often than not, users will find this annoying and look to get past it as quickly as possible. Online, the need is for speed; to get to the point.

Where animation is the main feature, as it would be with an animated cartoon or a screencast, then it makes sense to organise the content into short modules which users can access easily from a menu. You'll also need to make it easy to replay any animation.

If you're using an animation to draw attention to something new or important, then don't loop endlessly, because this becomes irritating and distracting.

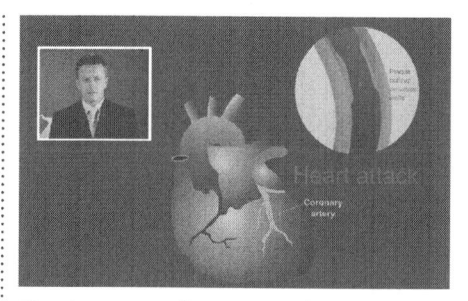

Here the presenter talking to camera distracts the user from the animation, which in this case should be the user's visual focus of attention.

Combining animation with other elements

Animations combine particularly well with audio, which allows the eye to maintain attention on the animation, while the verbal content is communicated aurally. Text is an option, but then the eye has to switch back and forth.

Animations do not combine well with a second visual source such as live video. If you want the user to focus on the animation, then it's best to turn any video off.

How animations are represented online

In the early days of the World Wide Web, the only available animation format was the 'animated GIF'. This allows a series of images in the GIF format to be sequenced and looped. Animated GIFs are still used, noticeably for advertising banners, but the format is too bulky and inflexible to use for any serious animation tasks.

Later versions of HTML and JavaScript (the formatting and scripting capabilities

Working with the basic media elements

```
<script type="text/javascript">
function starttimer()
{
  d=new Date()
  for (count=0;count<imagemax;count++)
  {
    yyy = yp[count]*Math.cos(rx)-
zp[count]*Math.sin(rx);
    bbb = bp[count]*Math.cos(rx)-
cp[count]*Math.sin(rx);
    zzz = yp[count]*Math.
sin(rx)+zp[count]*Math.cos(rx);
    ccc = bp[count]*Math.
sin(rx)+cp[count]*Math.cos(rx);
    xxx = xp[count]*Math.cos(ry)+zzz*Math.
sin(ry);
    aaa = ap[count]*Math.cos(ry)+ccc*Math.
sin(ry);
    zzz = xp[count]*-Math.sin(ry)+zzz*Math.
cos(ry);
    ccc = ap[count]*-Math.sin(ry)+ccc*Math.
cos(ry);
            // PERSPECTIVE
            xxx=xxx*(perspective/
(zzz+perspective));
            yyy=yyy*(perspective/
(zzz+perspective));
            aaa=aaa*(perspective/
(ccc+perspective));
            bbb=bbb*(perspective/
(ccc+perspective));

    line(image[count],320+xxx,240+yyy,320+aaa,
240+bbb)
  }
  ry-=(mouse_x-320)/5000
  rx+=(mouse_y-240)/5000
  timer=setTimeout("starttimer()",10)
}
function stoptimer()
{
  clearTimeout(timer)
```

Animations can be created using programming languages, such as JavaScript above, but to do so requires the specialist expertise of a web programmer.

supported by all web browsers) have evolved such that there are now quite a few ways to build transitions, animted buttons and drag-and-drop facilities into standard web pages, without recourse to third-party plug-ins. However, these facilities require expert coding and are still not adequate for more advanced purposes.

The emerging HTML5 looks like it will provide most of the animation capabilities that you are likely to require, but as yet the tools are not in place to make it possible to generate animations without coding.

Macromedia introduced the Flash format in 1996 as a way of adding animation capabilities to web pages. Because Flash stores graphical elements in vector format, the animations (stored as Flash 'movies') are small in size and can be scaled up or down without losing quality.

The Flash format has grown enormously in sophistication and popularity since then and, in its current form, now under the wing of Adobe, it is capable of driving complete websites and applications as well as smaller interactive multimedia elements within standard websites.

Artists and designers can work directly with the Flash tool (and its associated scripting language ActionScript) to create bespoke animations, games, simulations and applications. However, the technology is also accessible to less specialist users through much simpler third-party applications which export in the Flash format. Examples include screencasting tools, game engines and many e-learning authoring tools.

Interactive 3D environments are not supported directly on the World Wide Web but some, such as this simulation created using the Thinking Worlds tool, can be displayed using the Adobe Shockwave plug-in.

www.onlignment.com

Most but not all browsers can run Flash. Where not, this is usually because of the IT policy of a particular organisation, rather than the capability of the computer or browser. It makes a difference which version of Flash is being used, because earlier versions have much reduced functionality.

3D environments are not supported directly within HTML or Flash, although some applications (such as Caspian Learning's Thinking Worlds tool) will work in a standard browser with the aid of the Adobe Shockwave plugin. More commonly, 3D games and worlds have to be downloaded and delivered as separate applications.

Non-interactive animations, such as cartoons and software sims, can also be rendered as videos. This increases the range of situations in which the animations can be accessed (principally because some mobile devices, such as the iPhone, do not support Flash), but restricts the ability to scale the animations without quality loss.

Video

And so we move on to the final media element, video. What contribution can video make? In which situations is it less effective? How is video best delivered online?

What video is good for

Video excels at depicting real-life events. So, assuming that a particular event is of interest, if it moves and you can point a

Video requires more bandwidth than any other media element. Without adequate bandwidth, video downloads will be frustratingly lengthy and it will not be possible to display live video at an acceptable frame rate.

camera at it, video really is your medium of choice. As another real bonus, audio is recorded automatically at the same time in perfect synch, meaning video is really two media elements packaged as one.

Because the visual and audio content of a video is constantly changing, it attracts and maintains attention. Just think how your eye gets drawn to the TV, even when the sound is turned off.

Video can do more than show what a camera can capture; it can also be used as a simple alternative for displaying a wide range of multimedia material, including screencasts, narrated PowerPoint presentations, scenes from virtual worlds or Flash animations.

When video is not so suitable

Video is not self-paced. Although you may have the facility to rewind and fast forward recorded video, you cannot control the speed at which the audio content is delivered. Because video is not self-paced, it provides the viewer with less opportunity for reflection or note-taking.

Working with the basic media elements

Pre-recorded video is best organised into short modules. In this example, an interview has been divided into a number of short sections, each of which can be easily accessed using a YouTube playlist menu overlay.

Video is the most bandwidth-hungry of all media elements, so users with bandwidth constraints will be denied online access. In these situations, video can still be delivered offline, from a DVD, memory stick or hard drive.

Clearly video has little to offer when the content is not visual in nature or when there is little movement in the visual content.

Optimising video for online delivery

Because online video is typically displayed in a small window, it works best when the subject matter does not contain a lot of fine detail. In years to come, when bandwidth ceases to be much of an issue, then this constraint will drop away and online high-definition playback will be normal. Of course, HD is available now, but typically only through satellite or cable TV or when the video is viewed offline.

With pre-recorded video, it makes sense to organise the content into short modules which users can access easily from a menu. In YouTube, you can organise a collection of modules into a playlist with a single URL.

Video can be captured on a portable recording device (a camcorder, a stills camera with a video capability or a phone) or directly into a computer via a webcam. In the case of the latter, it pays to frame the subject carefully and make sure it is well lit. If your material is only ever going to be played back online, there is little to be gained by recording in high definition.

You'll usually benefit from carrying out some editing of your content. There are free tools such as Microsoft MovieMaker and Apple's iMovie, very capable low-cost versions of professional tools, such as Adobe Premiere Elements and, of course, the professional tools themselves, such as Avid, Adobe Premiere and Final Cut Pro. In most cases, the free and low-cost tools are more than adequate for the simple editing required for online video.

Note that, to accommodate those users who have a visual or auditory impairment, you will need to provide a transcript of any important video material.

Combining video with other elements

Video obviously combines well with audio, because this allows the eye to concentrate on the visual material, while the verbal

www.onlignment.com

83

DIGITAL LEARNING CONTENT

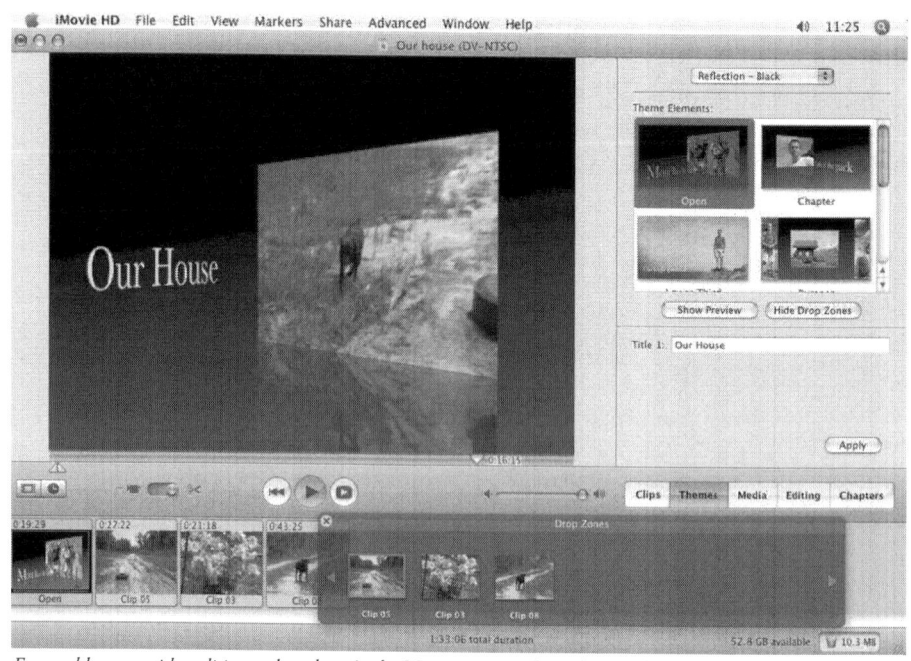

Free and low-cost video editing tools such as Apple iMovie are more than adequate for the post-production of video that's intended for delivery online.

content is communicated aurally. It would not work to display text alongside a video; if audio really is not feasible, perhaps because users' computers are not fitted with sound cards, then the text should be superimposed on the video, like sub-titles.

Video does not combine well with a second visual source. Whichever is not the primary focus of attention should be turned off or removed.

How videos are represented online

Video quality is determined by the resolution (the number of pixels making up the image) and the frame rate (the speed at which the picture changes). As a guide, standard definition TV is displayed at 720x576 / 25 frames per second (fps) in Europe or 720x480 / 30 fps in the USA. High definition has between two and five times better resolution.

Digital audio quality is determined by the sample resolution and frequency and the number of channels (see the previous section on audio).

Video can be recorded and edited in a wide range of digital formats, but will typically require extensive compression before it is suitable for online delivery. The most common file formats for online video distribution are:

Working with the basic media elements

- **MP4** (MPEG-4 / H.264) – the user must have Adobe Flash or Apple Quicktime installed

- **FLV** (Flash video) – the user must have Adobe Flash installed

- **WMV** (Windows Media Video) – the user must have Windows Media Player installed

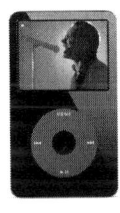

The trend in recent years has been towards using Flash video, not least because this is what YouTube uses. For delivery on iPods and similar devices, MP4 is the most common. Expect to see changes in coming years as video is directly embedded in the new HTML5.

Video can be delivered in such a way that it can be downloaded by the user and played offline, or streamed continuously to the user with no opportunity for download. To accommodate streaming, a streaming media server is required. As an example, YouTube streams its video, whereas iTunes makes videos available for download.

Most video editing software will be able to export in a wide variety of compression formats.

www.onlignment.com 85

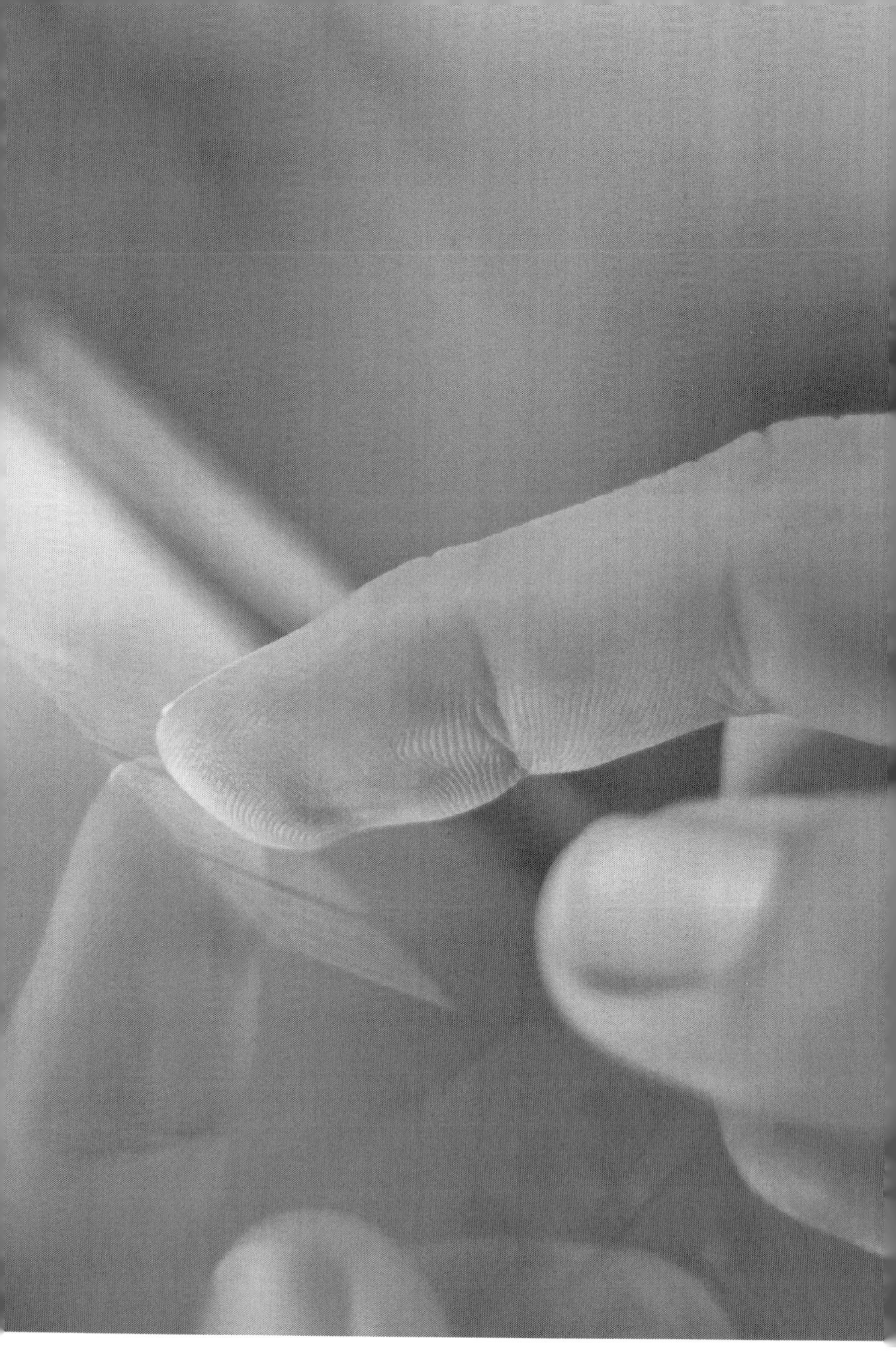

8
Distributing your content

8
Distributing your content

We leave the world of offline media behind

Before Sir Tim Berners-Lee did us all a big favour some twenty years ago by inventing the World Wide Web, the distribution of content was a very physical process. Regardless of the format – book, CD, DVD or whatever – some form of 'master' would be produced and this would be used as a basis for the manufacture of the finished goods. These would then be boxed up and physically distributed to wholesalers, retailers and eventually end customers. The books and CDs would end their journey neatly lined up on shelves or in racks, ready for consumption.

How quaint this process is beginning to look now.

While there is still a market for 'offline media' (the sort you can use without an internet connection), it is fast dwindling. Sales of printed media, CDs and DVDs are dropping rapidly as the price of computer memory drops and bandwidth increases. Why would anyone clutter up their valuable living space with piles of dusty books and CDs when they can store as many as they could possibly consume in a lifetime on a Kindle, on an iPod or somewhere in the cloud? Why indeed? No-one under thirty would even consider it.

Learning content obeys the same rules. Why burden employees with huge ring binders full of hand-outs and reference manuals which sit unopened on their shelves when the same information can be made available online at the click of a mouse? Information that can be easily maintained, indexed, searched and cross-referenced; and which costs nothing to replicate or distribute.

In the old world, learning content was a bit of an after-thought. The classroom was central to all learning activity. Your course manual was not much more than a trophy; something to display in your office to show everyone how much you had supposedly learned.

With the shift from 'courses' to 'resources,' content becomes critical. No-one expects anymore to have to struggle to absorb large volumes of information during a course. Yes, they want insights into important new concepts and principles. But the rest they want to be able to access quickly and easily if and when they need it. How you distribute learning content is now central to the potential success of any intervention.

Perhaps it's time to get a Kindle

Choosing a format for your content

Learning content can be distributed online in a number of formats:

Native document

By this we mean the output format of a proprietary application, most commonly Word, Excel or PowerPoint. These applications have sophisticated editing and formatting capabilities, but were never really designed as a means for distributing finished content. The consumer has to have their own copy of the application that was used to prepare the original document and often needs a particular version. The documents can be bulky to download because their file formats are not optimised for online use. They are slow to display, because the application has first to be loaded into memory. Perhaps most annoyingly, it is all too easy for multiple versions of a file to be in circulation at any one time.

There will be exceptional circumstances when the native document format must be maintained, perhaps because learners will be required to edit the documents, perhaps because the functionality of the native format is critical (you could be using Excel as the platform for a simulation), but more often than not, you will be better off using one of the other formats below.

PDF

This is the Portable Document Format as developed in 1994 by Adobe, but now an open standard. It's original purpose was to

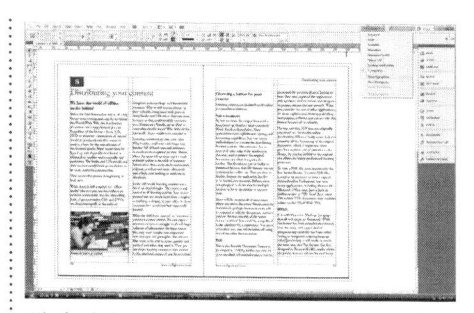

The book that you are now reading was laid out using a desktop publishing package called Adobe InDesign. It was then converted to PDF format for both printing as a paperback and viewing on-screen. Either way, the layout stays precisely constant.

get round the problem of users having to have their own copies of the applications and typefaces used by writers and designers to prepare documents and artwork. When you consider the cost of office applications, let alone sophisticated desktop publishing and graphics software, you can see why this format has proved so valuable.

Having said this, PDF was not originally conceived as a format for online distribution. Where it really scores is that it preserves all the formatting of the original document, which is important when you have applied a lot of expertise to the design. By staying faithful to the original, this allows for highly professional-looking print-outs.

To view a PDF file, users require only the free Adobe Reader. To create PDF files, it used to be necessary to own a copy of Adobe Acrobat Professional, but now many applications, including those in the Microsoft Office suite, have a built-in facility to save to PDF. As of 2011, some

DIGITAL LEARNING CONTENT

Use	When
Native documents	You want users to be able to edit the documents
	You want to preserve some unique functionality of the native format, e.g. modelling in Excel
PDF	You expect users to print the content
	You need to preserve the exact look of the original document
HTML	You want to provide the easiest possible access to your content
	You want to be able to edit the content easily
Flash	Your content is multimedia-rich
	Your content incorporates interactivity that is not easily achievable in HTML

Which format to use and when

150 million PDF documents were available online on the World Wide Web.

HTML

It is with Hypertext Mark-up Language that all web pages are formatted. While the format has been extended enormously over the years, and a great deal of programming capability has been added (using an integrated scripting language called JavaScript), it still works in much the same way that Tim Berners-Lee first designed it.

Because HTML resides within the public domain and can be used freely by anyone, it has been widely adopted as a standard on just about every computing device that can access the internet.

While HTML has many capabilities, it has not until recently had much functionality to offer in terms of animation, audio and video, a gap that has been filled largely by Adobe Flash. However, the next generation of HTML, version 5, promises to remedy these deficiencies and could eventually lead to the demise of Flash.

Flash

Flash was developed originally as an animation tool called FutureSplash Animator. It was acquired by Macromedia in 1996 and by Adobe in 2005. Flash grew in popularity as a way of providing sophisticated animation and multimedia facilities on the World Wide Web and has proved particularly popular for games, adverts and e-learning.

Flash files, or 'movies,' can be created using Adobe's own Flash Professional application, or by any number of e-learning authoring tools. The movies are then embedded into HTML pages for viewing online by any user who has the Flash plug-in installed (which is just about everyone).

While not as versatile as pure HTML for everyday internet use, Flash excels when sophisticated multimedia and interactivity

Distributing your content

are critical. This would explain why the overwhelming majority of e-learning materials are distributed in this format.

Having said that, the future of Flash is currently in question, largely because of the refusal of Apple to allow Flash on its iPhone and iPad. With a future that looks increasingly mobile, many e-learning authoring tool vendors are now shifting their focus to HTML5.

Choosing a platform for your content

Whichever format you choose for your content, you need a way to make this accessible to learners. As ever, there are plenty of options:

Use your intranet or internet web site

A relatively simple option is to make your content available directly on your web site. It's probable that your organisation uses a content management system (CMS) of some sort (such as Microsoft SharePoint) as a platform for the website, in which case you can work directly within this.

As well as inputting HTML content, you'll need to upload any additional files such as Flash movies, audio, video, PDFs and native documents and either embed these in the HTML or link to them for download. This may sound complex, but it won't take long before you know your way around the CMS.

An advantage of having your learning content on your website is that it will be easily searchable and linkable alongside all your other website content. However, while you will be able to track the number of users of your content, you will not normally be able to identify them by name, nor will you be able to record the progress they have made with your materials.

Use a learning management system (LMS)

If you need to catalogue and make available large volumes of formal learning content and to track learner scores or progress, then you are going to require some form of LMS or virtual learning environment.

These systems are compliant with e-learning standards such as SCORM, AICC or IMS, which provide important functionality, such as the ability to track learner scores and progress, describe content with metadata (descriptive labels) and specify the sequence in which learning content should be presented.

None of these features are going to work unless your authoring system is also compliant with the standards, but if you are working with a dedicated e-learning tool then this will not be an issue.

The SCORM standard was developed at the US Department of Defense's Advanced Distributed Learning Labaoratories. It has been adopted by every major authoring tool and LMS.

www.onlignment.com

91

DIGITAL LEARNING CONTENT

Use	When
Your internet or intranet web site	You want users to be able to easily search for and link to your content from within your website
	You don't want to have to set up a new platform for your content
An LMS	You want to include your content within formal courses
	You need to record learner progress and scores
A content sharing site	You want your content to act as a catalyst for peer-to-peer user interaction
	You want users to be able to upload their own content
An app store	You want your content to be specifically tailored for mobile use
	You want to provide the quickest possible access to your content

Which platform to use and when

Use a content sharing site

Another way to make your content available is by using a site specially designed to allow users to share content. This could be a public site, such as YouTube (for video) or SlideShare (for presentations), or a system offering similar functionality but sitting inside the firewall.

Content sharing sites are designed to achieve much more than delivering top-down, formal learning content: they allow users to rate, tag (label and categorise), recommend and comment on the content they view; more importantly, they allow users to upload their own content.

Clearly a content sharing site is much more informal and collaborative in nature than an LMS, but the two can work happily side-by-side; indeed a number of LMSs now include content sharing modules.

Distribute through an app store

Smart phone and tablet users can access content on any of the platforms described above through their device's own web browser. In many cases this will be adequate. However, content distributed this way is rarely formatted with the mobile user in mind and may be slow and cumbersome to access.

For regularly used content, a much more elegant solution is to create applications which can be downloaded using the device's app store and then opened with a single touch.

Given the technical differences between the various mobile devices, this may for now seem a rather complex way to distribute your content, but the process of app development will inevitably become much simpler as new tools become available.

In the meantime, some forms of content can be made available for mobile devices without being formatted as apps. Podcasts and vodcasts can be distributed via Apple's iTunes software for use on iPods and other Apple devices. Reference manuals and books can be formatted for use on e-book readers such as the Kindle or Sony Reader, or for smart phones and tablets.

Establishing copyright

Traditional copyright law allows content authors to reserve all rights. While this is still going to be appropriate in many cases, you now have the opportunity to make your content much more accessible to those who want to copy, distribute, edit, remix or build upon your work. If you are comfortable with granting some or all of these rights, you can do so using a Creative Commons license. You specify the terms on which you want to make your content available and then provide the appropriate Creative Commons license alongside your content. Doing so makes absolutely clear to learners what they can and cannot legally do. How far you go will, of course, depend entirely on your business model and your educational philosophy.

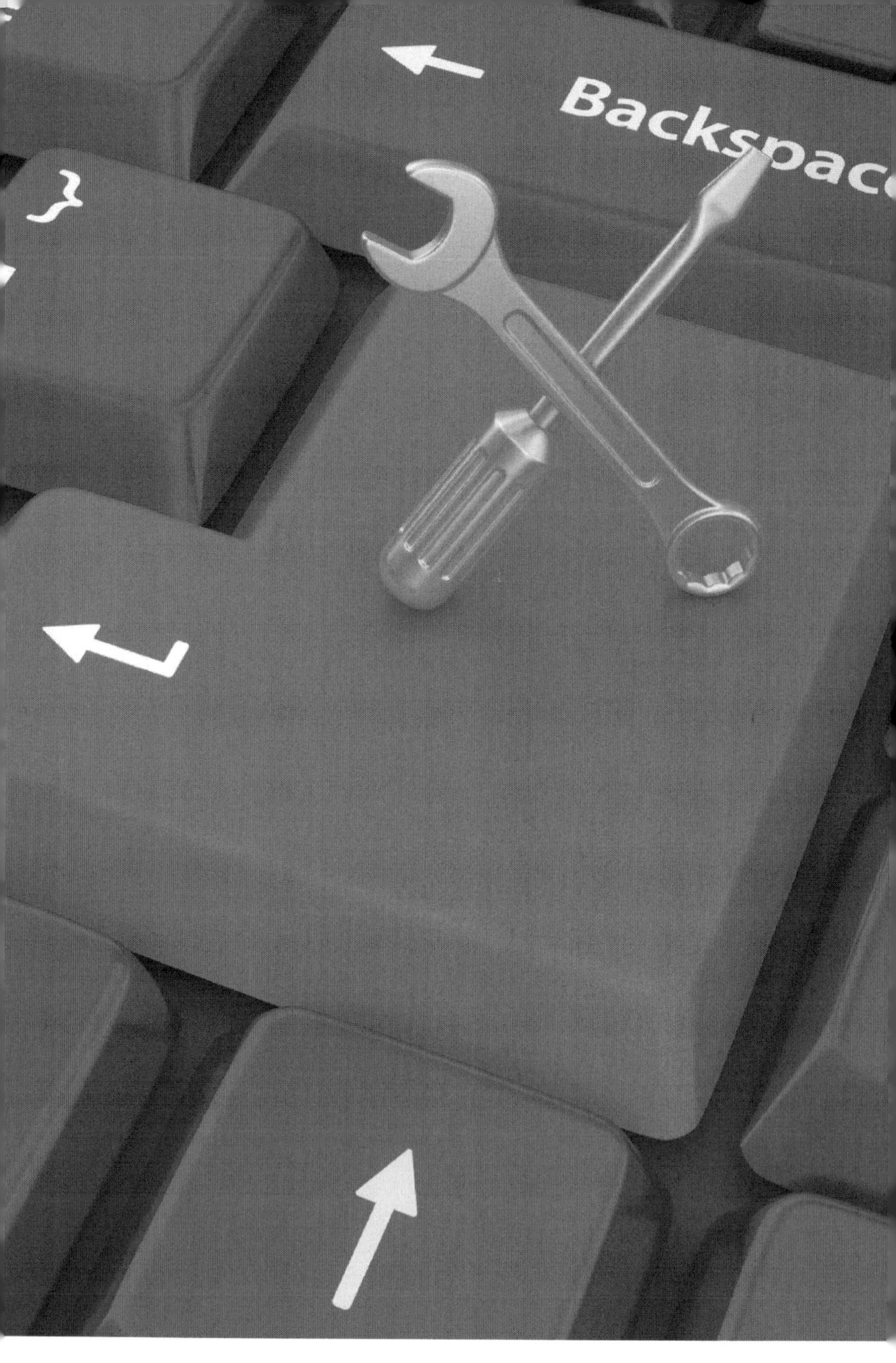
Backspace

9
Assembling your toolkit

9

Assembling your toolkit

Every content creator has the task of assembling their toolkit, the software applications they need to support them in their work. The composition of your particular toolkit will depend on the roles you are expected to play in your team. Are you primarily responsible for design, or are you expected to take your projects forward into development? Is yours a specialist role or do you find that you get involved in just about everything?

Whatever contribution you will be making, this chapter will give you an idea of the tools you'll need. What you end up with, however, may ultimately depend on your negotiations with your boss, your IT department or your bank manager!

Basic tools that everyone needs

Office suite

It's hard to imagine that you could get by very long as a content creator without a suite of office applications. The most essential element of this is going to be a Microsoft Word-compatible word processor.

Even if you do most of your own writing online or in some other application, you're almost bound to get material sent to you in Word's .doc or .docx formats. If you don't want to pay for the Microsoft suite, Mac and iPad users have the option of Apple's iWork apps, and there's also the free OpenOffice.

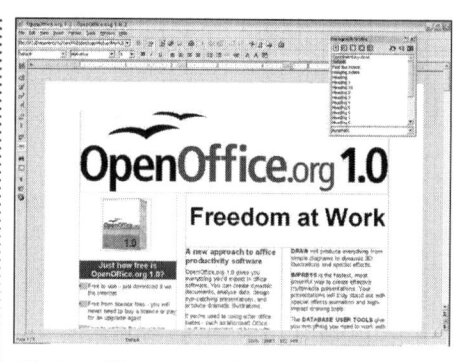

The OpenOffice suite provides compatibility with Microsoft Office but its presentation software is not as powerful as PowerPoint and won't accept add-ins such as Articulate Presenter.

If you are going to be creating slide-based material, then you must have PowerPoint. You can produce e-learning materials in PowerPoint alone, but more likely you will be using an add-in, such as Articulate Presenter, that converts your work into a more web-compatible format like Flash or, looking to the future, HTML 5.

Be careful, because these add-ins only work in PowerPoint itself, not compatible programs, and then only on Windows, not Mac.

A bonus is that, if your content development is going to centre on PowerPoint, you may not need a separate image editor. Recent versions of PowerPoint (2007 on) have fantastic imaging capabilities that may mean you'll never need to work with another program.

Asembling your toolkit

Image editing

Assuming, like most content creators, that your work will extend beyond PowerPoint, then you will definitely need some basic image processing capability. Let's start with photo editing. You must be able to crop, resize, flip and rotate, adjust exposure, white balance, tone and colour, as well as remove red-eye. A little more functionality can also come in handy, like isolating a figure from its background, correcting blemishes, creating photo montages, adding frames and shadows, and superimposing text.

There is only one professional choice for photo editing and that's Adobe Photoshop, although Adobe's much cheaper consumer offering, Photoshop Elements, has almost as much capability. If you have no serious graphic design pretensions, then almost any other photo editing tool will do everything you need. There are plenty of free tools, including Windows Live Photo Gallery and iPhoto for the Mac and iPad, as well as open source options such as Gimp.

Low-cost software like Apple's iPhoto will provide all the functionality you'll need for everyday photo editing, at a fraction of the cost of Adobe Photoshop.

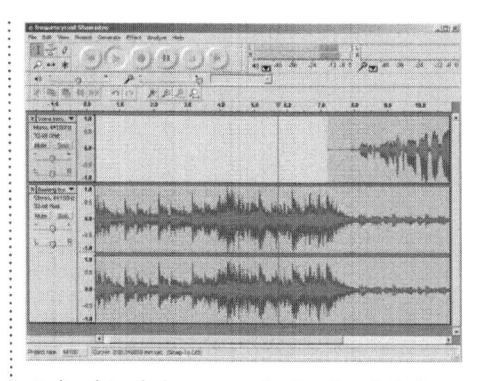

Audio editing looks more complex than it really is. In practice it's no harder than working with text.

Of course your graphical work is unlikely to be restricted to photos. Most photo imaging tools, including Photoshop, also have excellent capabilities for producing diagrams and charts, as does PowerPoint. Serious illustrators have their own specialist tool in Adobe Illustrator and web designers laying out interfaces and creating icons are likely to turn to Adobe Fireworks, but if you just need to dabble from time to time there's absolutely no need to spend any serious money.

Audio editing

It's possible that audio plays no part currently in your content plans, perhaps because you have severe bandwidth limitations, but without doubt that will change over the next few years. Audio editing might seem complex, with all those intimidating-looking waveforms to manipulate, but in practice it's no harder than working with text. You need a tool that will allow you to record audio from a microphone, edit this audio to remove bad

www.onlignment.com

DIGITAL LEARNING CONTENT

takes and hesitations, adjust and equalise the volume and then save to a variety of different file formats. Any audio editor will do this, including those built in to many authoring tools.

It is possible you'll want to go further than just capture a single voice. You may want to record from several different microphones at the same time, perhaps mix in music and sound effects, maybe even record and mix your own music. In these cases you will need a dedicated audio editor. The free option is Audacity and this is a very capable tool. Professionals and enthusiasts will undoubtedly want to go further and use a tool like Steinberg's Wavelab, Sony's Sound Forge or Adobe Audition.

E-learning authoring tools

If you're looking to develop interactive learning materials then you'll need to find an authoring tool that suits your purpose. It's important to take some care in choosing this tool or you could easily find yourself with all sorts of frustrations and a lot of wasted effort. Your tool will have to meet all of the following criteria:

It has the functionality required for you to produce the type of content you need

You might expect this to be a given, but in fact different tools tend to be geared to different types of content. While some tools, such as Adobe Captivate, Lectora and Articulate Studio, are relative all-rounders, some are more specialist. For example, Camtasia is a great tool for

Some authoring tools are aimed at specialist tasks. Caspian Learning's ThinkingWorlds, shown here, allows you to create immersive 3D simulations.

producing screencasts, Caspian Learning's Thinking Worlds lets you develop immersive, 3D learning environments, and the new Articulate Storyline is geared to the development of learning scenarios. There are many other tools to choose from, all with their particular strengths.

It works the way you want to work

Most of the tools mentioned above are desktop applications, licensed for use on individual computers and these are by far the most commonly used.

However, other tools, such as Kaplan's Atlantic Link, Rapid Intake's Unison, Edvantage's CourseBuilder and the new ZebraZapps, run online in the cloud and are geared towards a team approach to authoring. These tools are more likely to be licensed on an enterprise-wide basis, so that all members of a content development team, from project managers to designers, subject experts to graphics specialists, can work together collaboratively.

Asembling your toolkit

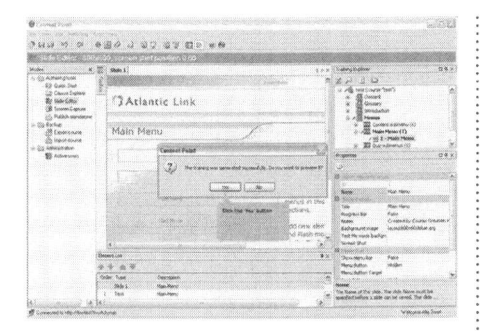

Online authoring tools, such as Atlantic Link, above, operate in the cloud, making it much easier for development teams to work together collaboratively.

With an online authoring tool, all project data is stored in a central database, accessible from any web browser on any device; components, from images to complete learning modules, can be easily shared between projects; reviews and tests can be conducted online and comments stored alongside the content for actioning by other members of the team; versions for different devices and languages can be exported from the same core material.

You can expect to see a wide range of new online authoring tools appearing in the coming years, as more and more of our computing switches to the cloud. For large teams working on building substantial content libraries, the benefits will be obvious.

It has legs

There is nothing more frustrating than having to re-develop a whole load of material because the tool you used to originally develop the content is no longer supported or available. If you go out on a limb and purchase an esoteric tool from a little-known vendor, you are taking a real risk.

That risk is even greater if you're working in the cloud. At least with a desktop tool, you can still make changes because the app and your data are sitting there on your computer; when an online tool is closed down, your work vanishes without trace.

There is no kudos to be gained by using the same tools as everyone else, but you will sleep better.

It outputs in the right formats for you

Before choosing a tool, you need to be aware of all of the devices that might be used to access your content and the formats that are supported on these devices. If your tool outputs in Flash and this is not supported on your users' PCs, or you want to deliver on iPhones and iPads, then you've got the wrong tool.

Tools that output in multiple formats, such as Rapid Intake's Unison, above, provide you with more options, particularly when you're looking to go mobile.

www.onlignment.com 99

DIGITAL LEARNING CONTENT

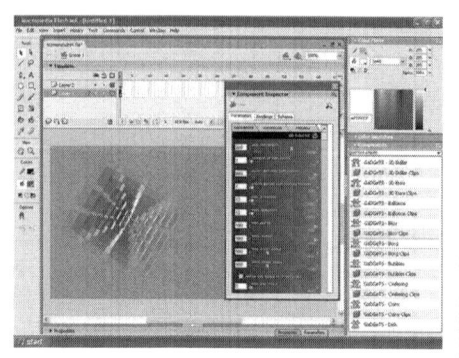

The tool of choice for serious animators is Adobe's Flash Professional.

Tools for special occasions

Creating animations

There is nothing trivial about creating animations and this is usually a job for specialists. Those who don't count themselves in this category can still produce quite decent results in PowerPoint, but this will only be of benefit if you are going to deliver your end product in PowerPoint or you are working with an authoring tool that will convert your work – including the animations – into Flash.

Specialist animators will almost certainly choose to work with Adobe's Flash Professional software, which is designed specifically for the job. As the name implies, your animations will be output as Flash 'movies', which can be imported into most e-learning authoring tools or embedded directly into web pages. You also have the option of exporting your animations as clips to use in videos, although you will have to sacrifice any opportunities for interaction.

Video editing

If video is part of your mix then, at very least, you'll need the ability to import all your video clips into a project, select the ones you want to use, trim them and place them in sequence. You may also want to add music or a voiceover, superimpose captions, and apply effects or transitions.

Luckily, all of this can be accomplished quite easily with low-cost or free tools such as Windows Live Movie Maker, Adobe Premiere Elements or Apple's iMovie. Serious users will opt for one of Adobe Premiere Pro, Avid Xpres Pro or Apple's Final Cut Pro.

Like audio, video is surprisingly easy to work with and it should not take more than an hour or two to become familiar with all the most common operations.

Desktop publishing

Desktop publishing tools are normally used to lay out high-quality print publications such as brochures, newspapers, magazines, books and reports, but these days you'll probably want to make this content

You can even carry out simple video edits on a smart phone as seen here by Apple's iMovie app.

www.onlignment.com

available online as well as in print, almost certainly in PDF format.

If so, although you can get by with standard word processing tools, you will almost always get much more professional-looking results with a specialist desktop publishing package, such as Adobe InDesign, Quark Express or Microsoft Publisher. Where these score over normal word processing packages is the compete flexibility you have over how you lay out text and graphics on each page. Look at a typical magazine and compare it with a typical Word document and you'll soon see the difference.

Getting started

We could go on. There are tools for creating cartoon books and others for building 3D models; there are tools for developing games and yet more for capturing screens from software packages.

Some tools you will use every day, some perhaps just once. But to get started there's no way you're going to need them all. So, start by kitting yourself out with the basics and then add to your collection over time, as you find opportunities opening up and your skills and creativity beginning to develop.

10
Creating learning podcasts

10
Creating learning podcasts

The simplest way to look upon a podcast is as an audio recording. Strictly speaking, podcasting is a more sophisticated concept than this, which involves a user subscribing to an on-going series of recordings, which are then automatically downloaded to the user's computer as they are released, and then copied to the user's iPod or similar MP3 player for listening to as and when the user wishes. In practice, once you have produced a learning podcast, you don't really mind how it is accessed.

You can listen to a podcast as well from a laptop as you can from an iPod

Yes, lots of users will find it convenient to listen to the recordings on their iPods while they commute to work, walk in the park or workout in the gym, but they might find it just as useful to listen to the podcasts directly from their PC or even from an audio CD.

Media elements

A podcast can employ only one media element and that's audio. Although, in general use, podcasts will often contain music, for learning purposes the primary component will usually be speech.

As an alternative verbal channel to text, speech benefits because it conveys tone of voice as well as words, but the listener is not able to control the pace at which the words are delivered. Delivery of the spoken word is much slower than the speed at which a person can read, which makes a podcast an unsuitable tool for reference information.

Although audio does have limitations as a stand-alone medium, it allows the listener to maintain visual attention on the environment around them, which they would certainly need if they were on the move.

The fact that a podcast is an audio-only medium leaves the eyes free to concentrate on other things

Interactive capability

A podcast is a passive medium with no interactive capability except simple navigation. As such, its use is limited to the following learning strategies:

www.onlignment.com

Creating learning podcasts

- *Exposition* – required listening as part of a set curriculum
- *Exploration* – as developmental material for use by learners at their own discretion

Podcasts could also act as supporting material within other strategies – *instruction* and *guided discovery* – but only as one element in a blend.

The power of audio can be easily demonstrated by the enduring success of radio

Applications

While limited in terms of media elements and interactive capability, podcasts have a great many applications. You should be encouraged by the success of radio over more than eighty years. Radio has the same limitations – audio only, no interaction – yet continues to entertain and inform hundreds of millions of people daily.

While it is easy to think of podcasts as a way of delivering monologues – such as lectures – you will rarely find this technique in use on the radio. The best applications employ multiple voices and a lively, informal style. Consider using podcasts for interviews, panel discussions, debates and drama. Wrap these up in familiar radio formats such as news shows, plays, talk shows, reports from the field, journalistic investigations and so on.

Pre-production

A podcast needs a plan. Even if you are intending just to thrust a microphone in front of an unsuspecting interviewee, you need to know what questions you are going to ask and who would be best equipped to answer them. As mentioned previously, radio is an excellent model here. The presenter of the programme would have researched the topic, got to know a little about their guests and prepared their questions. They would be mindful of how long each segment of the programme was intended to last.

Scripting: As a general rule, a script is only needed for a monologue and monologues should only be used in moderation. Listeners tune out when the

Listeners will tune out if the same voice goes on for too long

www.onlignment.com

same voice goes on for too long, however interesting the speaker. On radio, it would be extremely rare to hold on a single voice for more than a few minutes. But if a monologue really is required, think first about whether a script is absolutely essential.

Professional voiceover artists are very good at reading a script so it doesn't sound like they're reading a script. By and large, the rest of us aren't. If you're going to be doing the voice as well as preparing the script and you feel confident enough to work directly from your outline, then go for it. An alternative is to do a trial recording with you improvising from the outline, then convert this to a full script, ironing out the less successful elements. That way, you'll end up with a tight script that sounds natural.

A professional voiceover artist can make reading from a script sound natural

When scripting, it's hard to avoid slipping into report writing mode. Keep reminding yourself that the words you are writing will be read aloud, not from the screen. Try speaking the words yourself and keep revising until you can put them across effortlessly.

Whatever you do, avoid what Cathy Moore calls 'corporate drone'. Write as you would speak. That means short sentences, simple language, active voice ("The cat ate the mouse" not "The mouse was eaten by the cat") and contractions ("I can't remember …" not "I cannot remember …"). You can also help yourself by making absolutely clear, perhaps in bold type, which words need special emphasis.

Production

Professional recording: When it comes to recording your podcast, nothing beats a recording studio. Here you will be able to record in perfect conditions, in a specially-prepared room without excessive reverberations or extraneous noise, with an engineer who handles all the technical stuff allowing you to concentrate on communicating, and with the right microphones and editing equipment to ensure a perfect recording.

So, if you can, choose this option first. Studios are nowhere near as expensive as you might think and there are lots of them around. If you prepare well, so you can get on with the recording without delay, you probably only need to book for one or two hours.

Creating learning podcasts

You can't beat a professional recording studio for quality

You can use a single hand-held mic to record interviews

At the end of the session, have the engineer provide you with all the digital files in their highest quality format, i.e. as they were recorded, ideally with all the obvious mistakes and pauses edited out. If you do ask the engineer to convert the files into their final, compressed format, then make sure you are also provided with copies of the originals, so you can easily make changes in the future.

Doing-it-yourself: Of course it will not always be possible to use a professional recording studio, either because of budget or because you haven't got time to get it all organised. If you're going to do the recording yourself, then with a little care you can still obtain excellent results.

Working with one microphone is always going to be easier. Of course if you're recording a monologue, then one mic is all you will need, but even with an interview you can still manage:

- You can direct the mic at the interviewee to record all the answers to the questions, then record your questions on your own again later. This will mean that you have to edit the questions in, which will require some cutting and pasting.

- You can use a hand-held mic and direct it at whoever's speaking at the time. This will work fine as long as you don't talk across each other.

Although almost any microphone will deliver reasonable results when recording speech, it pays to use a decent one. Assuming you don't want to hand hold the mic and you're recording directly to a computer, then you should look at a USB condenser mic. There are now lots available and you shouldn't have to pay over $100.

A USB condenser mic

www.onlignment.com

Portable soundproofing and pop shield

If you record with multiple mics, you'll need a mixer

It helps to add a pop shield, an inexpensive accessory that stops the signal level exploding whenever the letter 'p' is spoken (and yes, this does make a real difference). If you want to get recording studio quality, you might also purchase portable soundproofing materials for deadening the sound.

However good the microphone, you need to ensure a good quality signal. That means positioning the mic 4 or 5 inches away from whoever is speaking and setting the input level on your computer or recording device as high as you can without suffering 'clipping' (digital overload) when someone speaks loudly.

Multiple mics: If you are running a panel discussion or want to conduct an interview without worrying about who's got the mic and when, then you'll need more than one mic. That makes things a little more complicated, because you'll then need some sort of 'mixer' to sit between the mics and the computer or recording device. The mixer allows you to plug in multiple mics, balance the volumes, position the various inputs in the stereo mix and provide a single, combined signal for recording. If all this is too much for you, you probably are better off using a professional facility.

Post-production

It could be that, when you listen to your podcast recording, it sounds great and you're happy to release it as is. Perhaps you recorded it in a studio and the engineer has supplied you with a perfect master. Even if not, sometimes a 'rough and ready' approach is all that's required and the priority is to get your podcast out as quickly as possible. However, a little care in editing could make your recording sound very much more professional, so it's probably worth getting to know what is possible.

First priority is to delete unwanted 'takes', cut out any silences and remove any obvious mistakes. To do this, you'll need

Creating learning podcasts

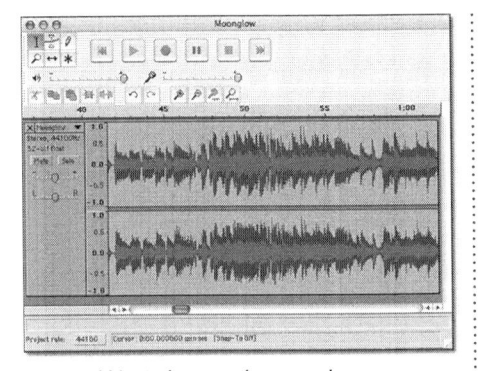

Use a tool like Audacity to edit your audio

some audio editing software. If you have access to professional quality software and know how to use it then great, but you'll only need basic functionality and a simple editor like the free Audacity is all that you really require. Audio edits are achieved using simple cut, copy and paste functions, just like word processing, except here you'll be editing an audio waveform rather than blocks of text. This is easier than it might sound, because the waveform indicates quite clearly where in the recording there is speech and where there is silence. If you're finding it hard to locate exactly the point in the recording that you wish to edit, you can easily zoom in and enlarge the waveform.

You might like to consider including a short piece of music at the beginning and end of your podcast, just like you'd hear on a radio programme. If it's not your own music, then you'll either need to pay a royalty or use a clip from one of the royalty-free audio sites.

If the audio volume levels in your recording vary too widely, you can either select the offending pieces and raise or lower the volumes, or apply a 'compression' effect. Compression automatically reduces peaks and boosts low signals, so there is less difference between the loudest and softest parts.

If your podcast is lengthy, i.e. more than ten minutes, you might consider chopping it up at this point into a number of shorter 'episodes'. This will obviously involve you in some more file manipulation, but it will also reduce the size of each podcast file, thus speeding up download, as well as making it easier for listeners to access the content that they are most interested in.

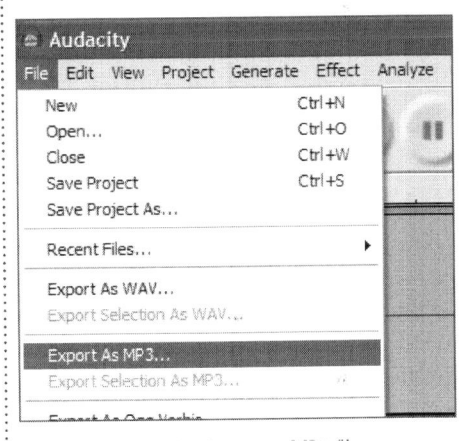

Export your finished podcast as an MP3 file

When you are completely happy with your recording, your next step is to convert your file to MP3 format for distribution. Assuming the main content of your file is the spoken word, you can safely export to MP3 at 64Kbps / 44.1Khz / mono. Don't worry if you don't understand these technicalities – you just need to choose

www.onlignment.com 109

DIGITAL LEARNING CONTENT

the right option from the list! If you're unhappy with the quality, try upping the bit rate to 128Kbps. You might want to use the stereo option if your podcast contains an interview or panel discussion, but only if you recorded it in stereo!

Distribution

So, your podcast is ready. Now all you need to do is make it as easy as possible for people to listen to it. You have plenty of options:

- Send it round as an email attachment.
- Attach it to a forum or blog posting.
- Upload it to your learning management system or virtual learning environment.
- Make it available on your web site or intranet.

Listeners could themselves, if they wish, import your podcast into iTunes and allow the software to copy the file over to their iPod for listening on the move. This involves you in no work, but is not the friendliest option, particularly if you are going to be releasing a series of podcasts. Much better to set up your podcasts so users can subscribe to the whole series. That way, each time you release a new podcast, iTunes will automatically

Your podcasts can be listed in the iTunes Podcast Directory

Creating learning podcasts

download it and copy it to the user's iPod at the next available opportunity. For this to work, your podcast needs to be made available with an RSS (Really Simple Syndication) feed. All blog posts work with RSS, so this is one way of setting up the feed – simply set up a new blog and attach each new podcast to a new post.

Alternatively, use one of the many available podcast hosting services. Make sure you label your RSS feed with an appropriate title, author name and description – for more details, see Apple's own guide to Making a Podcast.

Happy podcasting!

11

Creating learning slideshows

11
Creating learning slideshows

In a learning context, slides have traditionally been used as 'speaker support' – visual aids to support live presentations. However, slide shows produced using Microsoft's PowerPoint or Apple's Keynote also provide a useful way to deliver packaged content for self-directed learning. This chapter explores the potential for packaged slide shows as a learning tool and describes the many ways in which these can be developed and deployed.

Media elements

A slide show can incorporate all major media elements. Although the dominant forms are always likely to be still images and text, presentation software also makes it possible to animate the text and images on slides, as well as to import audio and video.

Interactive capability

As we shall see, there are many ways of distributing slide shows. Many of these are essentially passive – you watch the slide show as you would a video. Although some formats – including native PowerPoint – have the potential for quite sophisticated interactivity, this is not the normal use of packaged slide shows and we will not be examining this feature in any detail in this chapter.

As passive media, the use of packaged slide shows is largely limited to the following learning strategies:

Slides have traditionally been used primarily for speaker support

- *Exposition* – required viewing as part of a set curriculum

- *Exploration* – as developmental material for use by learners at their own discretion

Slide shows could also act as supporting material within other strategies – *instruction* and *guided discovery* – but only as one element in a blend.

Applications

While limited in terms of interactive capability, slide shows have a great many applications. Even without narration, they can provide a visually-dynamic and engaging way to present relatively small chunks of learning content. Where they are less suitable is in presenting large bodies of text. Text is much more satisfactorily handled on a web page or in a PDF, both of which more easily allow the reader to search and scan.

Creating learning slideshows

What your slides must achieve

If your slide show is going to be packaged with an audio narration, then your slides have very much the same function as they would do in a live presentation – they convey the visual element, while a voice delivers the words. In this context, slides are visual aids.

With photographs, illustrations, diagrams and charts, they capture the viewer's attention, clarify meaning and improve retention. With the sparing use of on-screen text, they can also help to reinforce key elements of the verbal content, but the prime purpose is always visual.

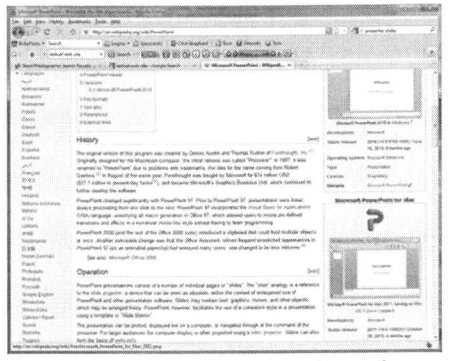

If you want to present lots of text, you're better off using a web page

When combined with an audio narration, slide shows take on many of the characteristics of video, allowing the learner to maintain visual focus on a sequence of images while these are explained in audio. Obviously if the intention is to depict actual events, in full motion, slides will not do as well as material captured with a video camera.

Without narration, your slides have to accomplish both roles – the visual and the verbal. In this respect they need a very different design focus to a live presentation.

	Animation?	*Interactivity?*	*Narration?*	*Easy distribution?*
Native PowerPoint/ Keynote	Yes	Yes	Yes	Yes if users have the application used to create the presentation
PDF	No	No	No	Yes
Flash (using tools such as Articulate and Adobe Presenter)	Yes	Yes	Yes	Must be uploaded to an LMS/web server
Video	Yes	No	Yes	Yes but large files
SlideShare	No	No	Only with special Slidecasting facility	Yes if users have internet access. You can embed the presentations in blogs and web pages

You have a wide range of distribution formats to choose from, each with its own distinct capabilities

www.onlignment.com   115

DIGITAL LEARNING CONTENT

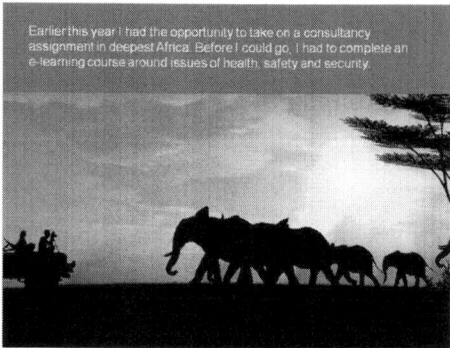

When there is no narration, the slide must be amended to include the verbal information

Take the example above of a slide taken from a live presentation that was converted to stand alone, without narration, on slideshare.net. A section of the slide has been allocated to a running textual commentary, essentially a much simplified version of the original presenter's words.

Not that this is the only way of displaying the verbal content. If, rather than converting a live presentation, you were designing a stand-alone and un-narrated slide show from scratch, you could use all sorts of devices to display the words, like the speech bubbles used in this example:

There are many ways to incorporate the narrative into the slides

Another consideration is the distance from which your slides will be viewed. In a live presentation, your audience is likely to be some way from the screen, whereas when the slides are used for self-study, they will be up close. Whether this matters depends on the device the audience will be using to view the presentation (this could be anything from a smart phone to a large PC monitor) and the size of the window in which your presentation will be displayed. You may be able to get away with displaying more detail than you would when live, but this needs testing.

An argument for imagery

Only an expert wordsmith can conjure up with words what a person, object or event actually looks like. Only an expert teacher can explain a concept or process clearly using words alone. And only a wonderful presenter can make a lasting impact on an audience without the use of imagery. As the saying goes, "a picture is worth ten thousand words". Pictures show, quite effortlessly, what things really look like.

116   www.onlignment.com

Creating learning slideshows

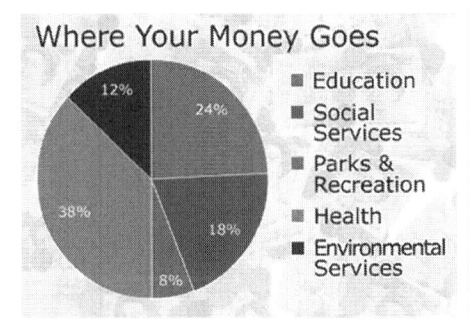

Charts clarify numeric data that might otherwise be indigestible

They clarify concepts and processes. They stick in the memory. All you have to do is use them.

Pictures come in a variety of forms to suit different situations. Photos portray what things look like; diagrams clarify concepts and processes; illustrations make the abstract more memorable. Software such as PowerPoint makes it easy to employ pictures in all these forms. Your task is to avoid the lazy option – clip art – and to find the picture that really does tell a story.

Break the mould

It's all too simple to use the standard templates provided by your presentation software, but these won't always do justice to your images. Take the examples below:

The title doesn't have to be centred at the top of the screen – it can be positioned to complement the image

Again, with a little care you can break the mould. Here the image has been tinted blue.

www.onlignment.com

DIGITAL LEARNING CONTENT

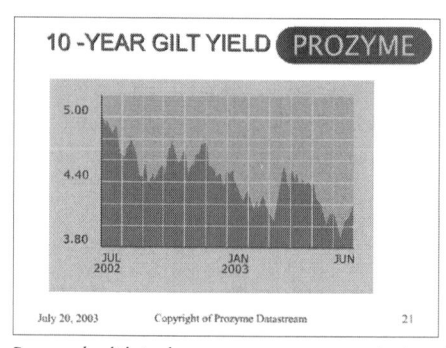

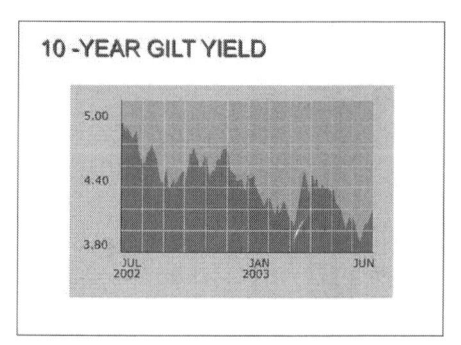

Remove the slide junk – your corporate communications department doesn't always know best

You can definitely do without the slide junk – the logos, headers and footers that appear on every slide. There's a place for your logo and that's on the title slide (OK and maybe at the end as well). And you don't really need all that clutter at the bottom of each slide – you're producing slides, remember, not a report.

Text is also OK in moderation

You've probably heard of the expression "death by PowerPoint". You've probably experienced it.

Well, by far the biggest complaint you will hear from presentation audiences is that the slides contain too much text. In his book *The Great Presentation Scandal*, John Townsend relates how he counted the number of words and figures on every slide at a conference he was attending. The overall average was 76. That's right, 76.

Given this, you may find it surprising that we could be recommending the use of text as a visual aid when the real problem is that there's far too much of it. This is a fair point, but text can be useful as a visual aid,

Admit it, you've been there ...

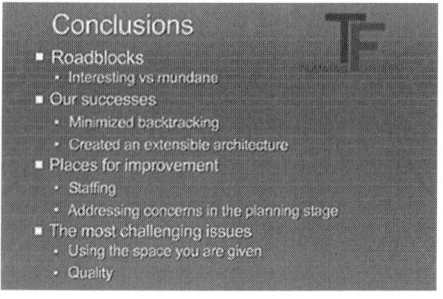

If you've got two levels of bullets then you've no longer got a visual aid

when you need to highlight the start of a new section, emphasise a key point, list a number of related points or present data in the form of a table.

If you do keep the amount of text on your slides to a minimum, it will have that much more impact when it does appear; particularly if you know when to use it and how to lay it out like the professionals. If you obey a few simple guidelines, that's what you will achieve.

Use your slides to tell a story

A presentation is much more than a collection of independent thoughts accompanied by visual aids – however interesting the thoughts and however brilliant the visuals. Just like a novel, a radio play or a film, it has a beginning, an end and a carefully planned route in between.

Too many presentations look like they have been constructed by simply extracting slides from previous presentations. Although re-using slides is fine, if they are appropriate to the task in hand, this is never going to be enough to do the job. Like a film director, you have to look at the big picture, using words and images to manipulate your audience's attention and their emotions. There is no black art to this; you just need a little imagination and a simple structure.

Packaging up a live presentation

The way you approach the narration will depend on whether you are (1) packaging up a presentation that you have previously delivered live, or (2) creating a stand-alone slide show from scratch. In the case of the former, the presentation will most likely represent you and your perspective on the topic in hand – you will want to record the voiceover yourself and retain as much of the personality of the original presentation as possible. That means keeping it natural and informal. Assuming you didn't read from a script when you presented live (and let's hope that's the case), then you won't want to read from a script now. Try to capture the buzz of the live presentation by imagining you are presenting to a live audience. Or why not record it live? You can always edit it down afterwards to remove any superfluous elements.

Designing specifically for stand-alone use

On the other hand, you may be designing a slide show that will only ever be used as a piece of learning content. It is not intended as a personal statement and it won't be

If you are packaging up a presentation you delivered live, you'll want to retain its personality

attributed to you. In this case you are almost definitely best off writing a script and you should seriously consider using a professional voiceover artist to deliver this. Why? Because professional voiceover artists are very good at reading a script so it doesn't sound like they're reading a script. As we've mentioned before, the rest of us aren't.

Script for speaking

Few of us have experience of writing a narration script. Most, if not all, of the writing we do is for documents that will be printed or displayed as text on a screen. There is a difference. Try reading out your script and you'll soon find out whether it works or not. If you can't speak it effortlessly, you've got more editing to do.

Use a conversational tone

The secret is to write your script using the same style and language that you would use in ordinary conversation and certainly

Remember your script will be read aloud, not as a report

nothing like a business report or brochure. Use short sentences, simple language and wherever possible the active voice. You will help the narrator if you also mark up your script to make clear which words require particular emphasis.

Don't duplicate your voiceover as on-screen text

Your learner's brain can cope with one verbal channel (in this case the voiceover) but not two. If words are coming at you from two places at once, you'll just overload. If absolutely necessary, emphasise key points and headings with on-screen text, but please don't display your whole script verbatim.

Let's move on to explore what's involved in getting your slide show out there in front of as many eyeballs as possible.

Keeping it simple

Your first option is to send round your presentation in its native PowerPoint format or to make this available for download. This will work as long as everyone who is likely to want to view the slides has their own copy of PowerPoint and are able to view the slides in the format in which you have saved them (for example, to view presentations saved in the pptx format, viewers must have PowerPoint 2007 or later).

Presentations saved in native PowerPoint format will be bulky but they can still be edited by the recipient (if you regard this as an advantage).

Creating learning slideshows

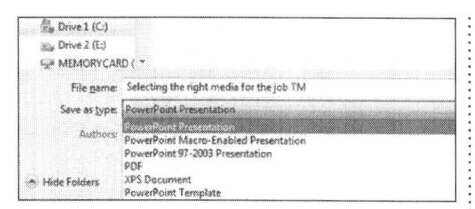

PowerPoint allows you to save in a number of backwards-compatible formats but also as PDF files

This presentation has been converted to Flash for delivery online

A simple alternative is to save your slides directly from PowerPoint into PDF format. This reduces compatibility problems as most people have a PDF reader. It will also reduce file size. However, the files will no longer be editable.

Converting to Flash

You can achieve a more polished and web-friendly result using one of a number of tools that will convert your presentation into Flash format, along with a host of useful additional features. Perhaps the best-known of these tools are Articulate Presenter and Adobe Presenter. Both work similarly in that they sit within PowerPoint itself as an add-in, with their own ribbons or drop-down menus (depending on the version of PowerPoint).

Using these tools you can add narration, organise your slides into sections and sub-sections, insert additional media such as Flash animations and videos, and then publish into Flash for upload to your intranet, learning management system or other web site. Actually these tools can do a lot more in terms of adding interactivity, but that goes beyond the scope of this chapter.

Exporting to video

If you just want your slides to be viewed in a linear fashion, from start to finish, and you are prepared to add an audio narration, then you should seriously consider distributing in video format.

One attraction is the ease with which you can upload video to sites such as YouTube. Another is the fact that nearly all mobile

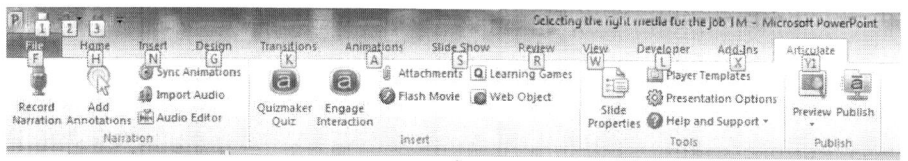

The functions of Articulate Presenter are available as a ribbon in PowerPoint 2007 and 2010

www.onlignment.com

121

DIGITAL LEARNING CONTENT

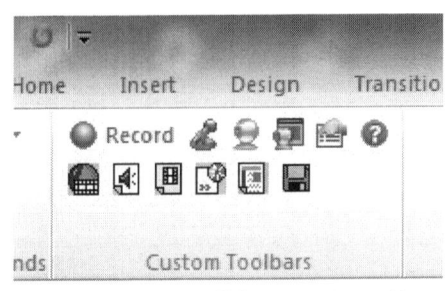

Camtasia can also be installed as a PowerPoint add-in, allowing you to access the Camtasia controls direct from the ribbon

devices will support video, whereas Flash can be a problem, particularly on Apple hardware.

You need a tool which will capture your slides, allow you to add narration and then publish to a suitable video format. If you are happy to go with the Windows Media Video (WMV) format, then you can do this directly from the latest version of PowerPoint. If you want a bigger choice of formats and more editing flexibility, try using a tool like Camtasia.

Once you have captured your slides (including any embedded animations and videos), the Camtasia Studio software allows you to make edits and export to a wide range of video formats.

Camtasia Studio

www.onlignment.com

Publish on SlideShare.net

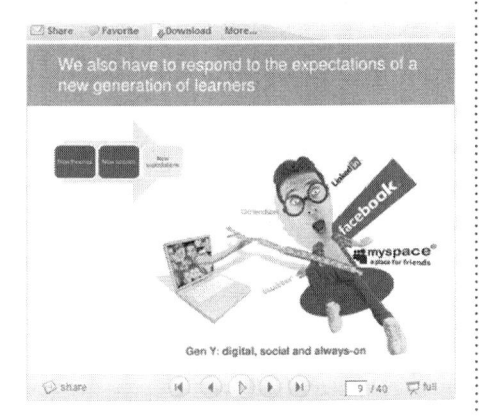

Another option to consider, if you want your presentations to have the widest possible online presence, is to publish to a site like SlideShare.net. What YouTube is to videos and Flickr is to photos, SlideShare is to presentations.

The process is really simple. You set up an account and then upload your PowerPoint or Keynote slides, which are then automatically converted into SlideShare's Flash-based format. Users can view and comment on the slides on the SlideShare site or you can embed the slides in a web page, blog or forum posting.

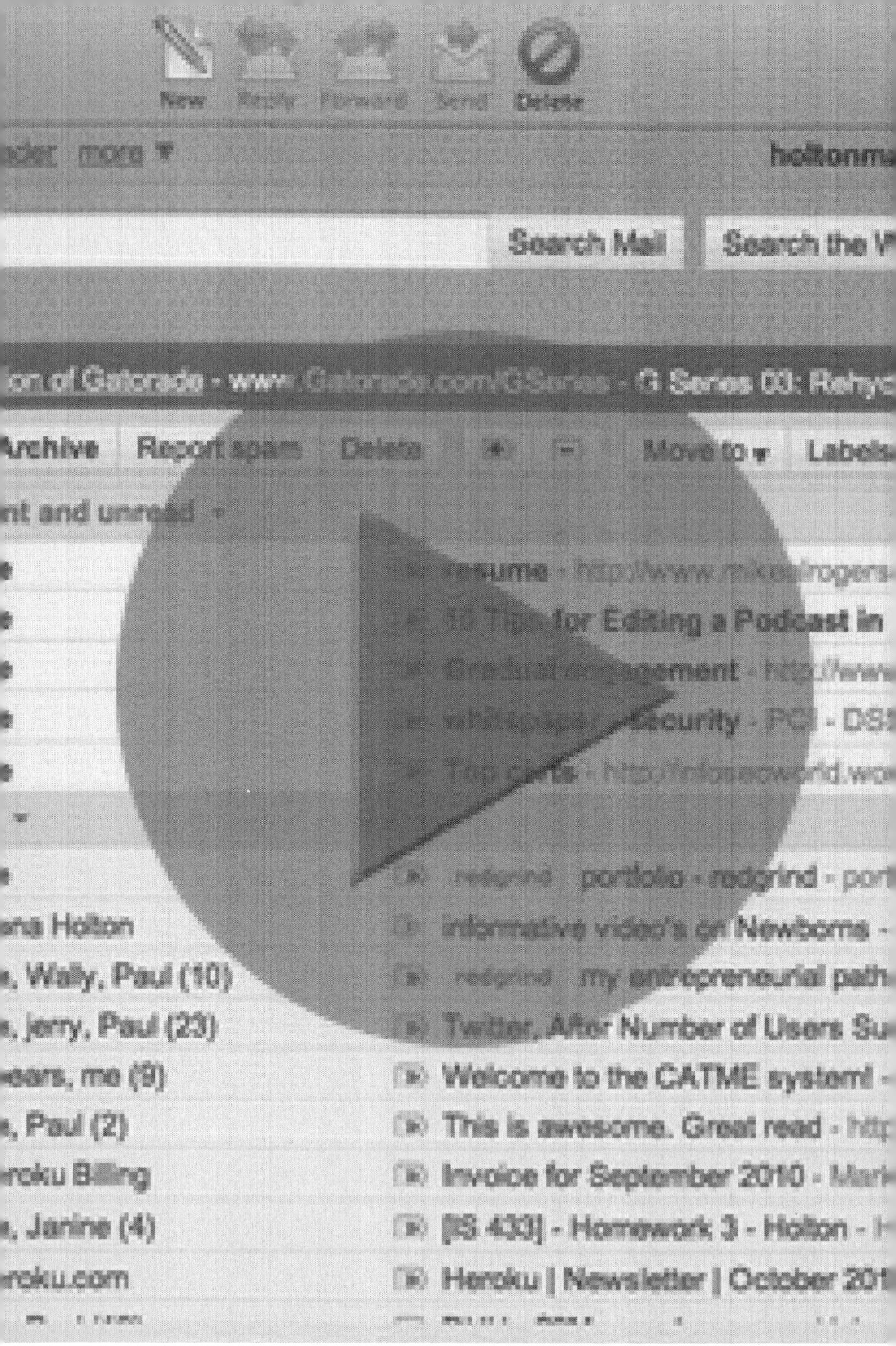
New
Delete
more ▾
Search Mail
Archive
Report spam
Move to ▾
resume
10 Tips for Editing a Podcast in
portfolio
informative video's on Newborns
Wally, Paul (10)
jerry, Paul (23)
Twitter, After Number of Users
Welcome to the CATME system!
Paul (2)
This is awesome. Great read
Invoice for September 2010
Janine (4)
[IS 403] - Homework 3 - Holton
Heroku | Newsletter | October

12
Creating learning screencasts

12

Creating learning screencasts

A screencast is a demonstration of a task carried out in a software application or on a web site for use as a learning aid or for reference.

To create a screencast, you simply carry out all the operations involved in completing the task and the software records this as an animation. This animation can be annotated with text labels, accompanied by an audio narration or both.

Some authoring tools allow you to go beyond offering simple demonstrations, to provide the learner with opportunities to try out the tasks for themselves using a simulation of the original software.

In this chapter, we explore the potential for screencasting, describe the different types of tools available and provide some tips on how to make a good job of your own screencasts.

Media elements

A screencast contains one essential visual element – an animated software demonstration – supplemented by a verbal explanation, presented either as a series of pop-up text labels, an audio narration or as a combination of the two.

Typically screencasts are presented as short, self-contained modules or in short sections, to make it easy for the learner to access the material in small chunks and often to practise as they go.

Interactive capability

Many screencasts are passive, presented as short videos which the learner can review quickly and then try out for real. Others incorporate simulations of software tasks which allow the learner to practise without having to leave the screencast and use the real application.

In their passive form, the most likely strategy for the use of screencasts is *exploration*, as material for use by learners at their own discretion, typically for reference.

When you incorporate simulated tasks into a screencast or when you combine a screencast with other activities that allow the learner to practise what they have learned, the screencast can also play a key role in an *instructional* strategy.

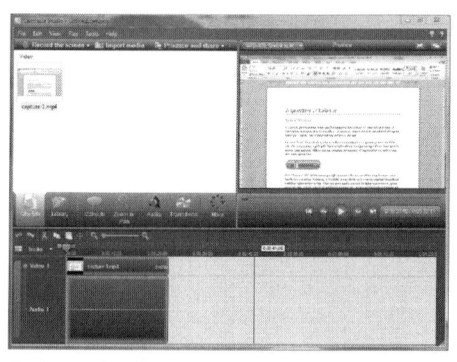

Desktop tools such as Camtasia provide much of the functionality of a video editor and an elearning authoring tool

Applications

Screencasts have two very obvious applications: they can be used as part of a formal training programme to introduce a new or revised software application or web site, or as reference material for people who are already users.

Screencasting tools

Some screencasting tools have been around for many years, long before the term 'screencasting' had been coined. These tools, like Techsmith Camtasia and Adobe Captivate, are desktop applications with sophisticated functionality. Over the years, their capabilities have been increased to support many forms of digital learning content, not just screencasts. These tools allow many ways for the learner to interact with the screencast and to undertake assessments. They also allow the author much greater control over the way in which the screencast is displayed.

Simple online tools such as screenr allow you to produce screencasts in one take

Other, much more recent tools, such as screenr and screenjelly, operate 'in the cloud'. They allow you to create simple software demonstrations 'all in one take' and then publish these online.

Let's start by taking a closer look at the online tools.

Choose an online tool

There are plenty of free online screencasting tools – you'll find them listed in Jane Hart's Directory of Learning Tools. To get your search started, you could do worse than take a look at screenr, screenjelly and screencast-o-matic.

Why use an online tool?

Here are some arguments for going the online route:

- If they're not free, then they're certainly inexpensive.
- You don't have to download an install yet another desktop application.
- They come with all sorts of nifty connections to other online tools, particularly social media.
- The tools come with very basic functionality, so you'll be up-and-running in minutes and won't spend ages tinkering.

As you probably guessed, there are some drawbacks:

- There may be security issues having

DIGITAL LEARNING CONTENT

your organisation's applications and sites shared online.

- You need good internet connectivity.
- Because you only get the one take and can't edit your work or add extra functionality, you may not be able to achieve all you want.
- If the vendor goes bust, bang goes your content (assuming you haven't downloaded copies).

Choose your topic

All-in-one-take screencasts make great resources for just-in-time use or as elements in a blended offering. They need to be short (under 5 minutes) and highly practical. Don't just work through all the functions in your application or on your site, regardless of whether anyone's interested – describe how to do something really useful and not obvious. Everyone loves practical tools and tips.

Prepare

You'll want to think through carefully what you want to show and how. If necessary,

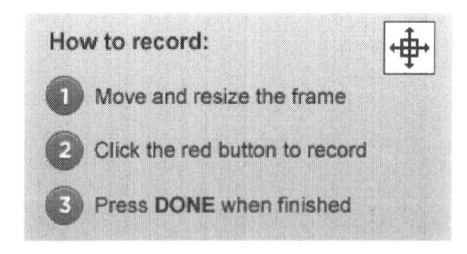

The instructions for screenr won't take long to read!

The screenr toolbar is typical of all these tools. You can set the capture dimensions, choose your mic and then start, pause and stop the recording.

practise a few times until you feel confident that you can perform the task fluently. In most cases best advice would be not to script – the best screencasts are simple and conversational in tone. If you really must script, then edit the words carefully to make sure they sound completely natural.

Setting up

Typically you will be asked to select the area of the screen that you want to capture or to pick one of a range of standard sizes. Remember that the screencast is likely to be viewed at less than the original size, perhaps much less if on a smart phone, so focus in on what's really relevant. A few tests should help you to find the most appropriate arrangement.

If you have more than one microphone on your system, then you'll have to specify which one you want to use. As with all audio, quality does count – if you have a quality mic (ideally with a pop shield) then use it. If not, use what you have, but try to ensure there's not a lot of background noise.

Record

First, briefly introduce yourself and explain what it is you will be showing and why viewers will find this useful. Then commence your live performance (no

Creating learning screencasts

Screenr allows you to share your screencast in a number of ways or download to use locally

pressure then), pausing where necessary. If you make minor stumbles, don't stop, because chances are no-one will notice or care. Obviously if you make a complete hash, there's no problem in starting again.

Sharing

Depending on the tool, you're likely to have plenty of ways to share your screencast:

- Provide a link in an email, tweet, blog post or forum post or on your intranet, web site or LMS. The user will be taken to the vendor's website to see the screencast.

- Alternatively play the screencast directly in a web or forum posting or on a web page by embedding the HTML code supplied by the vendor.

- Download the screencast as a video. You can then upload it to your website, intranet or LMS, or send it out as an email attachment.

- Publish the video on YouTube.

Choosing a desktop tool

Desktop screencasting tools have been around for well over a decade. Over time, two tools have emerged as clear front-runners – Adobe Captivate and Techsmith Camtasia. However, other tools can definitely do the job, including the free Wink.

There are also much higher-end performance support tools as well as applications designed specifically to support screencasting for ERM systems such as SAP and Siebel.

What you can do with these tools

Desktop tools will give you much greater functionality than online tools. Whether you need this functionality or not only you can decide. For example, Camtasia will allow you to:

- Record a webcam stream alongside the screencast. This feature requires some care, because it could just create visual noise.

- Edit your screencast just like a video.

- Record narration quite separately from the recording of the software demo.

www.onlignment.com

DIGITAL LEARNING CONTENT

Camtasia allows you to output to a wide range of formats, especially video

- Not use an audio narration at all, focusing instead on the use of text labels and highlights.
- Share your output in a wide variety of ways including CD-ROM, a YouTube-ready format, or as an MP4 video for Apple mobile devices.

Although you can add interactivity to Camtasia screencasts, including quizzes, the product is heavily orientated towards video as an output. In this respect, it differs quite noticeably from Captivate which, as well as allowing you to add narration, labels, highlights or any combination

of these, also permits you to achieve the following:

- Have the learner interact with the simulated application (in Training Mode) rather than just watch and listen to your presentation (Demo Mode).
- Assess how well the learner can carry out a software task on their own, without prompts (Assessment Mode).
- Output to Flash (with SCORM wrappers if you're deploying on an LMS).
- Output to F4V (Flash video), or as a handout in Word/PDF format (any of which will lose you your interactivity).

And, of course, Captivate is much more than a screencasting tool. It has all the functionality needed for creating general-purpose e-learning modules.

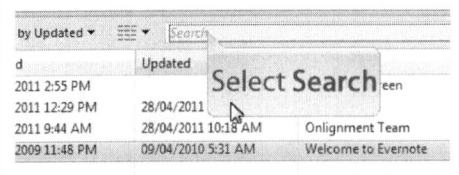

Captivate can generate captions automatically, although these can always be edited later

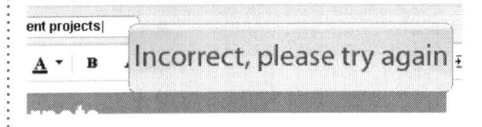

Captivate also allows you to provide the user with feedback based on their interactions with the simulated software

130   www.onlignment.com

Start with a plan

However impulsive you may be, it will save time in the long run to think through carefully what you are trying to achieve from your screencast:

- If your screencast is going to be used for reference, then a demo is probably all you need ("show me").
- If you're looking to build competence, then have the user interact with the simulated software ("try me").
- If you need to measure competence, then build in an assessment ("test me").

Also consider the topic for your screencast. Don't bother teaching functionality which is pretty obvious anyway – concentrate on those tasks which you know users are having trouble with. And rather than talking about the functionality in abstract, much better to tell a story, to demonstrate how the software is used to solve real world problems.

Reference information is best kept short and sweet. If you have four aspects of a system to describe, create four screencasts. If you really do need to build a more elaborate piece of content, then make sure you add a menu that enables users to get to the information they want without delay (but remember menus are of no use if you are exporting to video).

Scripting

The more elaborate your screencast becomes, particularly in terms of interactivity, the more you will benefit from designing it in detail before you commence production, and that is likely to include a script for the narration. As ever, the key to success here is making sure the narration comes over as natural and conversational. Much of that is in the writing (write for the spoken voice, not for the screen) and the editing (try reading it aloud and if this causes you any difficulty, keep working on it), but delivery counts too. Not everyone will come over well as a narrator. If, even with practice, you can't deliver the script confidently and convincingly, ask someone else to help or, best of all, hire a professional.

Recording

With an online tool, you record the whole screencast in one take. If you make a mistake, you have to start again. With desktop tools, you are under much less

Recording options in Camtasia

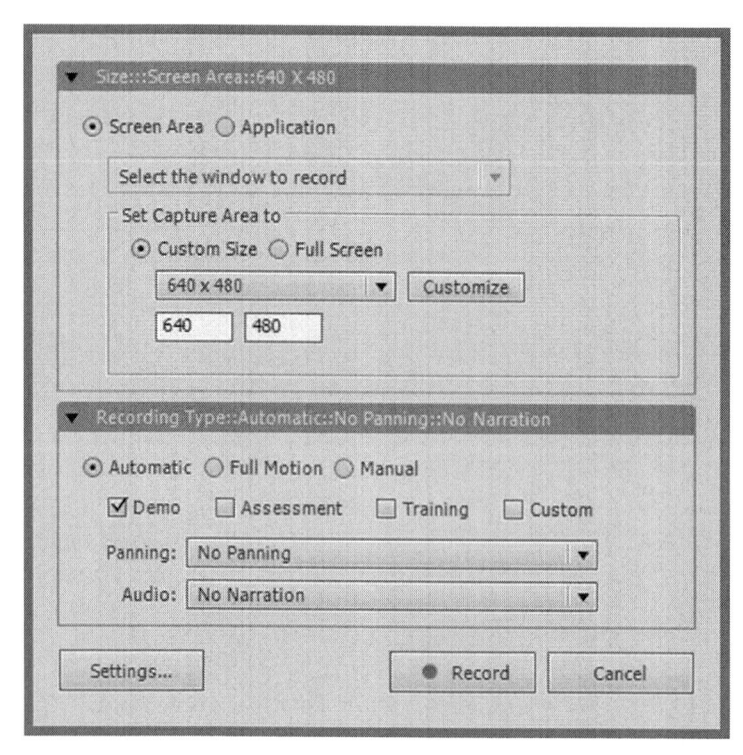

DIGITAL LEARNING CONTENT

The dialog for setting recording options in Captivate

You can edit just about any aspect of your screencast in a top-line tool like Captivate

pressure. You can record your demos piece by piece and assemble them together later. Mistakes can easily be edited out.

However, you still have to make some major decisions like the size of the capture window. Be mindful of the device and the software your audience will be using to view your screencast – if necessary focus in on a small area of the application.

Editing

Here's where desktop tools come into their own. You'll find that just about any aspect of your screencast can be changed to suit your requirements. You can supplement your recordings with titles, menus, captions, highlights, interactions and much more.

Software such as Captivate or Camtasia provide timeline tools which allow you to make very precise timing changes.

Don't rely on your own judgement. Test every aspect of your screencast out with colleagues or, better still, typical users, at each step in development. Don't get precious about sticking to your original design – what matters here is that it works!

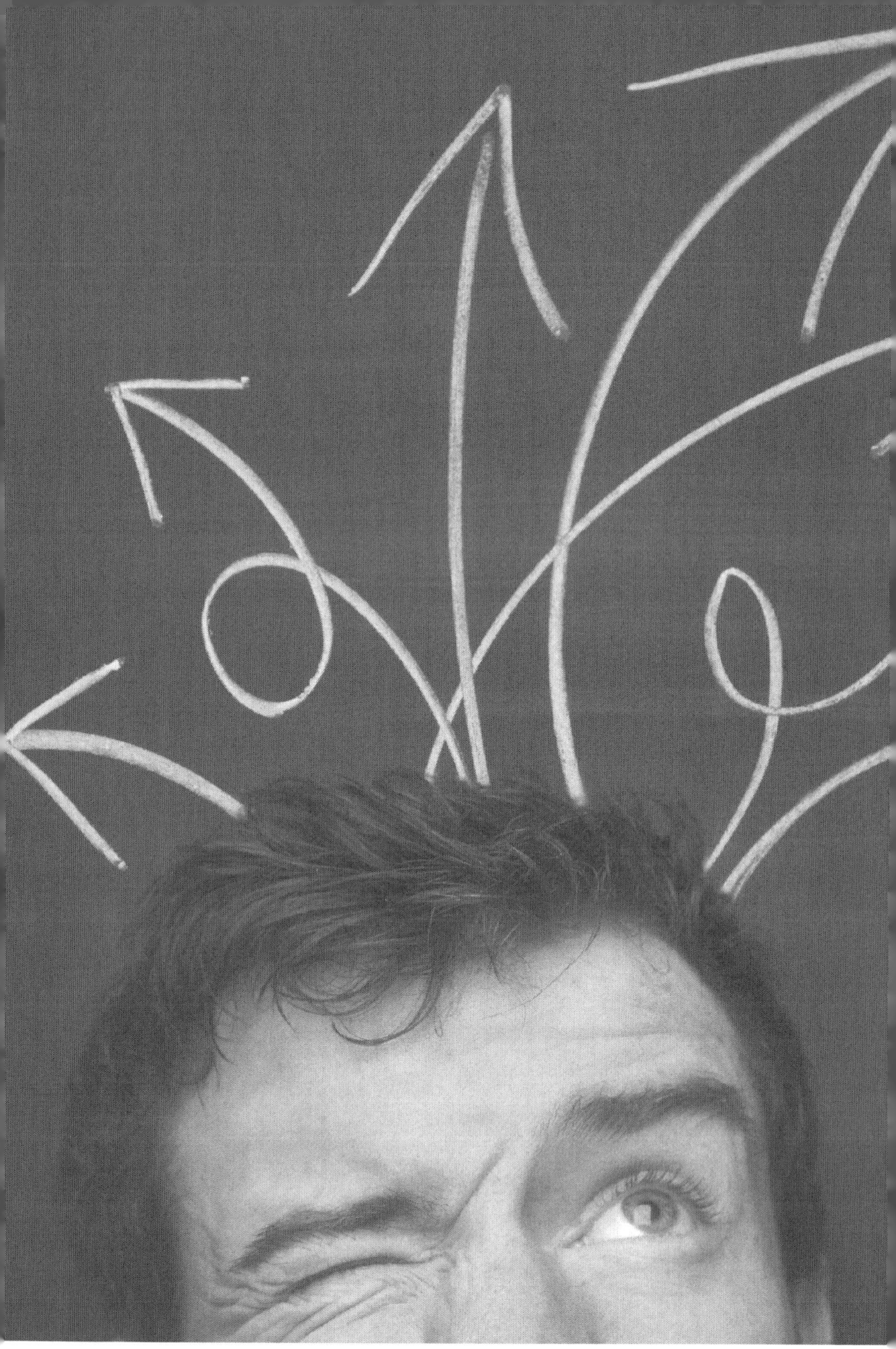

13

Creating learning scenarios

13
Creating learning scenarios

A learning scenario consists of a description of a realistic situation (usually fictional), accompanied by one or more questions that challenge the learner to respond to some aspect of that situation. At its simplest, a scenario could consist of a single description followed by a single question, but it could also develop in stages with one or more questions at each stage. In the case of a branching scenario, the information depicted at each stage will vary depending on the answers the learner made at previous stages.

The information that describes a scenario could be presented using a wide range of media elements, including text, images, animations, audio and video, in various potential combinations. What is more important than the media mix is that the situation described to the learner seems relevant and authentic.

Although, in theory, a variety of different question formats could be employed to challenge the learner about aspects of the situation, the most common and the most versatile is the simple multiple-choice question, as shown in the example below.

Note that scenarios can be presented in the third person, as below, where you are an

> Meet Denise. She's a learning designer in the Learning and Development department of Applied Utilities. She's sitting down to prepare a presentation she has to give next week. What do you think she should do first?
>
> ☐ Identify how her points can be visualised
> ☐ Clarify her goal for the presentation
> ☒ Structure her points
>
> Hold on a minute. First she has to know what she's trying to achieve. Try again.

This simple scenario is presented as a short text statement with an accompanying picture. The learner then has three options from which to choose. Feedback is provided simply in text depending on the option selected.

observer to the situation, but they can also be delivered in the first person, with you as an active participant in the situation:

What would you do first?

Feedback plays a very important role in a learning scenario. This could be explicit and immediate, as in the example above, but in a branching scenario, the feedback occurs implicitly, by what happens next – you learn by seeing the potential results of your decisions.

In this section, we'll be exploring scenarios in all of these forms.

Media elements

As we have seen, a scenario has three core components:

1. A description of a situation
2. A question with various options
3. Feedback on the options selected or, in the case of a branching scenario, a jump to the next stage in the scenario

The first and third of these could be presented in a wide variety of forms:

- Simple text
- Text with one or more images
- Audio with images or animations
- Video

The question and options will normally be presented textually, to provide the learner with as much time as they need to reflect on their decision.

Interactive capability

A learning scenario is by nature interactive – a case study with questions built in. Although, in this section, we are focusing on fully-interactive scenarios, it is worth mentioning that very similar results could be obtained by combining a more conventional case study with some means for collaboration, such as a forum, a blog or a classroom discussion.

Applications

Principle-based tasks: A learning scenario is most commonly used to help a learner gain insight into key principles that influence the problem-solving and decision making elements of their work.

The focus in this context is on tasks that cannot always be accomplished through the application of a few simple rules – there is a need for a critical judgement to be made.

In these cases, a strategy of *guided discovery* is usually applied. The scenario is positioned early in the solution, before the formal presentation of learning material. It provides a chance for the learner to experiment with different approaches and to reflect upon the possible outcomes.

Rule-based tasks: However, a scenario could also be used as a means for practising a simpler, rule-based task. Here the strategy is more likely to be *instructional*, with the scenario coming later in the solution, after the rules have been explained.

DIGITAL LEARNING CONTENT

Scenario-building tools

Scenarios can be produced quite simply in tools such as PowerPoint, using hyperlinks to jump from slide to slide depending on the learner's selections. Further functionality can be added by converting the slides into Flash, using tools such as Articulate Presenter or Adobe Presenter.

For maximum flexibility, you'll want to use a fully-fledged desktop e-learning authoring tool, such as Adobe Captivate, Lectora or Articulate Storyline. Alternatively, you could use an online tool, such as Rapid Intake's Unison.

Designing simple principle-based scenarios

We move on now to look in more detail at the steps involved in creating simple scenarios to support learners in understanding the principles underlying everyday problem-solving and decision making. Scenarios are well suited to this type of learning problem, because they provide learners with the opportunity to experiment with different responses to the sorts of situations that they could encounter in their jobs and to gain insights into the dynamics that can determine success and failure.

Justin decides that his only practical option is to create an e-learning module. The next problem is deciding how.

So, how should Justin go about creating this e-learning module?

- Put the work out to a contractor
- Use the in-house training team
- Do it himself

This might be possible, if the training team had the necessary skills, was available to do the work and was capable of both learning what they needed to about the new product and turning the job round in such a short time.

Unfortunately they fall down on all these counts (although you weren't to know).

So what else can Justin do?

This scenario was created using Microsoft PowerPoint

Creating learning scenarios

Principle-based tasks require you to make judgements rather than simply follow rules

When we talk about 'principle-based tasks' we mean those jobs that cannot be accomplished by following simple rules of the type 'if this happens then do that'. Principle-based tasks require you to make judgements on the basis of the particular situation you happen to be facing. They require you to understand cause and effect relationships, for example:

- Projects with unclear objectives are more likely to fail.
- Irritable behaviour can be caused by lack of sleep.
- You'll find it easier to cope if you don't look at each email as soon as it comes in.
- An impolite greeting will turn the customer against you before you've begun.

Principles such as these are relevant to just about any job you can imagine, although clearly some more than others. Principles are rarely black and white – in fact they are often the subject of differing opinion. Principle-based tasks, therefore, require a very different treatment and this is where scenarios come into their own.

Step 1: Decide which principles you want to bring out through the scenario

A scenario needs a clear purpose – don't use it just to lighten up what would otherwise be a boring piece of e-learning. Be realistic about what you can achieve in one scenario. You may be able to tackle a simple principle with a single question, but often a whole series of questions will be required to bring out all the elements and to compare different perspectives. A lot depends on your learner. Novices will want to look at a single issue at a time, whereas more experienced practitioners will feel comfortable immersing themselves in a complex situation with all sorts of competing pressures. If in doubt, keep it short and simple.

Step 2: Develop a storyline

Your next task is to develop a storyline that will bring out the principles you have chosen to focus on. It is really important that this storyline is credible with your audience. They must be able to relate to the situation and the characters. If you are struggling for ideas, ask a sample of your potential learners to describe the situations they face in their own day-to-day work. As with TV drama, be careful not to base your plot too closely on a real-life incident in case you reveal the identity of the protagonists.

The problems that you set should be challenging yet achievable. Remember that what is challenging for a beginner may

www.onlignment.com

DIGITAL LEARNING CONTENT

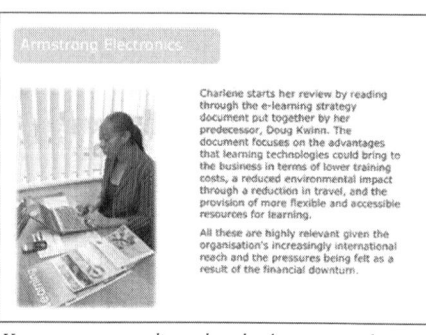

You can use any media to describe the situation, but text and graphics will often suffice

This scenario is presented as a dialogue shown as a series of pictures with speech bubbles

be completely obvious to an old hand, so adapt your scenario to your audience. With beginners, start with relatively routine problems, and move gradually to the more complex cases in which right and wrong is not so easy to establish.

Step 3: Develop your script

Use whatever media are necessary to convey the storyline. More often than not text will do the trick, but some situations will be hard to get across without richer media.

Without doubt, your hardest job will be to develop plausible options for your questions. Every option should be tempting to at least a minority of your target audience. Throwaway options, which are clearly not going to work, will devalue the whole process.

Assuming this is not a branching scenario (and we'll be dealing with these later), every option should have its own feedback. Writing this feedback will not be as simple as "Correct – well done" or "Sorry, incorrect." Every answer deserves a considered response, weighing up all the pros and cons.

Each of the options you present needs to be plausible, at least to a minority of your target audience

140   www.onlignment.com

Creating learning scenarios

If the feedback won't fit on the same screen as the question, jump to a new screen where you have the room. Remember that this feedback will be the primary source of new learning, so it shouldn't be wasted.

Again, assuming you are not creating a branching scenario, you should allow the learner to explore any and all of the options before moving on. A scenario is not an assessment, so don't follow assessment rules.

Step 4: Test and revise then do it again

You've probably got the message by now that a scenario needs to be authentic. The only way you will tell whether you've got this right is to try it out with typical learners. Bring them in early. Have them provide a verbal commentary to you as they attempt the questions. Act on their feedback and then test again. You are not admitting a mistake by changing your script – you are showing how much you want to make it work.

Designing simple rule-based scenarios

Although scenarios are usually thought of as tools to support more complex problem-solving and decision-making, as we shall see, they can as easily be used as a technique for practising more routine, everyday tasks.

When we talk about 'rule-based tasks' we mean those activities that can be carried

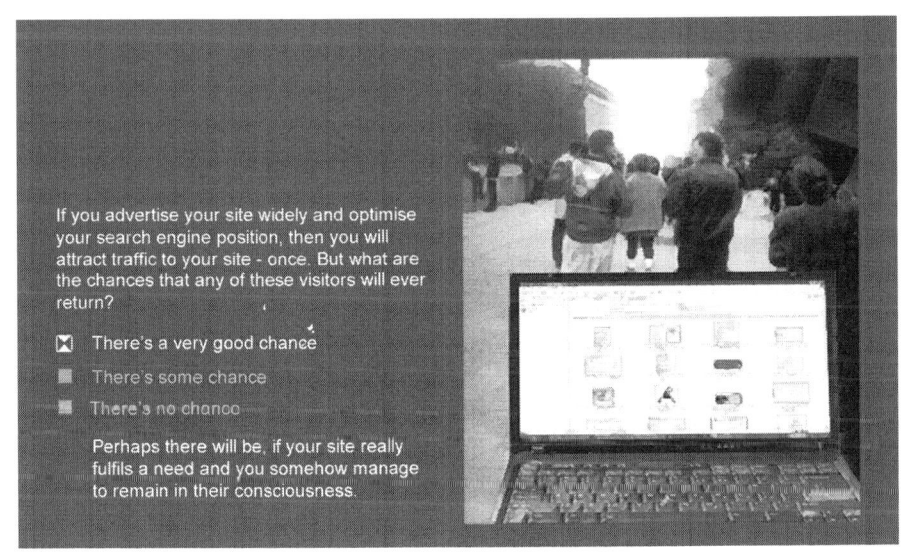

Each option here has its own feedback, written to bring out the pros and cons of the learner's choice. Learners are free to select as many options as they like.

www.onlignment.com

141

DIGITAL LEARNING CONTENT

Rule-based tasks don't require you to make judgements, just to follow instructions

out repeatedly according to clearly laid-out instructions. The job holder is not required to make a judgement, just to follow the rules – if this ... do that.

In the developed world, it would be fair to say that less and less tasks are of this nature, because routine tasks that obey strict rules can often be undertaken by robots or computers, transferred off-shore where the labour is cheaper or just looked up from some reference source as and when needed. Having said that, everybody's job involves some rule-based elements, and some tasks simply can't be carried out by a machine or at a distance.

Step 1: Teach the rules

Principle-based scenarios are typically used as an element in a process of guided discovery. The scenario brings out issues that can then be reflected upon and discussed, hopefully resulting in learner insights.

A task-based scenario is much more likely to be used within an instructional strategy – you teach the rules, then have the learner practise applying them in realistic situations.

So, before building the scenario, be clear about what the steps are in the procedure you want to teach and the rules that need to be applied at each step. Then create some content to get all this across:

- provide an overview of the task and why it is important
- demonstrate each step, explaining the rules that need to be applied and why these are necessary

Don't over-teach. The idea is to provide the minimum information necessary for learners to be able to have a go themselves. The detail can be filled in later, either as feedback within the practice scenarios or as further reading.

Step 2: Develop a storyline

You can then set about designing your scenarios. The idea is to provide the learner with the most realistic experience of the task that you can.

For more difficult tasks, start with a simple initial practice that will allow the learner to build their confidence by applying the most basic rules. Then move on to provide more difficult scenarios that require the learner to apply more complex rules.

Creating learning scenarios

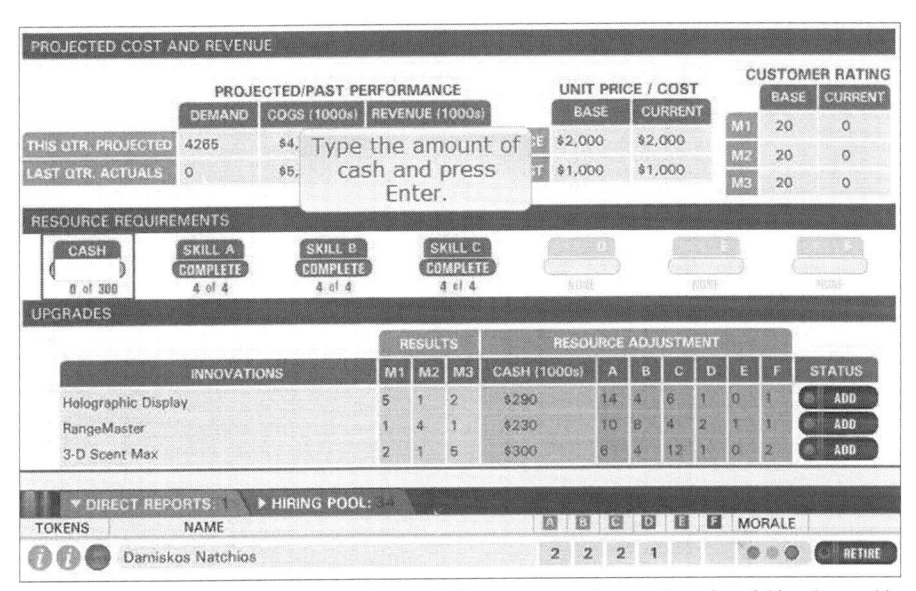

If you can, make the interaction match the task. Here the learner is required to complete a form field as they would in a real software application

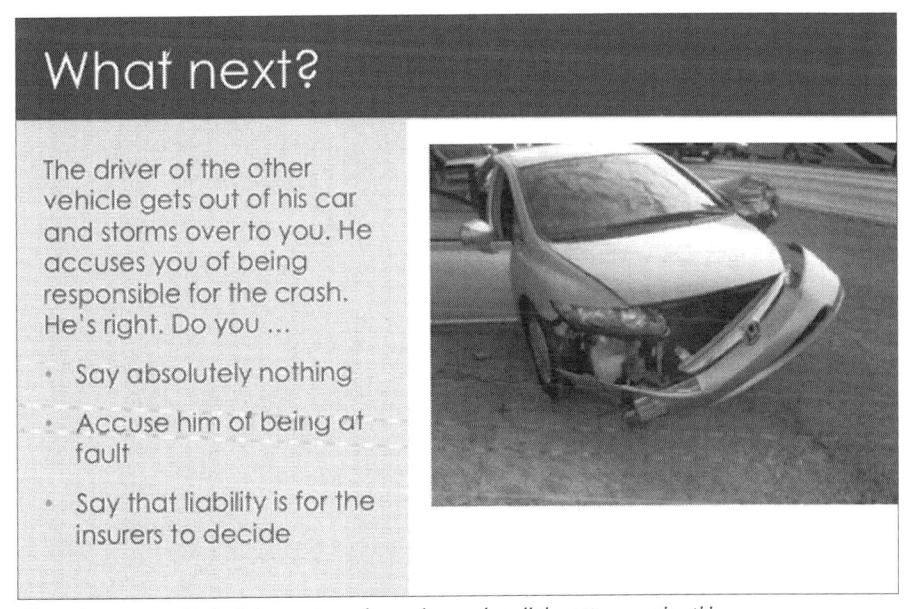

What next?

The driver of the other vehicle gets out of his car and storms over to you. He accuses you of being responsible for the crash. He's right. Do you ...

- Say absolutely nothing
- Accuse him of being at fault
- Say that liability is for the insurers to decide

If you plan to use multiple-choice questions, then make sure that all the options are plausible

www.onlignment.com   143

DIGITAL LEARNING CONTENT

Aim to provide enough opportunities for practice that any learner will be able to gain confidence in applying the rules to real tasks.

You will not always be able to provide completely authentic practice opportunities. Sometimes your scenarios will be just a first step to be followed up by more realistic practice away from the computer.

Step 3: Develop your script

As with principle-based scenarios, use whatever media are necessary to convey the storyline. Text and images will often suffice, but if you need a more realistic experience, you have the option of richer media – perhaps even 3D graphics.

As ever, your hardest job will be to develop suitable questions. Where possible, these should match the real-life experience; so if the real task requires someone to type a code into a form field on a computer, then have them do the same thing in your scenario.

Ideally every option should have its own feedback. This allows you to correct any misunderstandings that might have led to an incorrect answer and to add little details that you might have held back from your initial demonstration.

Step 4: Test and revise

As early as you can, have some sample learners try out your scenarios. Find out from them whether the scenarios

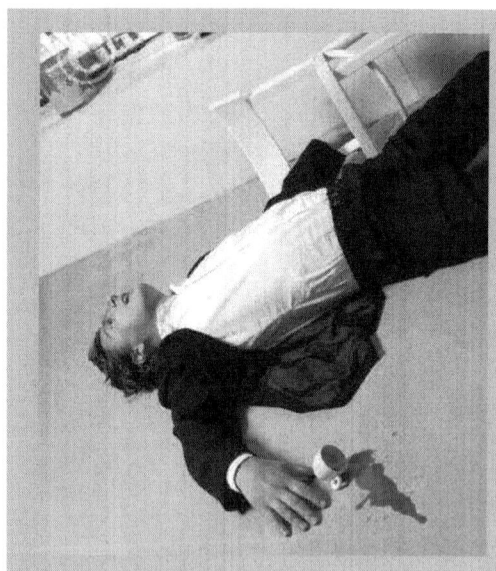

You check and it seems the patient has a pulse but is not breathing.

What would you do first?

■ Provide resuscitation

■ Call for an ambulance

■ Check whether anything is blocking the mouth or windpipe

That is important but you have a more urgent task to fulfil first. Feel inside the mouth with a finger to see if there is anything blocking it or the windpipe and remove any food or other objects. Provided that dentures are not broken, it is better not to remove them

The feedback you provide can be used to correct any misunderstandings and to add extra detail

are sufficiently realistic, whether they understand clearly what they have to do, whether the questions are set at the right level of difficulty, and whether the feedback is helpful. Be prepared to make lots of refinements until you get it right.

Designing branching scenarios

We turn our attention now to branching scenarios, which provide a more immersive approach to learning principle-based tasks.

Why branching?

To understand the value of branching, you first need to understand how a scenario looks when it doesn't branch.

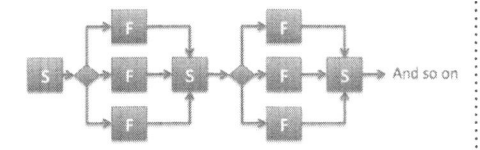

The diagram above shows the learner being presented with a situation (S) and three choices. The learner is then immediately provided with feedback (F), related directly to the choice that they have made, pointing out positive aspects and correcting any misunderstandings or errors. All learners then proceed to the second stage of the scenario.

Although the feedback can be considered to be branching, the overall path is linear.

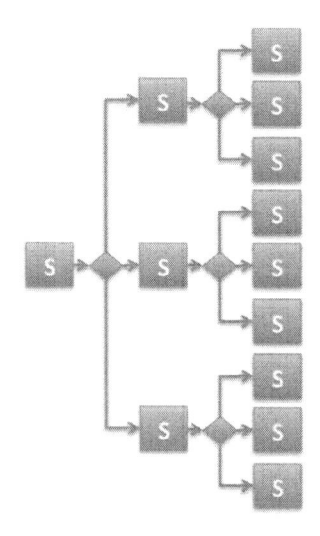

While a linear scenario works well in many situations, it doesn't resemble real life, where you get to experience the results of your decisions, for better or for worse.

With a branching scenario, it will be possible for different learners to progress along different routes through the scenario and to experience different end points. Where you arrive depends on the decisions you make along the way.

The diagram above shows only the initial two stages in the scenario – there could, of course, be many more. As you can imagine, if at every stage the scenario trebled in size (assuming three choices) it would soon become unmanageable.

In practice, many branching scenarios return to a common narrative at key points or kick the learner out early if their initial choices represent fatal mistakes.

DIGITAL LEARNING CONTENT

> I need a course on branding for my sales reps.

What's the best question to ask now? Click your choice.

A. What kind of course do you need?

B. Why do you need the course?

C. What do you need to cover?

Order taker — Instructional designer

Sales reps will understand branding.

This scenario aims to help you make the transition from order taker to instructional designer and the meter at the bottom left gives you an update on your progress.

146 www.onlignment.com

Creating learning scenarios

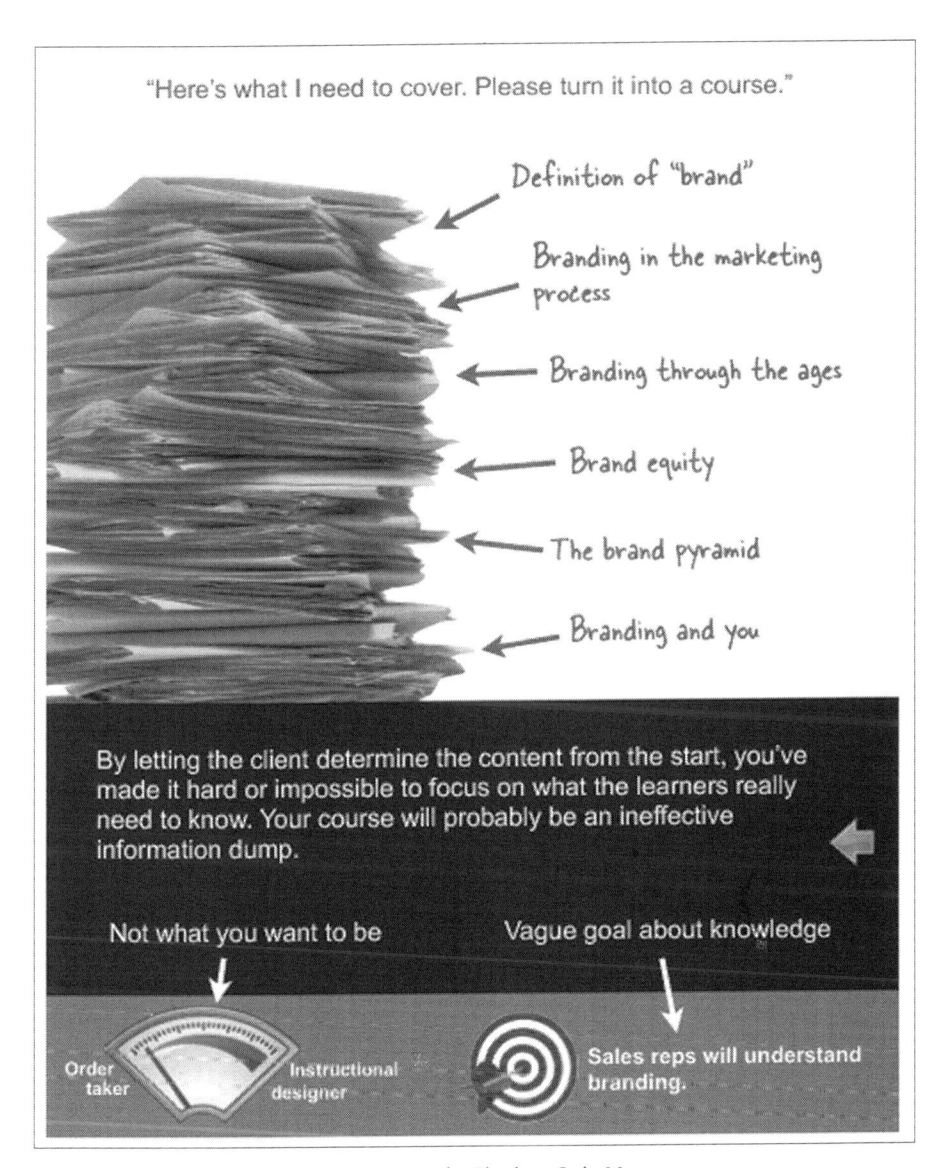

"Here's what I need to cover. Please turn it into a course."

- Definition of "brand"
- Branding in the marketing process
- Branding through the ages
- Brand equity
- The brand pyramid
- Branding and you

By letting the client determine the content from the start, you've made it hard or impossible to focus on what the learners really need to know. Your course will probably be an ineffective information dump.

Not what you want to be — Order taker / Instructional designer

Vague goal about knowledge — Sales reps will understand branding.

Here is an example of the feedback the scenario provides. Thanks to Cathy Moore:
http://blog.cathy-moore.com/2009/10/how-to-steer-your-client-away-from-an-information-dump/

DIGITAL LEARNING CONTENT

This scenario uses an eye-catching comic strip approach, achieved by converting photographs into illustrations. This extract is part of the scene setting.

Still using the comic strip approach, the learner is presented with a situation and a number of options for action.

148 www.onlignment.com

Creating learning scenarios

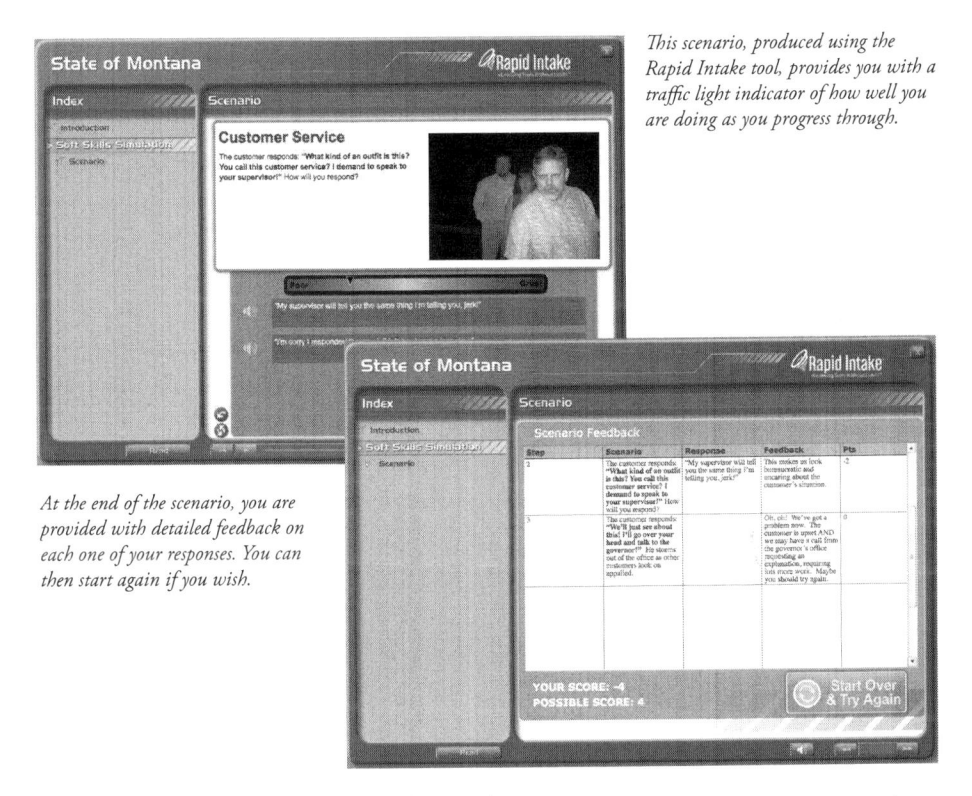

This scenario, produced using the Rapid Intake tool, provides you with a traffic light indicator of how well you are doing as you progress through.

At the end of the scenario, you are provided with detailed feedback on each one of your responses. You can then start again if you wish.

Providing the learner with feedback

Looking at the second flow chart on page 145, you might wonder where all the feedback went! Well, first and foremost, feedback is implicit in the branching that occurs. If you shouted at the customer in situation 1, you'll get your payback in situation 2.

Another way that feedback can be provided is with some sort of visual indicator, as in the example above.

Deciding on the look and feel

You can use any combination of still images, text, audio and video to present the situations in your scenarios, although the evidence is stacked against using text and speech simultaneously.

Your decision is likely to be made on the basis of (1) how much realism is needed to adequately convey the situation, and (2) how much time and money you have got available to you.

Cathy Moore, along with her friends at Kinection, turned to a comic book approach for the acclaimed Haji Kamal scenario, seen on the left.

Enjoy your story-telling.

www.onlignment.com

149

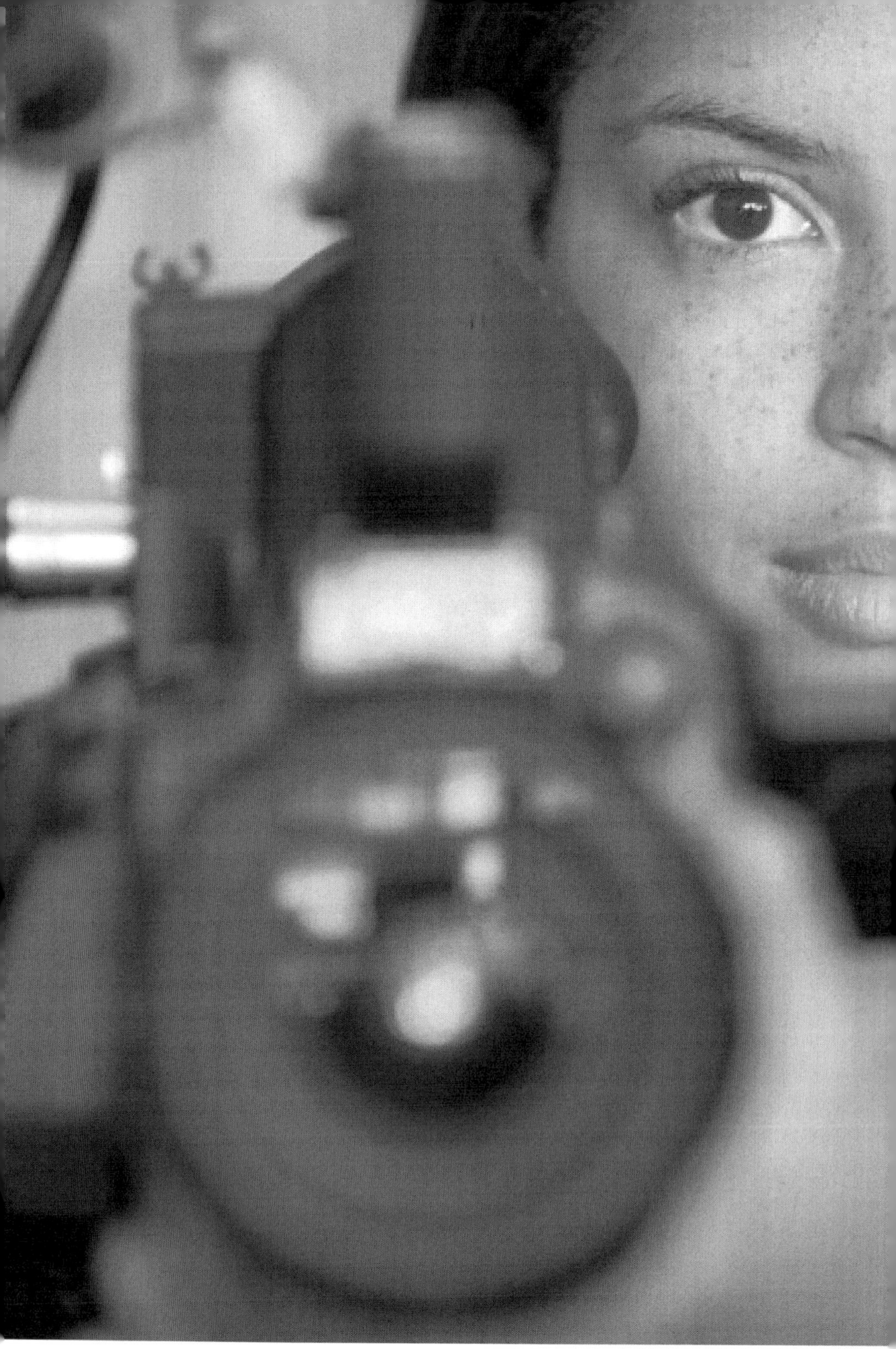

14

Creating learning videos

14
Creating learning videos

Video is very much the medium of the moment. Not only do we spend many hours each day watching it on our TVs, it has become an integral part of the online experience. An ever-increasing proportion of the population does not only consume video, it creates and shares it with a world-wide internet audience. Whereas once video cameras cost many hundreds, if not tens of thousands of pounds, they are now integrated for no additional cost in computers, stills cameras and mobile phones. And where once video editing could only be carried out by skilled engineers in elaborate editing suites, it can now be accomplished, often with equivalent production values, with free or low cost software on PCs and even mobile devices.

In a learning context, video provides a compelling means for conveying content,

Gone are the days when, to shoot a video, you depended on the services of a full crew and expensive equipment

The same applies to the post-production process. What once required an edit suite can now be accomplished with a smart phone app

Creating learning videos

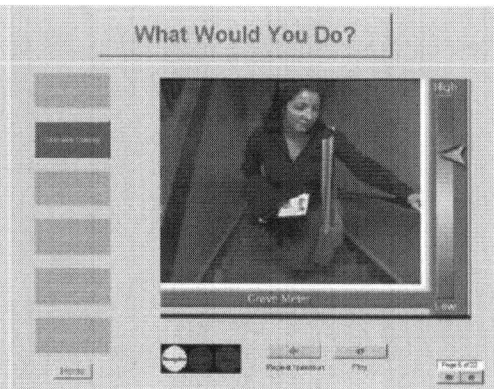

Although not the focus of this chapter, video can be used interactively using DVD, digital TV or online. It can also be used as an ingredient in an interactive scenario.

particularly real-life action and interactions with people. Amazingly, it can also be quicker and easier to produce than slide shows or textual content. Sometimes you just have to point the camera, press record, shoot what you see and then upload to a website. Obviously it won't always be that easy, but you should start with the attitude that "I'll assume I can do it myself, until proven otherwise."

Media elements

In its purest form, a video is a recording, in moving pictures and sound, of real-life action as captured by a video camera. In actual practice video goes way beyond live action, and is capable of integrating just about every other media element, including still images, text, 2D and 3D animation. At the heart of video, however, will always be moving images of some form and an audio accompaniment, whether ambient sound, voice, music or some combination.

Interactive capability

As a general rule, video is not interactive, other than in an exploratory or navigational sense. And for the purposes of this chapter we will be assuming no interactivity. Having said that, it is possible to build interactivity into video, whether that's on a DVD, a digital TV system or online; it's also possible to incorporate video material into what are essentially interactive media, such as scenarios and tutorials.

Applications

In its purely linear form, video can be useful for the simple *exposition* of learning content, such as lectures, documentaries, panel discussions and interviews. It can

www.onlignment.com

DIGITAL LEARNING CONTENT

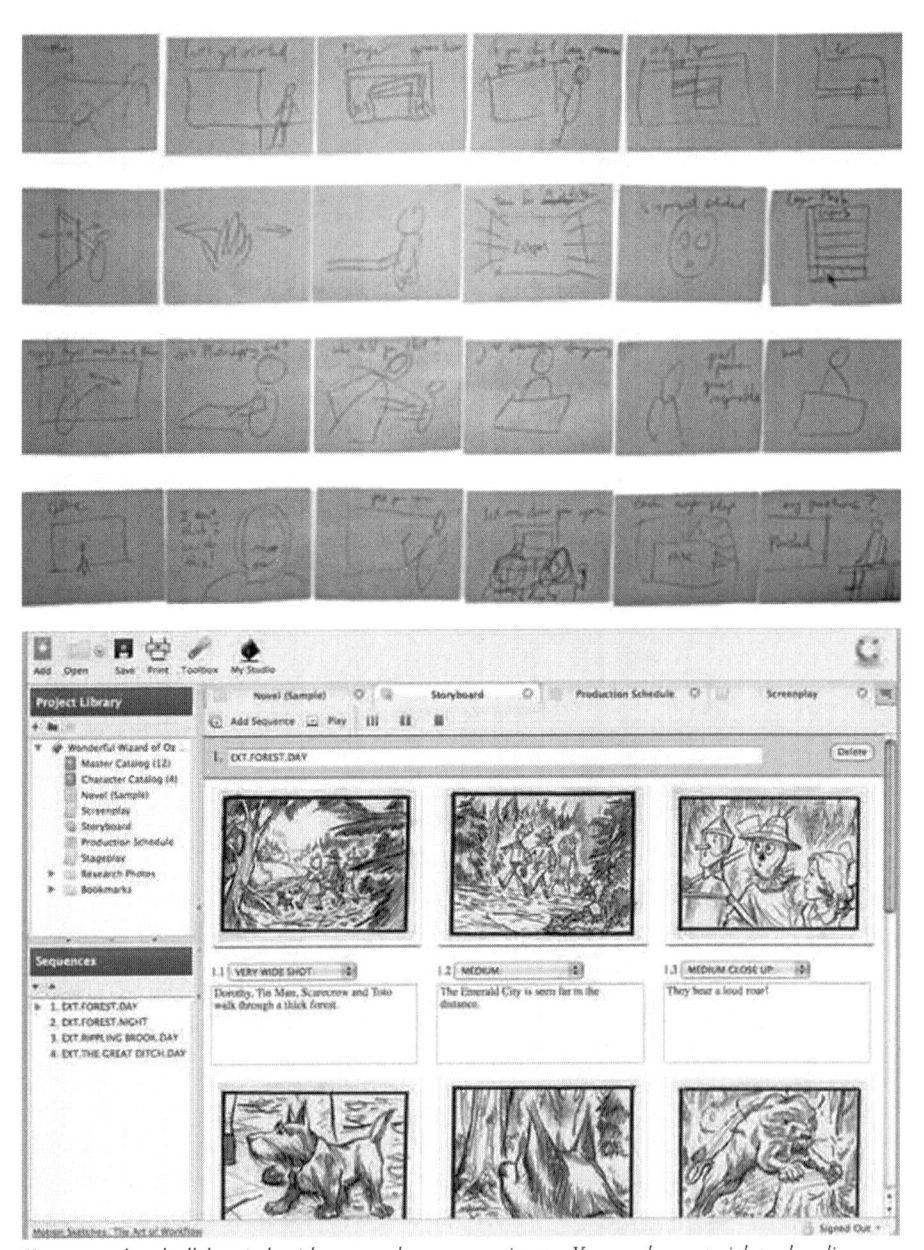

You can storyboard collaboratively with no more than some post-it notes. You can also use special storyboarding software.

154 www.onlignment.com

also function within a more learner-centred context, as a means for providing how-to information on demand, a facility that has been demonstrated with enormous success on YouTube.

As mentioned above, video also has a role to play within the more structured strategies of *instruction* and *guided discovery*, as a component within, say, interactive tutorials and scenarios. It is ideal for setting the scene for a case study or demonstrating a skill. It can also be effectively used as a catalyst for discussion in a forum or in a classroom.

Video is a rich medium in every sense. It is highly engaging and can portray real actions, behaviours and events more faithfully than any other medium. However, this comes at a price. Video is also data rich, and consumes vast amounts of bandwidth. On a CD or DVD this causes no problems, but your IT department will certainly want to know if you are going to be distributing video on a large scale over your company network.

Pre-production

We move on to the practicalities of getting a video made, starting with what the film and TV industries call pre-production – essentially all those tasks that need to be completed before you press record on the camera.

Seeing as we are concentrating on the absolute basics of video production, requiring the minimum of technical expertise and equipment, you might feel that pre-production is a bit of a grand topic on which to be spending much time. But even the simplest productions need some planning, as we shall see.

Develop your concept

You need an idea. You can't just press record and shoot the first thing you see. This idea must be compelling to some degree or no-one is going to take the time to watch. So, take the time to consider what you could contrive that would enhance the lives of your audience in some way. In a learning context, that could mean showing how to do something, explaining a difficult concept, or allowing people to share their thoughts and opinions on a matter of some importance.

If we're talking online video (and probably we are) then you have to figure out how to realise your concept in five minutes or less. That's not a long time, but it's all most viewers are prepared to spare. Keeping your video short also reduces the burden on you in terms of the more advanced production techniques you would need in order to sustain interest over a longer period.

Five minutes is not so long, but your video still requires a beginning, a middle and an end. Think this through up front – don't expect to be able to fashion all this in the edit.

Prepare a script or storyboard

If your video requires narration or acted dialogue then this clearly has to be scripted in advance. Even if you are conducting an interview, you'll need to prepare the questions and have some idea how you expect the interviewee to respond and for how long. You can prepare a script using Microsoft Word or similar word processing software, or use a specialist application such as Final Draft. Normally a video script will provide some information about the visual content in the left-hand column and the words on the right, although there is no law about this.

Whether or not your video is going to contain narration or dialogue, if you intend it to be visually rich, with many different scenes, camera angles, graphics or effects, then you should seriously consider preparing a storyboard. This goes beyond a script to provide a rough idea of how each shot in each scene should be composed. A storyboard will be a great help both in planning and directing your shoot, reducing the chance that you will have to go back to shoot important elements that got forgotten on the day. You may find you can storyboard adequately using a pack of post-it notes. For something more permanent and sharable, PowerPoint may do the job. And of course there is specialist software available, like the free Celtx.

Find a suitable place to shoot

There are probably four main considerations when selecting a location for your shoot:

1. Will it allow you to show what you need to show? If you were looking to demonstrate a task or act out a scene in an authentic setting, then this would be the over-riding issue. If a more contrived setting, such as a studio, will work equally well, then you have less to worry about.

2. Will the environment be quiet enough? Without the right sound equipment, a noisy location could completely scupper your chances. If you really must work in a lot of noise, you will need a highly directional mic as close as you can to whoever is speaking. Of course this will not be an issue in a studio.

3. Will there be enough light? Time was when every video shoot required dedicated lighting, but modern cameras – even the really cheap ones – cope remarkably well in low light. Having said that, you will always obtain best results when the scene is well lit, so if the ambient light is not likely to be good enough, hire some proper lights.

4. Is the location available when you want and at an appropriate price?

Decide what equipment you will need

Assuming you are intending to distribute your video online then, contrary to what you might think, the camera you use is not going to make a big difference to the quality of the end result. Why? Because practically all cameras – even webcams and the cameras built in to phones – provide adequate resolution for display on a mobile device or in a small window on a PC.

Amazingly, most cameras can now record in high definition, which is fine if you are playing back on an HD-compatible display, but pointless otherwise. Don't underestimate the processing power needed

Creating learning videos

Video cameras come in many shapes and forms, including smart phones, digital SLR cameras and low-cost dedicated HD video cameras

to edit HD video. Your computer will have to handle something like six times the number of pixels than it would with standard definition and up to 20 times the number you need for YouTube. If your computer can handle HD then fine, but don't expect it to make any difference to the end result.

If you really do need to record at high resolutions and to very high quality, then go for a semi-professional camcorder (you'll get something great for £1500) or one of the new digital SLR stills cameras with HD capability built in (the Canon EOS 5D sets the standard here). Otherwise there are plenty of excellent low-cost models to choose from, including what you have in your phone.

Much more important to the quality of the end result is the microphone. There will be one built in to the camera and this may be adequate, but if you want clear speech this has to be of good quality and highly directional. A much better option is to use an external microphone that can be positioned close to the subject. This could be wired or wireless, but does require that your camera has a socket to connect an external mic.

We've handled lighting already, which leaves the issue of a tripod. Some cameras have good integrated image stabilisation, but this can't perform miracles. If you really need a rock-steady camera then support it on a tripod. Simple as that.

Production

So, we get to the day of the shoot. Here are some hints and tips for the set ups you're most likely to encounter when producing learning videos.

The 'piece to camera' or PTC

We're all familiar with the piece to camera as a technique used in news broadcasts, but in the context of low-budget learning videos, we're more likely to use this approach to record a response to a question. The following tips will help you to do an effective job:

- Explain to the subject what you are going to do and what question you would like them to answer.

www.onlignment.com

DIGITAL LEARNING CONTENT

The piece to camera

- Make a note of the subject's name and check the spelling with them before you leave.

- Find an interesting setting, ideally one which will reflect the context of the topic.

- Position the camera at the subject's eye level, ideally on a tripod. Whatever you do, do not look down on the subject.

- Frame the shot so you don't leave lots of space above the subject's head as this will make them look short.

- Ask the subject to look directly into the lens.

- Don't rehearse if you want the subject's response to sound really natural.

- If you're feeling adventurous, add some movement by using an occasional slow zoom in and out.

The interview

The interview is one of the principle video formats and one that has real value for learning. In the ideal world you would shoot an interview with two cameras – one for the interviewer and one for the interviewee – and then choose the shots you would like to go with during the edit. However, this chapter is about what you can do with very little equipment and very little experience, so let's see what you can do with a single camera.

If you want to keep it simple, frame your shot to include both the interviewer and interviewee (see right). If at all possible you should use an external mic, which the interviewer can hold.

It's also possible to simulate a two-camera shoot and this will certainly provide you with a more interesting end result, particularly if the interview is extended. You'll need to set up at a number of different angles:

An over-the-shoulder shot establishes the scene

Creating learning videos

Your simplest option is to set up the camera on a tripod and leave it with interviewer and interviewee in shot

- A shot which shows both the interviewer and interviewee (a 'two-shot'), to establish the scene and prove that this interview really did happen with both parties present at the same time! Sometimes this is shot over the interviewer's shoulder (an 'OTS').

- Close-ups of the interviewee listening to the questions (which are being spoken off camera) and then giving their answers.

- Reverse shots of the interviewer listening intently to the responses (usually called 'noddies'). These can be useful in covering up any cuts you want to make in the interviewee's answers.

- Reverse shots of the interviewer asking the questions. Be clear that, because you have only one camera and mic, these are recorded separately from the interviewee's answers – you can safely ditch the original questions to which the interviewee responded.

The presentation

A video recording of a lecture or presentation is an invaluable way to extend the reach of the event beyond the initial face-to-face audience. Your simplest option is to record the presenter and any slides in one mid-shot. The camera will need to be on a tripod for stability.

If the presenter is using a mic then your best bet is to take a feed from this directly. If not, you'll need to provide your own, ideally a radio mic that the presenter can attach to his or her shirt. Don't rely on the mic built into your camera, as you'll be too far away from the presenter to get a clear signal.

If you don't mind doing a little editing later, then you could mix up the shots. A wide 'establishing' shot of the meeting room will set the scene. Then cut between a close up of the presenter and his or her slides. Don't shoot the slides at the time – get a copy of the presentation, save each slide off as an image and then import these directly into the edit. You might also like to get some cut-aways of the audience to provide more visual interest.

A simple technique is to shoot the presenter and the slides in one mid-shot, but you'll do well to make the slides clearly visible

www.onlignment.com

DIGITAL LEARNING CONTENT

You'll achieve a more interesting result by starting with a wide shot, cutting between a close-up of the presenter and his or her slides, and mixing in some audience shots

Post-production

And so to the final stage in the creation of a learning video – post-production. At this stage we collect together all the material that we shot at the production stage, select what we want to keep and what we can safely leave 'on the cutting room floor', edit all this together, add titles, graphics, music and effects, export as a finished product and distribute to our audience. This may all seem very technical but modern software has transformed much of this to a process of drag and drop, copy and paste. So let's get started.

Editing

Editing is not obligatory. There's nothing to stop you shooting something straightforward like an interview to camera and then uploading the results, without modification, to a site such as YouTube. But even the simplest videos will usually benefit from a little editing, even if just to trim the start and finish points and add a caption to inform the viewer who it is that's speaking. This sort of editing is a doddle. And while you're at it, why not add a title, perhaps with a little music behind? Yes, before you know it, you're putting

Creating learning videos

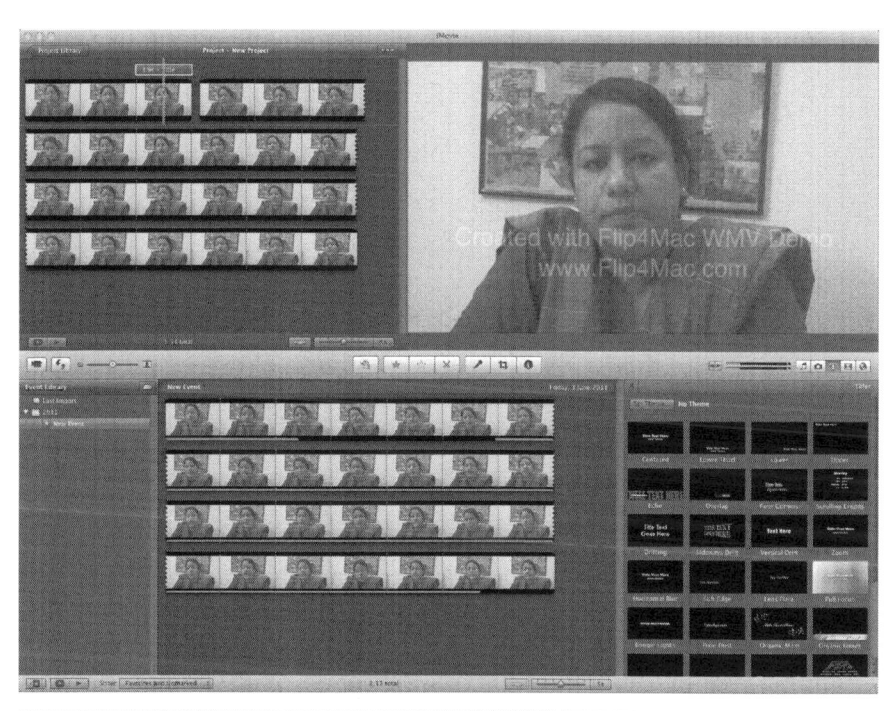

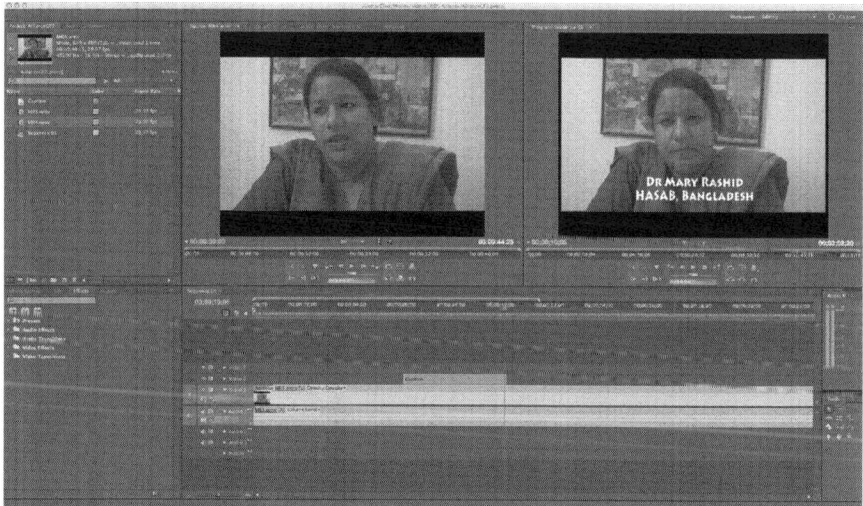

Editing software works much the same way whether it's a free program like iMovie (top) or a full professional package like Adobe Premiere Pro (bottom)

www.onlignment.com 161

DIGITAL LEARNING CONTENT

together videos that, while not quite professional in quality, don't annoy the viewer with their amateurishness.

The aim of editing is to be invisible. In other words, you want the viewer to be able to concentrate on the content of your video without becoming aware of any of the mechanics of production and post-production.

If you've done a good job, no-one will say what a good job you've done of putting it all together – they'll just thank you for a great piece of content.

Video editing software comes at three levels of sophistication: (1) the free programs that come with your computer, such as MovieMaker (Windows) or iMovie (Mac), (2) budget versions of the top-end tools, such as Adobe Premiere Elements (under $250) and (3) the top-end tools themselves, Final Cut Pro (Mac only), Adobe Premiere Pro and Sony Vegas Video Pro.

Although you wouldn't think so from the price tags, pretty well all video editing software is roughly the same. The free software will get you a long way and may be more than enough for all your future needs. If you love playing with software, you'll want more features and the mid-level tools will provide you with plenty of toys. The top-end tools are for pros and if you're one of them you won't be reading this guide.

Your basic editing tasks are as follows:

- Import your clips from your camera.
- Choose the clips you want to use and drag and drop them onto the timeline.
- Where appropriate, split clips up into smaller clips.
- Trim the start and end point of each clip.
- Arrange the clips into sequence.
- A simple cut between clips is usually best, but in some cases you may want to create a transition, perhaps some form of cross-fade. If you want your editing to be invisible, then avoid flashy transitions.
- Overlay titles and captions where appropriate.
- You may want to cut away to photographic stills or graphics. By contrast with your video clips, these could look overly static, so consider adding movement through some subtle panning or zooming.
- To help create the right mood, consider adding a music track, particularly in those sections where there is no speech.

With a little practice, these tasks will be simple enough to perform. If you want more help, there are plenty of great how-to videos on YouTube – which only goes to emphasise what a great learning tool video can be.

Look for inspiration on YouTube and on the TV. In particular, focus in on those programmes in which the editing is almost invisible and try to identify the techniques that were used to achieve that result.

Sharing

Now your video is ready to go, you'll want to get it into the right format for your intended audience. You'll probably want to distribute your video material in one of the following three ways:

- *On a DVD*: In this case your editing software will guide you through the steps needed to write a single disc or to prepare a disc image for duplication.

- *As an element within an e-learning module*: The key here is to find out what formats and resolutions are supported by your particular authoring tool. Obviously you'll want your video to be played back in the largest video window and with the best audio quality possible, but check out whether this will be realistic given the bandwidth available to your audience.

- *Through a video streaming service such as YouTube*: We all know how YouTube works and how well it adapts to the available bandwidth and the particular device you are using. You can upload to YouTube in quite a range of formats, but you should probably check out the most appropriate options on the YouTube site first. Your videos do not have to be made public – if you prefer you can restrict access only to those who are provided with the URL. Even so, if you need a completely secure service, YouTube may not be the answer. Check with your IT department or LMS provider to see what other options are available.

Don't be too put off by the thought of the burden you will be placing on your organisation's network by making video available online. Chances are your network is capable of supporting hundreds, perhaps even thousands of simultaneous users without undue strain. But do check first. You won't be popular if business grinds to a halt as scores of employees rush to sample your latest offering.

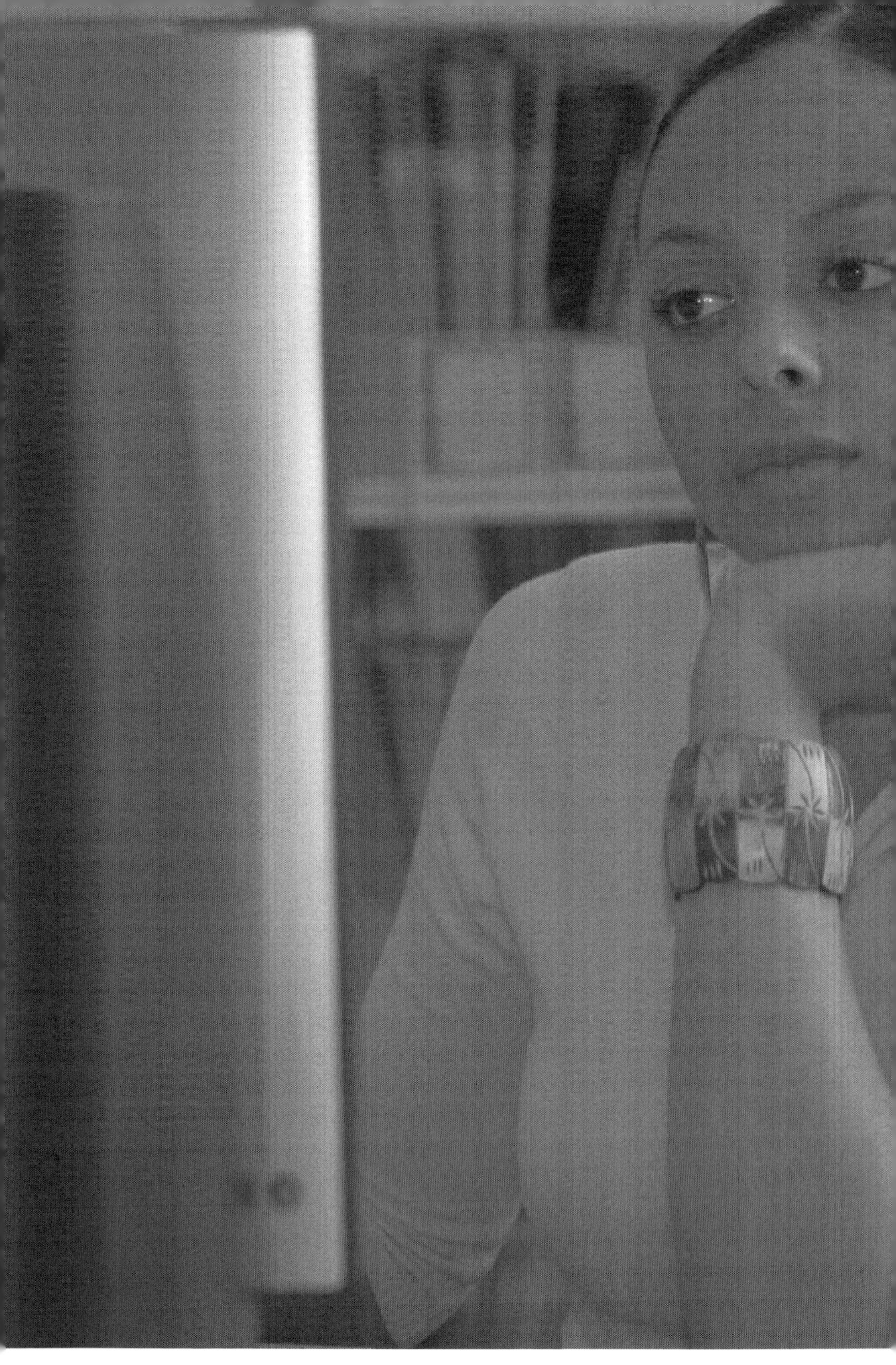

15
Creating learning tutorials

15

Creating learning tutorials

The digital learning tutorial is anything but a new concept. Almost as soon as computers became generally available, efforts were made to automate the process of teaching through the medium of self-study lessons. Under the guise of CBT (computer-based training), interactive video or e-learning, and on a variety of platforms from green-screen mainframe terminals to the early microcomputers, using videodiscs, CD-ROMs, web resources or smart phone apps, the format stays pretty constant – a carefully-crafted sequence of screens displaying learning material and providing opportunities for interaction.

The digital learning tutorial is not a new concept

Strange as it may seem, as a result of this long history, instructional designers (those who design these tutorials) are as much a part of the training establishment as those who've spent much of their lives in the physical classroom. A handful has been at this task for 30 years or more and they have learned a thing or two along the way.

In this chapter, we'll attempt to pass on some of the wisdom that has been handed down about the design of learning tutorials, while acknowledging that change is occurring very fast in learning and development and that, as a result, what worked in 1981 when the IBM PC was first launched may not be quite so appropriate in 2011.

So what is a tutorial? The Concise Oxford Dictionary defines a tutorial as "a period of teaching or instruction given by a tutor to an individual or small group." This hardly sounds like an efficient way of bringing about learning; indeed, only a select group of universities are still prepared to go to this much trouble for their students, and trainers are no different.

Luckily, the same dictionary provides another definition: "A tutorial is an

The digital learning tutorial is not a new concept

The traditional tutorial is free-flowing and interactive – its digital equivalent should be no different

166 www.onlignment.com

Creating learning tutorials

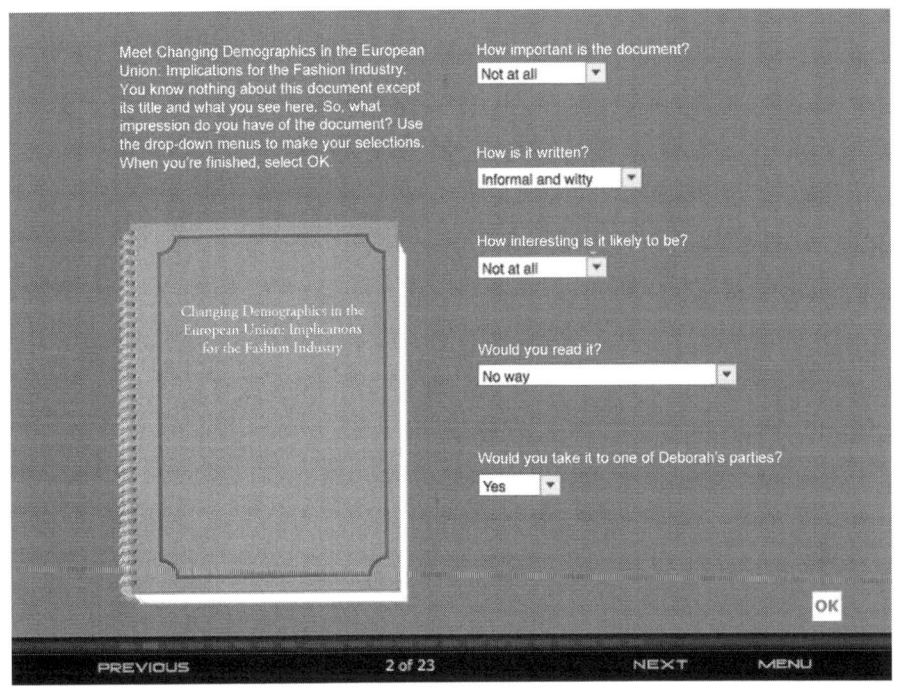

Interaction is integral to the tutorial

account or explanation of a topic, printed or on-screen, intended for private study." This is nearer to what we're looking for, but with some of the interactivity, perhaps, that we might find in the face-to-face tutorial.

Media elements

A digital learning tutorial can and frequently does utilise every available media element. Verbal material can be provided in textual form or as audio. Visual material can range from simple photos, illustrations and diagrams through to animations, 3D environments and video. The perfect combination is one that communicates the learning material clearly to the intended audience, while working within the constraints of the available technical infrastructure.

Interactive capability

A tutorial is essentially interactive. Screencasts, slide shows, podcasts, videos and all manner of other digital resources can be used effectively without any built-in interaction. Not so a tutorial.

Here interaction is the key to what is typically intended as a completely self-contained learning experience. An exposition of learning content followed by a quiz does not constitute a tutorial. To be effective, interaction needs to be integrated into every step of the learning process.

DIGITAL LEARNING CONTENT

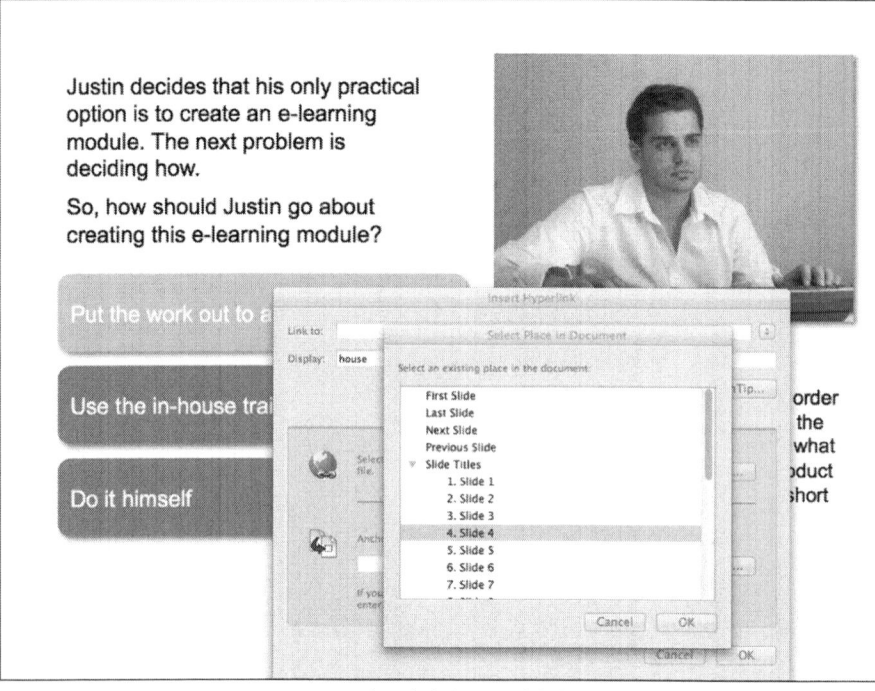

You can create interactions in PowerPoint using hyperlinks between slides but this is a laborious process and you are limited in what you can achieve

Applications

A digital learning tutorial is an instructional device. Instruction is guided by clear objectives. It uses appropriate strategies to support learners as they progress towards these objectives. It is responsive to the difficulties learners may experience along the way. It finishes when the job is done, not when time is up or when all the slides have been shown.

Instruction is particularly valuable when your goal is to provide essential knowledge or to teach rule-based tasks. Designed well, it is capable of providing consistent, measurable results. While those with higher levels of expertise in the topic might find this process laboured, even patronising, novices will be thankful for the structure and support.

So how do I get started?

It is possible to create learning tutorials with a general purpose tool like PowerPoint, but you will be severely limited in what you can achieve interactively (you can branch between slides using hyperlinks, but this is a fiddly method to use for anything other than the simplest interactions) and you will not have the functionality necessary to track progress in a learning management system.

The same applies if you use a standard web development tool like Dreamweaver (although, to be fair, Adobe do provide the additional functionality required for building tutorials in a special version of Dreamweaver available as part of their eLearning Suite).

Most people prefer to use a tool that is specially designed to support the development of e-learning. These come in desktop form (Articulate, Captivate, Lectora and many others) and also as online tools available through your web browser.

You'll be looking for a tool that's easy to use but that is also capable of delivering the level of interactivity that you require.

Meet Ewan. He's a project manager for a software development company working on important government contracts. He has just returned from holiday to find that one of his projects has encountered serious problems and looks like missing its deadline. The customer is extremely anxious and on the phone to Ewan and his boss continually. On top of this, Ewan has 450 emails in his inbox, an appraisal to do that afternoon and an important business trip scheduled for early the following morning.

Ewan loses his temper with his boss. Why wasn't this dealt with while he was away? How can he be expected to deal with this when he's only got a few hours before he goes away again? He returns to his workstation and presses Ctrl-A to select all the items in his inbox. His finger hovers over the Delete key as he wonders whether the undo function would give him a second chance.

This opening screen is designed to engage the learner with the topic – in this case managing stress at work. However, there is a lot of text here, which might be better presented over two screens and with more visual support.

Creating knowledge tutorials

Let's move on to uncover some strategies you can use to design tutorials that impart important knowledge.

Engage the learner

You cannot take for granted that the learner is interested in the information you want to convey. You have no automatic right to their attention. Your first task is to engage the learner in the tutorial by persuading them that the subject in question matters to them – not to people in general, but them.

You may be pretty sure that your learners will come to your tutorial motivated, but even then it makes sense to explain why the topic is relevant to their work and how they stand to benefit by sticking with you until the end.

In other cases you may need to make a greater effort, to somehow demonstrate the importance of the topic. This can be achieved through a simple but credible example – a case study, a scenario, a 'war story' if you like, ideally one with which the learner can easily identify. The storyline should demonstrate what the negative consequences might be if the learner was to remain in ignorance of the important information you have to offer. If you can't come up with a plausible storyline, ask yourself whether you really do have a learning need.

Explore the learning content

Learning happens as learners make connections and detect patterns. So all

DIGITAL LEARNING CONTENT

Let's see how good you are already at identifying mammals from other animals. Four of the animals below are mammals and belong, quite rightly, in the mammal house. Use your mouse to drag and drop the four correct candidates into the mammal house.

These interactions build on what the learner already knows rather than assuming they are complete novices

That's right. The cheetah is the fastest mammal. At its fastest (70 mph or 110 kph) it can keep up with all (legal) motorway traffic.

Every year more than one million Americans and many others around the world suffer a heart attack, about half of which are fatal. What do you think is the most likely cause of a heart attack?

A malfunction of the heart

Over-straining the heart through excessive exercise or stress

The build up of deposits in the coronary arteries

No. The heart may malfunction as a result of the heart attack, but this would not be the cause. Try again.

Creating learning tutorials

In this example, the learning content is explained diagramatically, using an animation, as well as in a simple, tabular form

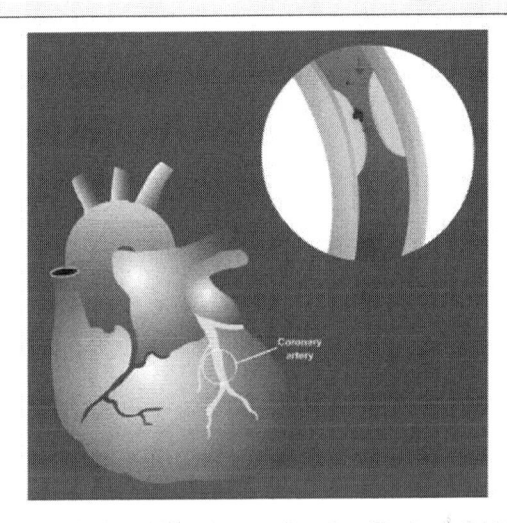

It is the rupturing of this plaque, rather than the simple build-up of it that is the main cause of heart attacks. A thrombosis (blood clot) forms that blocks the blood flow.

Here's a summary of what occurs:

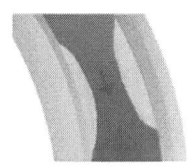

Fatty deposits called plaque build up in the coronary arteries over time.

The plaque ruptures and a blood clot forms.

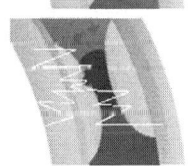

The clot blocks the artery, stops blood flowing to the heart and brings about a heart attack.

DIGITAL LEARNING CONTENT

> Let's take a closer look at the camera unit. As before, roll your cursor over the diagram to discover more.
>
> **Auto focus motor**
>
> The autofocus mechanism automatically adjusts for the distance that the subject you are shooting is away from the lens, to ensure a sharp recording.

This screen allows the learner to explore a piece of equipment by rolling their cursor over parts of the picture

learning is actually built on previous learning – it cannot occur in isolation. For this reason, just about all learners will benefit from relevant examples, analogies and metaphors. They might also surprise you by having some or all of the required knowledge already. Some of the most successful knowledge tutorials start by checking what the learner already knows and then work to fill in the gaps.

Sooner or later you will want to present what needs to be known, as clearly and succinctly as possible, making good use of visuals to clarify your points and improve retention. If you have some 'must knows' as well as 'nice to knows', then make absolutely clear what these are – don't expect learners to work these out for themselves. Even better, move the 'nice to knows' to a separate resource that the learner can access later.

Abstractions are not enough, so don't hold back – present as many examples as you can. If you're not sure how many examples to provide, simply ask the learner: "Would you like another example?"

Depending on the type of knowledge, you might want to provide the opportunity for the learner to actively explore the topic in more detail. This particularly makes sense

Creating learning tutorials

when you are explaining how something works or familiarising the learner with the layout of a physical space, an object or an interface.

Put the learning to work

The learner is much more likely to retain and recall important information if they are provided with plenty of opportunities to work with it, and in the context of a tutorial that's likely to mean answering questions. These serve not only to reinforce the learning but also to help you identify gaps that need to be filled.

The easiest way for you to fill the gaps is through the feedback you provide to the questions. Although many rapid authoring tools do not make this easy to accomplish, it helps if you can provide different feedback for every answer that the learner can make.

Use the feedback to correct any mistakes, not necessarily by repeating the same information from earlier in the tutorial but with a new form of words, perhaps a new example or a new memory aid.

You cannot be sure you have achieved your objectives for the tutorial just by asking a few questions and giving feedback. If the learner struggled with the first questions then you should ask some more to make sure the feedback has worked.

If in doubt, you could always ask the learner if they want to try more questions. To be honest, most tutorials do not go to this trouble, but then most tutorials are a little hit and miss.

Point to the next step

A knowledge tutorial is a catalyst. If you do your job well, you will have excited the learner's interest in the topic and provided them with a foundation on which to build. Unfortunately, new knowledge cannot be cemented in a single session. Your key learning points will need to be reinforced often before they really stick.

So, finish the tutorial by pointing the learner to the next step, whether this is a further tutorial, web sites that they can explore, a discussion forum or all manner of other resources.

```
By now you should be pretty clear about what it is that makes a
mammal a mammal. Just to make sure, here's a quick quiz. On
the screen are twelve examples of animals, eleven of which are
mammals. See if you can find the odd one out, without choosing
any wrong examples.

  ○ Wallaby
  ○ Gorilla
  ○ Koala
  ○ Walrus
  ● Lion
  ○ Wild boar
  ○ Seal
  ○ Shrew
  ○ Squirrel
  ○ Penguin
  ○ Donkey
  ○ Dolphin

No, the lion is the largest member of the cat family. Think
about the characteristics of mammals.
```

This example tests for understanding of a concept.

```
The first major implementation of Internet technology occurred
in the 70s with [arpanet] which linked research
establishments at US universities.

Type your response into the box. Then click OK.

[OK]

That's right. You have a good memory.
```

This one tests for factual knowledge.

www.onlignment.com

173

DIGITAL LEARNING CONTENT

Locate the microphone in this picture of a digital video camera.

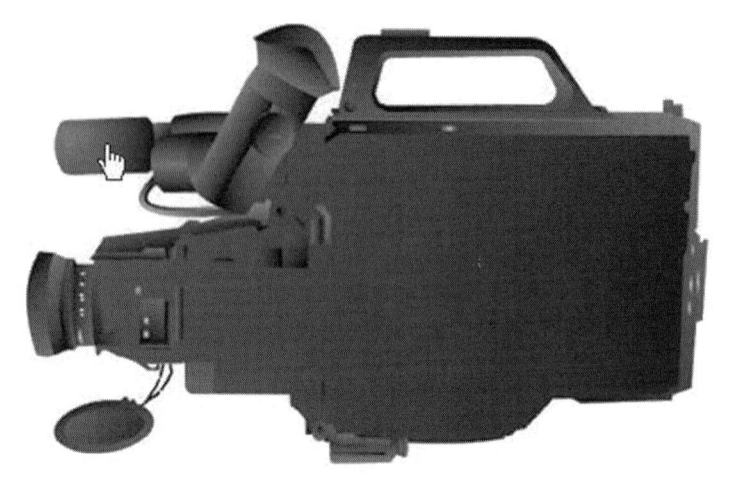

These two examples test for knowledge of the location of a part of a piece of equipment and for the name of a part at a specific location.

No, it looks like a microphone, but it's actually a stabiliser. Try again.

What is the name of the part highlighted in this picture?

Type your answer into the box. Then click OK.

| zoom mechanism | OK |

That's right, the zoom mechanism.

Creating learning tutorials

Creating how-to tutorials

Finally, let's look at how tutorials can be used to teach procedures.

Engage the learner

As we have already discussed, you cannot simply assume that the learner will come to your tutorial full of enthusiasm for the topic. Your task is to convey the importance of the topic and its relevance to the learner's job. The simplest way to do this is just to explain, but you can achieve a more powerful effect through some form of introductory activity.

Explain and demonstrate

Your next step is to provide a quick overview of the steps in the procedure. It will help the learner if you present the big picture before going into detail.

Then explain or demonstrate the procedure step-by-step, explaining any special rules that need to be followed at each step.

Provide an opportunity for safe practice

It's one thing to understand a procedure. It's quite another to be able to put it into practice. It takes time to turn knowledge

The opening is not only the first stage in a call, it's the most important. First impressions count and, on the telephone, the first impression you give is through your opening.

Listen in to this opening. Grab a pen and some paper, and make a note of any problems you detect.

This activity opens a tutorial on greeting a customer on the telephone. It demonstrates why the opening is so important.

www.onlignment.com   175

DIGITAL LEARNING CONTENT

Which of the following statements is true of your use of Microsoft Word?

I don't use Word at all

I can create, modify and apply Word styles to a document

I can apply Word styles to a document, but I can't create or modify styles

I make no use of Word styles

So you're already enjoying some of the benefits of Word styles. This tutorial will still be useful if you want to learn how to create and modify your own styles.

This activity, in a module that teaches how to use styles in Microsoft Word, aims to establish relevance of the topic.

The next step in the module is to demonstrate just how much time can be saved by using Word styles.

If you're not already a user of Word styles, take a moment to consider how many minutes you spend on a typical day carrying out the following tasks:

- applying formatting (text font, colour, size, emphasis, etc.) to blocks of text
- applying formatting (alignment, indents, spacing) to paragraphs
- setting up tabs
- setting up borders and shading
- configuring bullets and numbering
- changing any of the above for multiple instances in the same document

When you've got a figure, go to the next screen ...

So, assuming you carried out the exercise on the previous screen, how many minutes did that add up to?

12 [OK]

That's a lot of time if you multiply the figure up by the number of days in a year – time you could have been spending more profitably. Using Word styles will save an awful lot of that time and all you have to do is this short tutorial.

Creating learning tutorials

Here the five steps in the procedure are presented one at a time using simple animations and text. This is followed by a simple tabular summary, which could also serve as a job aid.

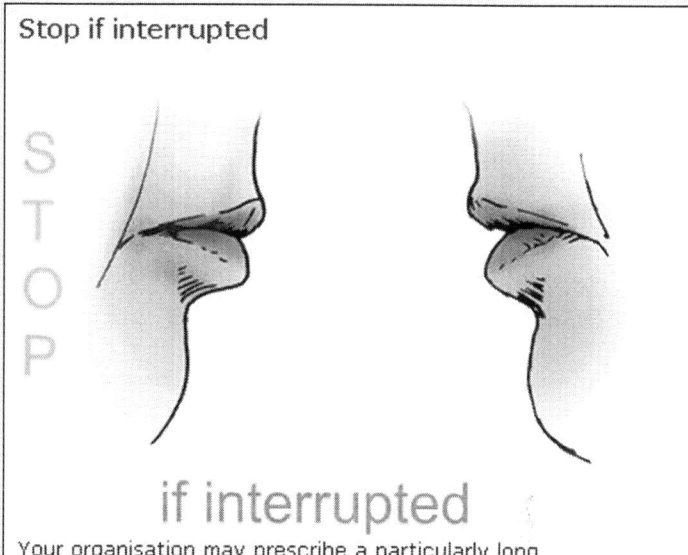

Stop if interrupted

S
T
O
P

if interrupted

Your organisation may prescribe a particularly long announcement, or maybe your caller's in a hurry. Either way, if you're interrupted by the caller midway through your announcement, don't carry on regardless. Remember, the caller is much more important than the announcement.

And here's a summary of the five rules for effective openings.

1	Wait for the call to connect	Allow for the time it takes for your organisation's call handling system to connect you with the caller.
2	Announce in the style of your organisation	If your organisation has a standard announcement, find out what it is and what room there is for variations.
3	Sound fresh each time	Don't be a robot. Make your caller believe he or she is your first call of the day.
4	Smile!	Remember, your caller can hear you smiling.
5	Stop if interrupted	Don't go through your whole routine if your caller wants to get on with the call.

www.onlignment.com

177

DIGITAL LEARNING CONTENT

Modifying a style

Sometimes you want something different from the styles available in the current document template. Here we're going to modify the 'Heading 1' style to change it from black to blue.

Word styles

A style is a set of form[atting]
change its appearance.
For example, you may
separate steps to forma[t]
one step by applying th[e]

In this example, screencasts are used to present each step. Again, the key points are also summarised in simple tabular form.

Modifying a style

Here's the procedure, in words:

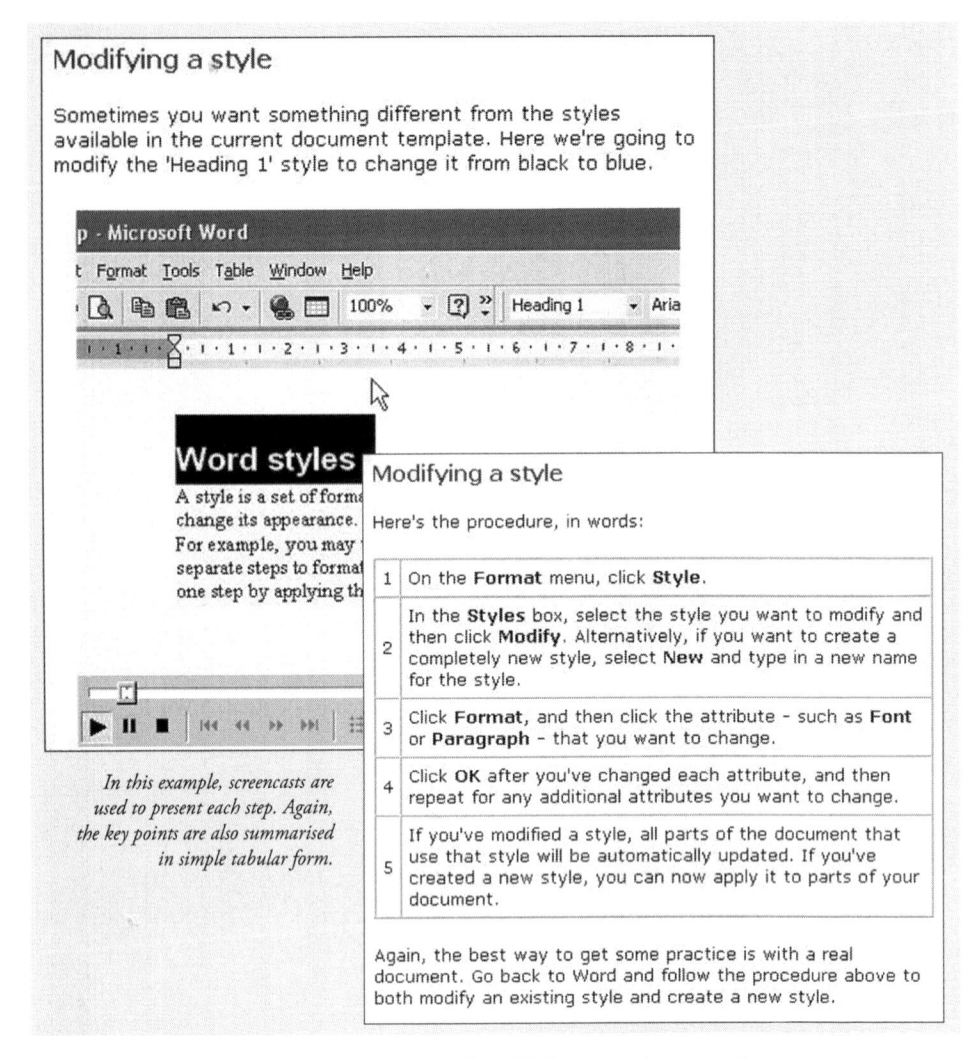

1	On the **Format** menu, click **Style**.
2	In the **Styles** box, select the style you want to modify and then click **Modify**. Alternatively, if you want to create a completely new style, select **New** and type in a new name for the style.
3	Click **Format**, and then click the attribute - such as **Font** or **Paragraph** - that you want to change.
4	Click **OK** after you've changed each attribute, and then repeat for any additional attributes you want to change.
5	If you've modified a style, all parts of the document that use that style will be automatically updated. If you've created a new style, you can now apply it to parts of your document.

Again, the best way to get some practice is with a real document. Go back to Word and follow the procedure above to both modify an existing style and create a new style.

into skill and it's unlikely that your tutorial will do much more than kick-start this process. It's your job to provide the learner with the opportunity to take their first step, with a simple yet challenging activity that mirrors the real world as closely as possible.

With a complex procedure, you may want to provide a practice activity at each step. In this case, it's likely that you'll cover each step in a separate tutorial. Don't forget to bring the whole procedure together at the end, as in real life steps are not carried out in isolation.

Creating learning tutorials

OK, I know, that was too easy. This time - **adding or modifying a style** - there are more steps. Drag the pictures on the right below, each representing a step in the procedure, into the boxes on the left, in the order in which the steps would be carried out in practice.

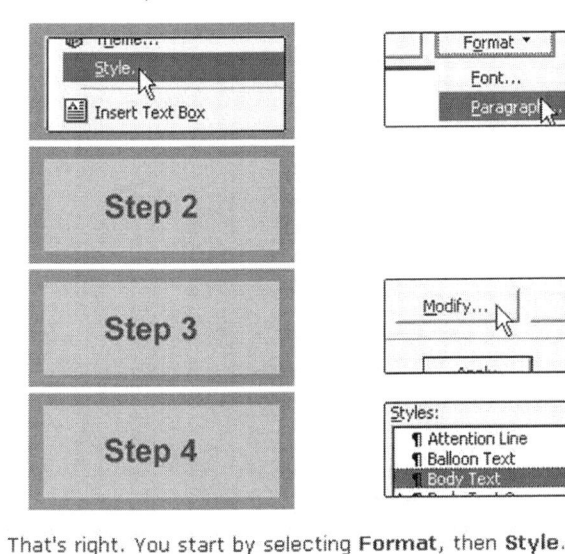

This drag and drop activity requires the learner to place the steps in the procedure into sequence. This is still not checking for the ability to apply the skill, so another activity will be needed which has the learner carry out a task using this knowledge.

That's right. You start by selecting **Format**, then **Style**.

Point to the next step

A how-to tutorial is the first step in learning a new skill. In many cases the learner will be able to take things on from there on their own, but where the skills require a great deal more safe practice before they are applied on-the-job, you may find you have to organise further practice opportunities using simulations, role plays and workshop activities.

www.onlignment.com 179

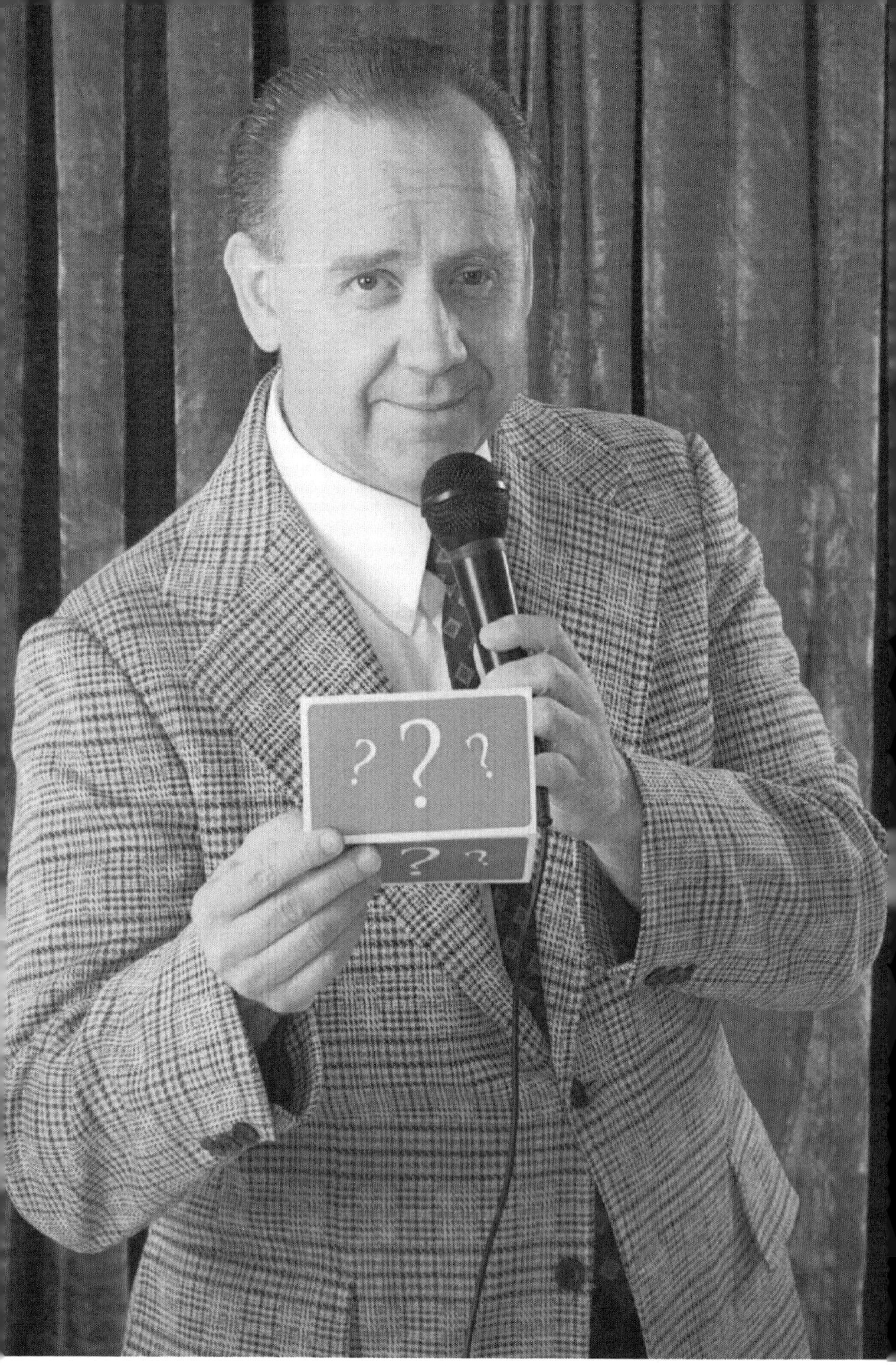

16
Creating quizzes

16

Creating quizzes

We all know what a quiz is. It's a test of knowledge, typically accomplished by asking a series of questions.

Quizzes are popular in the digital environment, not least because computers find it so easy to deliver the questions and score the answers. In fact, if you were in your first week of a programming course, you'd probably have a go at putting together a multiple-choice quiz. Quizzes are an entertaining diversion, particularly when delivered within the context of a game, with rules, levels, competition and prizes, but they can also play a useful role within a learning solution. A role that is often abused, perhaps, but the potential is there.

Media elements

Although many quizzes are primarily textual, the possibility is there to use every media element. Images can provide the basis for questions that test for recognition of people, objects or places or to locate elements within interfaces and other spaces. Video can be used to portray situations that test the learner's ability to make critical judgements. Audio can be employed to check for recognition of voices or pieces of music. A variety of media can also be used to introduce questions and provide feedback.

Interactive capability

Quizzes are essentially interactive. They serve their function in testing knowledge only by eliciting responses from learners. Just about any input device imaginable can be used as the basis for that interaction – key presses, mouse clicks, touches, the lot.

Applications

The most common application for a quiz is as a test of mastery. This is fine in principle as long as it really is possible for the knowledge and skills in question to

TV quiz shows make for good popular entertainment and similar formats can be used within computer-based quizzes

Creating quizzes

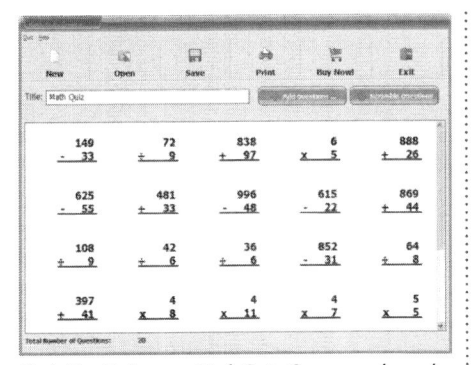

Tools like this low-cost Math Quiz Creator can be used not only for assessment, but to provide loads of valuable practice

be assessed by the sort of questions that a computer can deliver. To state the obvious, you might be able to check that a pilot understands the principles of aerodynamics using a quiz, but you can't check they can fly the plane. Some caution also needs to be taken in terms of when a quiz is delivered. If a quiz comes right after the delivery of content (and the learner knows it's coming), it is all too easy for the learner to hold on to enough of the information to get them through the quiz, but then forget it all the day after. We can probably all remember how possible it was to cram in information before an exam, only to see that evaporate almost as soon as we committed it to paper. A much more valid test of knowledge comes weeks, months or years after original exposure to the information.

Although their potential is rarely exploited to the full, quizzes can actually play a useful role at just about every stage in the learning process:

- As a way, right up front, for the learner to find out how much they already know and how much they need to know. This sort of diagnostic pre-test not only demonstrates the need for learning, it helps to direct the learner to content that is likely to be most useful.

- As a vehicle for delivering the learning content itself. One way to create an engaging lesson is to use a series of quiz questions to challenge and then build on the learner's prior knowledge. Every question alerts the learner to a gap to fill and all you have to do is oblige.

- As a means for repetitive drill and practice. Unlike teachers, computers never get bored asking questions and they don't lose their patience when the learner takes a little longer than expected to get the point. In the classroom, most knowledge is under-rehearsed and most skills under-practised. Quizzes represent a good way to remedy that.

So how do I get started?

There is no shortage of tools for creating quizzes. Most cover the usual range of questions types – multi-choice, multi-answer, free text response, sequencing, matching, selecting hotspots and all sorts of variations.

Most e-learning authoring tools come with a quiz making capability, plus there are specialist stand-alone tools, including ones that you can use for high-stakes assessments or for quiz games.

www.onlignment.com

Choosing the right question type

There is a variety of question formats, each suited to particular types of learning:

Factual knowledge

In an adult learning context, factual information is usually supplemental to the core learning objective and more often than not just for general interest.

However, some facts really do need to be known by heart: When was … ? What is … ? Who is … ?

If it is essential that the learner can recall the information without prompting, then you have little choice but to ask a question that requires them to type the answer in.

If it is only necessary for them to recognise the right answer, then various forms of multiple choice will do. See the examples opposite.

Conceptual knowledge

Concepts provide a common language for understanding a subject. Generally the aim is for the user to be able to identify the class or category to which given objects belong, whether these are tangible (like types of computer) or abstract (like schools of thought). The most common way of checking this knowledge is to provide the learner with examples and ask them to place these in the correct categories, as in the examples shown on page 186.

Process knowledge

A process explains how something works as a chain of cause and effect relationships. To check understanding of a process, you can ask questions about causes or about effects, as shown on page 187.

Spatial knowledge

In this instance our aim is for the learner to be able to identify the locations of parts of an object, device, physical space or system. The easiest way to check this knowledge is with a question that has the learner click on a given part as shown on page 188.

Procedural knowledge

Procedural knowledge is tougher because in many cases what you really want to test is whether the learner can actually carry out the procedure rather than just answer questions about it. However procedural knowledge is a first step and you can use a variety of questions to check learning. See page 189.

Writing good questions

Question writers are faced with two tricky problems:

1. They do not want to make the correct answers too obvious but, on the other hand, they don't want to leave these answers open to challenge. So, they put an awful lot of care into how they phrase the right answers, to make them absolutely clear. In the process, they often give the answers away.

2. They need to tempt the user with distractors (wrong answers) that are genuinely distracting. To be distracting, they must be plausible. The trouble is that plausible distractors – tempting but still unambiguously wrong - can

Creating quizzes

Quiz1
Question 1 of 10 ▾   Point Value: 10

In what year was the Battle of Hastings?

Score so far: 0 points out of 0   SUBMIT

Quiz1
Question 2 of 10 ▾   Point Value: 10

Place these Kings and Queens of England in the order in which they reigned:

1. James I
2. Charles I
3. Henry VIII
4. Elizabeth I
5. Mary I
6. Edward VI

Score so far: 10 points out of 10   SUBMIT

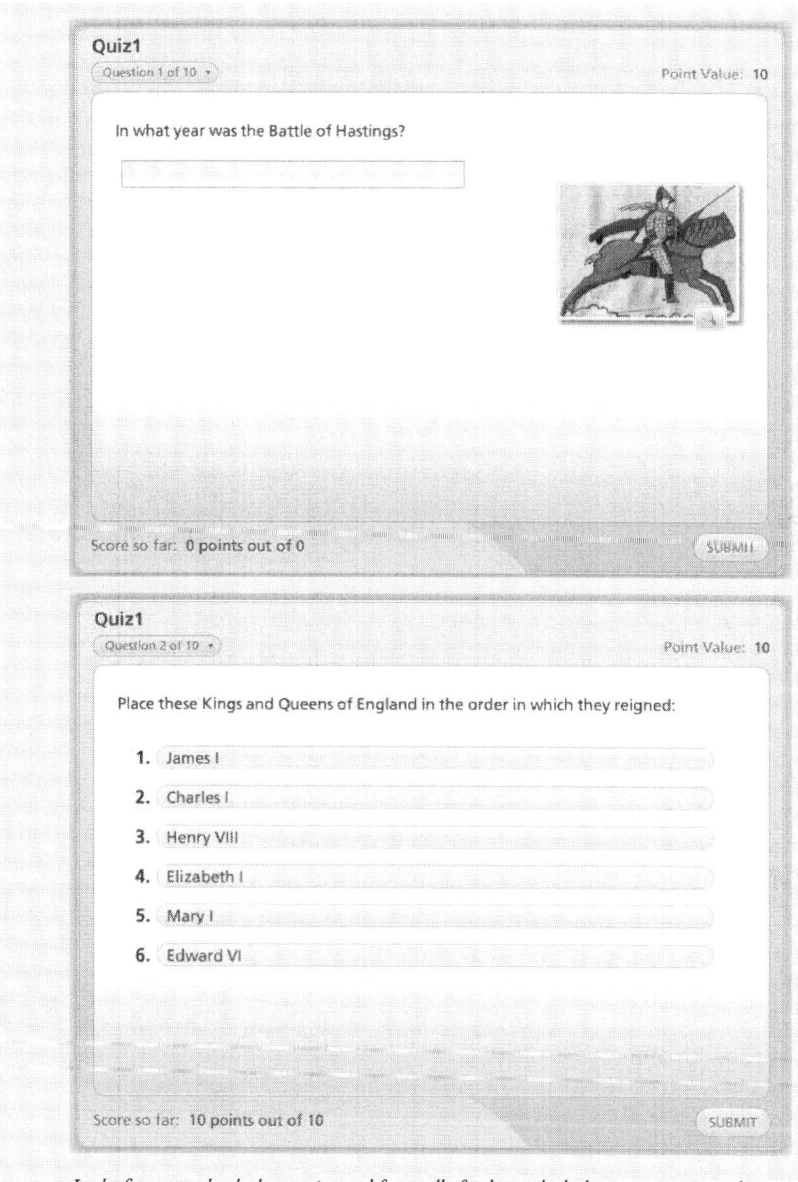

In the first example, the learner is tested for recall of a date, which they must type in to the text box. The second example also checks for recall, in this case of a chronological sequence.

DIGITAL LEARNING CONTENT

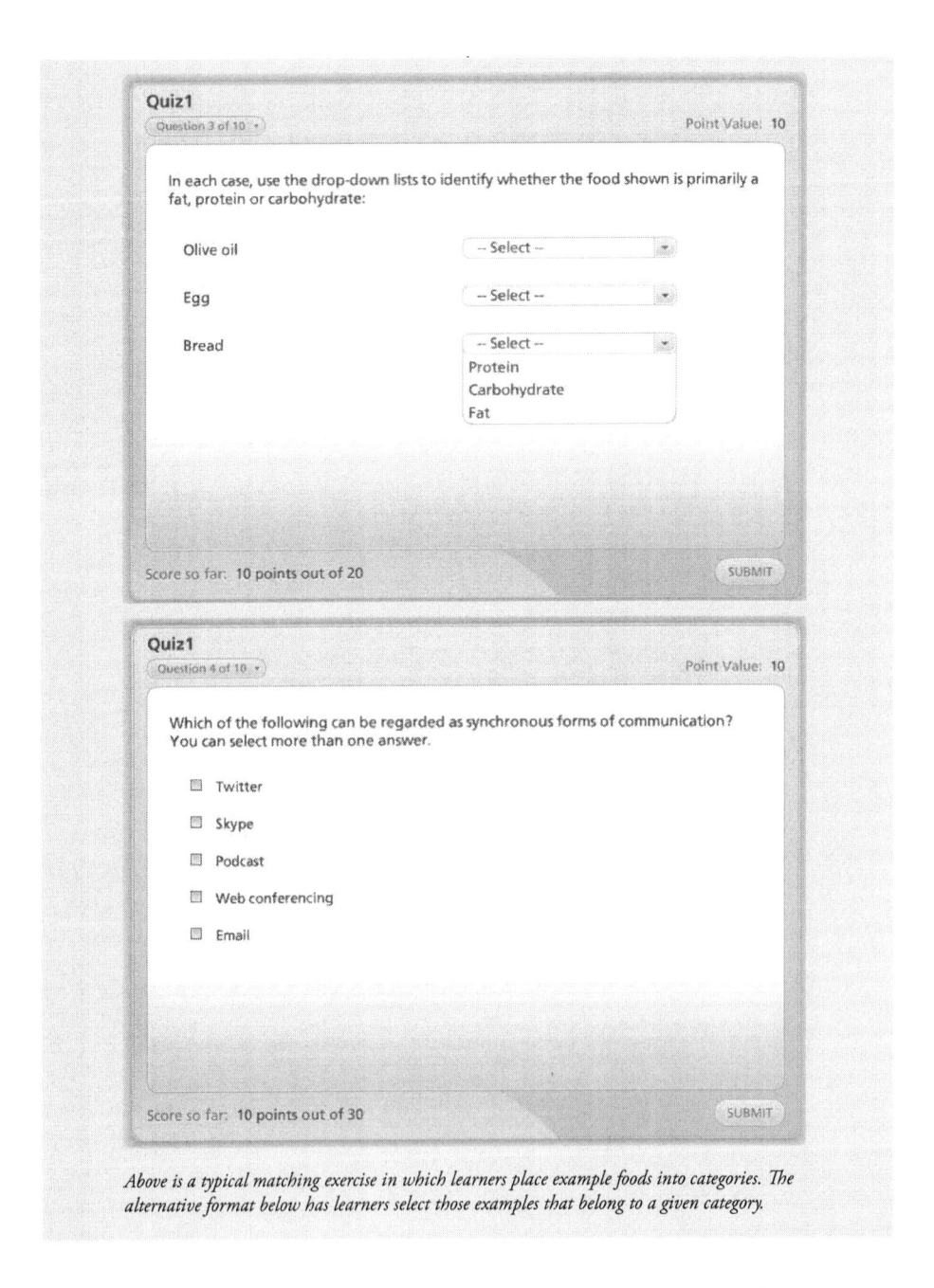

Quiz1
Question 3 of 10   Point Value: 10

In each case, use the drop-down lists to identify whether the food shown is primarily a fat, protein or carbohydrate:

Olive oil   -- Select --

Egg   -- Select --

Bread   -- Select --
                   Protein
                   Carbohydrate
                   Fat

Score so far: 10 points out of 20   SUBMIT

Quiz1
Question 4 of 10   Point Value: 10

Which of the following can be regarded as synchronous forms of communication? You can select more than one answer.

☐ Twitter

☐ Skype

☐ Podcast

☐ Web conferencing

☐ Email

Score so far: 10 points out of 30   SUBMIT

Above is a typical matching exercise in which learners place example foods into categories. The alternative format below has learners select those examples that belong to a given category.

Creating quizzes

Quiz1
Question 5 of 10 ▾ — Point Value: 10

Which of the following instances is most likely to trigger a central bank to increase interest rates? Drag your answer into the box.

- A growing balance of payments surplus
- A rise in inflation
- A fall in unemployment
- A rise in currency values

Score so far: 10 points out of 40 — SUBMIT

Quiz1
Question 6 of 10 ▾ — Point Value: 10

Which of the following is likely to result from lowering the tension of the strings on your tennis racquet? You can select more than one answer.

- ☐ You get more control
- ☐ You place less stress on your arm
- ☐ You get more power
- ☐ You get more spin

Score so far: 20 points out of 50 — SUBMIT

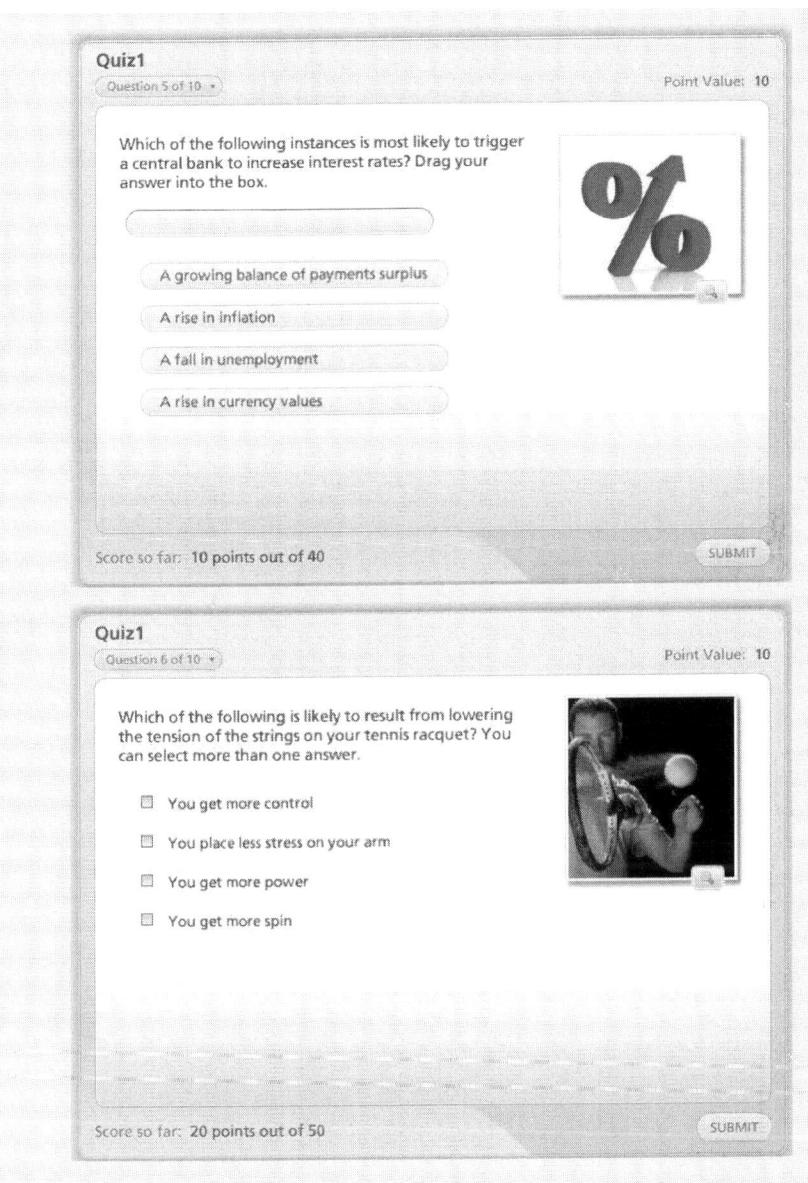

In the first example the learner identifies a probable cause. In the second, the learner looks at possible effects.

DIGITAL LEARNING CONTENT

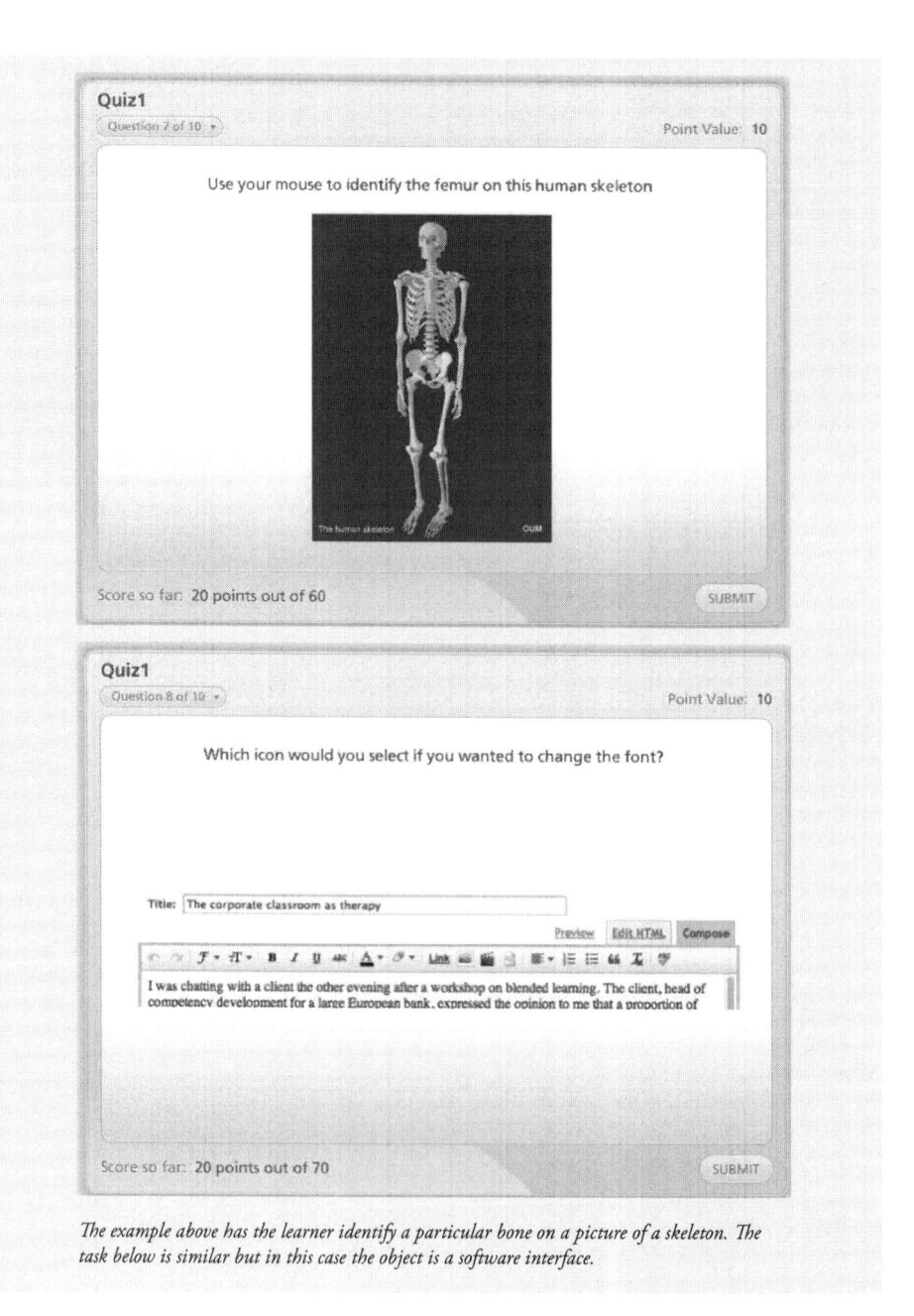

Quiz1
Question 7 of 10
Point Value: 10

Use your mouse to identify the femur on this human skeleton

Score so far: 20 points out of 60
SUBMIT

Quiz1
Question 8 of 10
Point Value: 10

Which icon would you select if you wanted to change the font?

Title: The corporate classroom as therapy

Preview Edit HTML Compose

I was chatting with a client the other evening after a workshop on blended learning. The client, head of competency development for a large European bank, expressed the opinion to me that a proportion of

Score so far: 20 points out of 70
SUBMIT

The example above has the learner identify a particular bone on a picture of a skeleton. The task below is similar but in this case the object is a software interface.

188 www.onlignment.com

Quiz1

Question 9 of 10 — Point Value: 10

What would you do if the SME insisted on including every piece of information in the module?

- ○ Accept on the basis that there is only so much you can do to influence the SME's opinion
- ○ Refer the issue to your supervisor
- ○ Refuse to work further on the project on the basis that to continue would compromise your professional values
- ○ Remind them once again that this will detract from the effectiveness of the module
- ○ Suggest a compromise solution, such as placing all the nice-to-know information in a separate document

Score so far: 20 points out of 80 — SUBMIT

Quiz1

Question 10 of 10 — Point Value: 10

Place these steps in the correct order

1. Implementation
2. Design
3. Analysis
4. Development
5. Evaluation

Score so far: 20 points out of 90 — SUBMIT

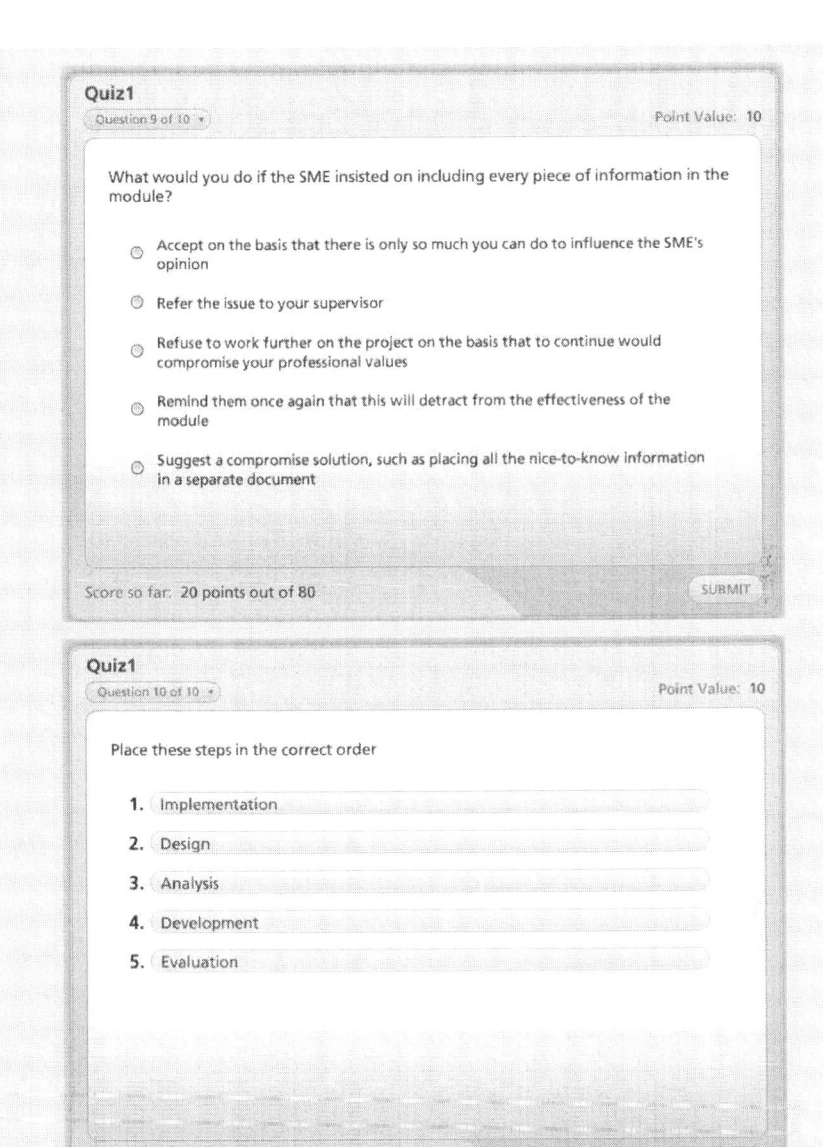

Rules and principles determine how a procedure is implemented in specific cases. The top example explores how different principles could be applied to a particular situation. The second checks that the learner knows the correct order in which procedural steps should be applied.

DIGITAL LEARNING CONTENT

be hard to come by, particularly when you're testing knowledge of rules and principles. Still sure you want to write quiz questions?

Let's explore both of these traps, with the help of some examples.

Obvious answers

In the first example, shown below, most learners will pick the fourth option. Why? Because it is the longest. That's because the question writer will spend a disproportionate time making sure the correct answer is absolutely precise. As a result, it stands out.

Also, the question writer was obviously struggling to come up with a plausible fourth option, which is why they threw in option 3 – an amusing throw-away, but certainly not a genuine distractor.

The second example, shown above right, is just carelessness. Only the word 'elephant' fits grammatically with the stem of the question.

Below right is another frequent mistake.

The absolute answers ('no men' and 'all men') are clearly less likely than the softer 'some men'. No learner is going to be fooled by these distractors.

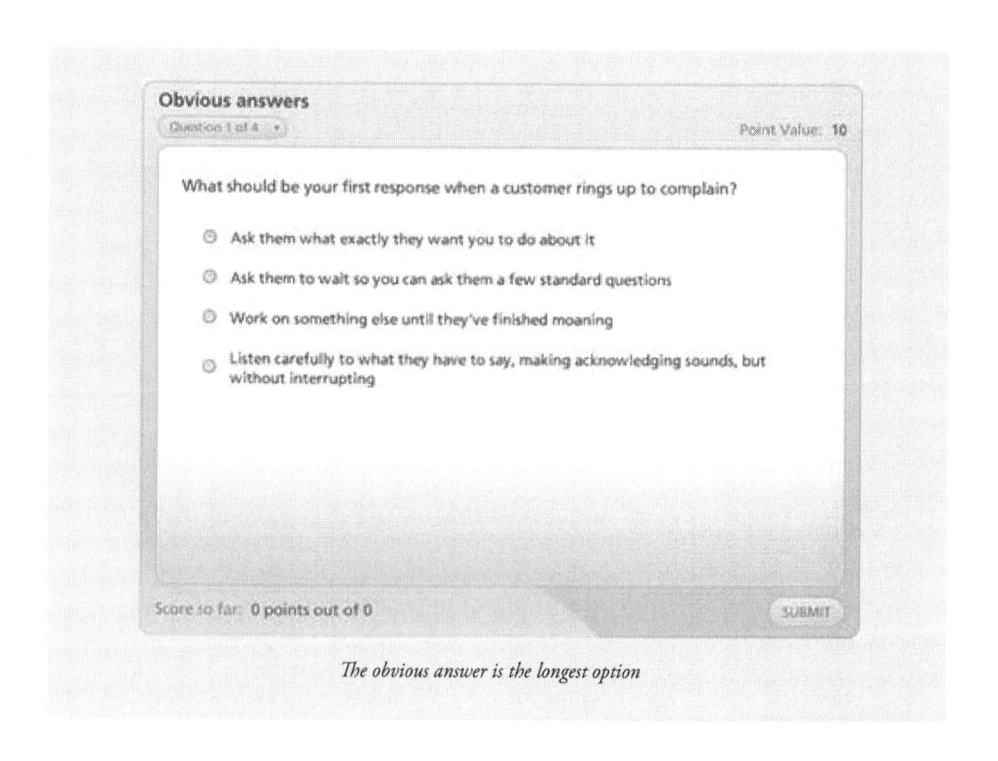

The obvious answer is the longest option

Creating quizzes

Obvious answers
Question 2 of 4 Point Value: 10

The largest land-living mammal is an ...

○ hippopotamus
○ elephant
○ giraffe
○ rhinoceros

Score so far: 0 points out of 10 SUBMIT

The absolute answers are clearly distractors

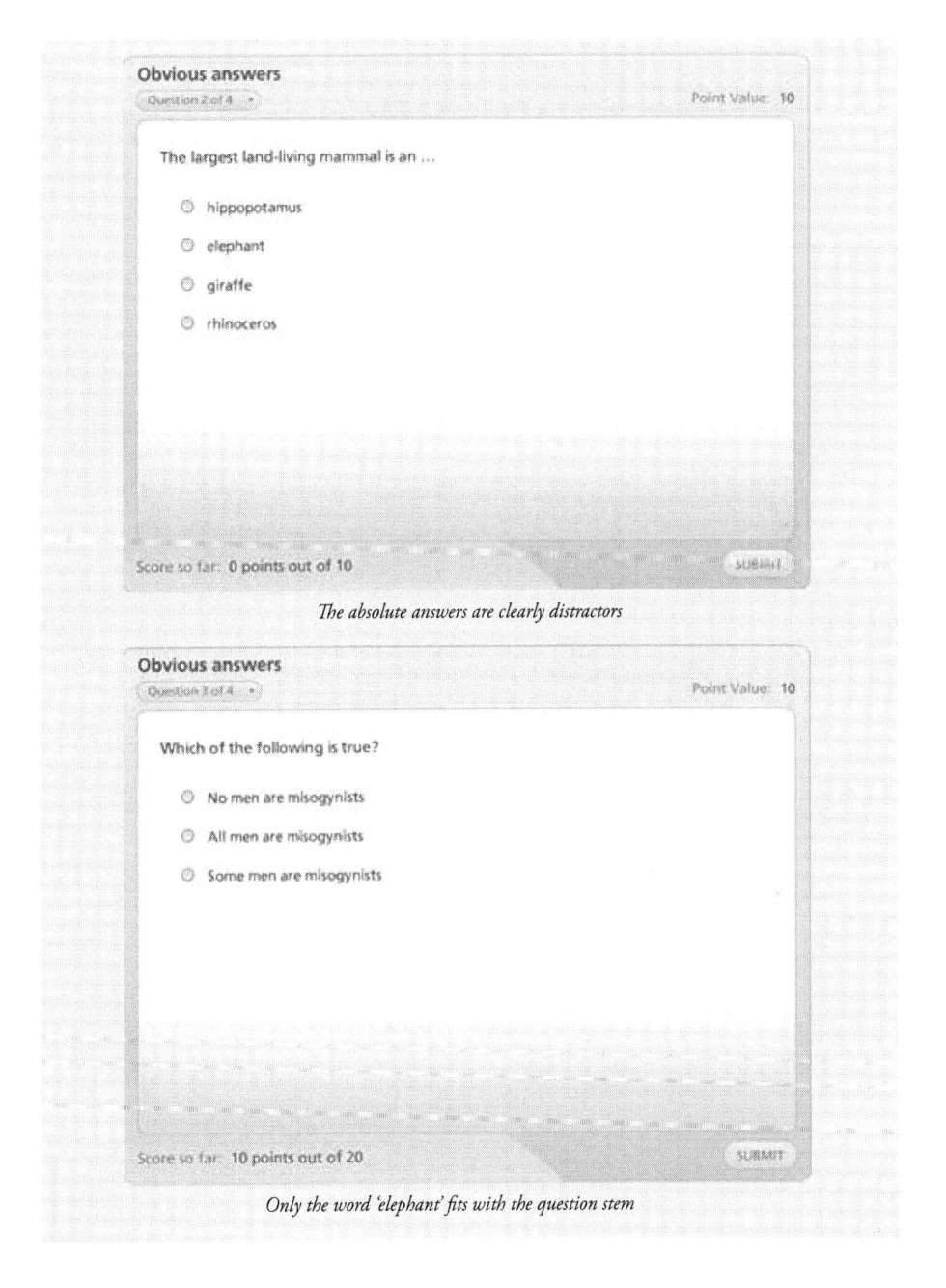

Obvious answers
Question 3 of 4 Point Value: 10

Which of the following is true?

○ No men are misogynists
○ All men are misogynists
○ Some men are misogynists

Score so far: 10 points out of 20 SUBMIT

Only the word 'elephant' fits with the question stem

www.onlignment.com

191
Void using 'none of the above' as an option

DIGITAL LEARNING CONTENT

Avoid using 'none of the above' as an option

Another lazy cop out is to use 'none of the above', as in the example above.

This is a way of telling the learner that you're having trouble phrasing a correct answer. And option 3 is another throwaway.

Confusing questions

Learners don't mind obvious answers, because it makes their job easier. But they will get annoyed if they are presented with questions that they don't understand.

Take the example shown at the top of the next page. It's bad enough having a negative in the question stem ("Which of the following is NOT …"), but a double negative such as "never unnecessary" makes the question really hard to fathom out.

There is no grammatical consistency in the options presented below right. Each option should be phrased in the same way and flow nicely from the question stem.

Looking overleaf, the problem here is that the learner could enter their answer in so many different ways: "CERN", "CERN in Geneva", "Switzerland", even "Centre Européen de Recherches Nucléaires".

Text input questions are fine, but you must make it absolutely clear what sort of answer you are expecting, for example, "In what city was the research establishment where the World Wide Web was invented?" Even

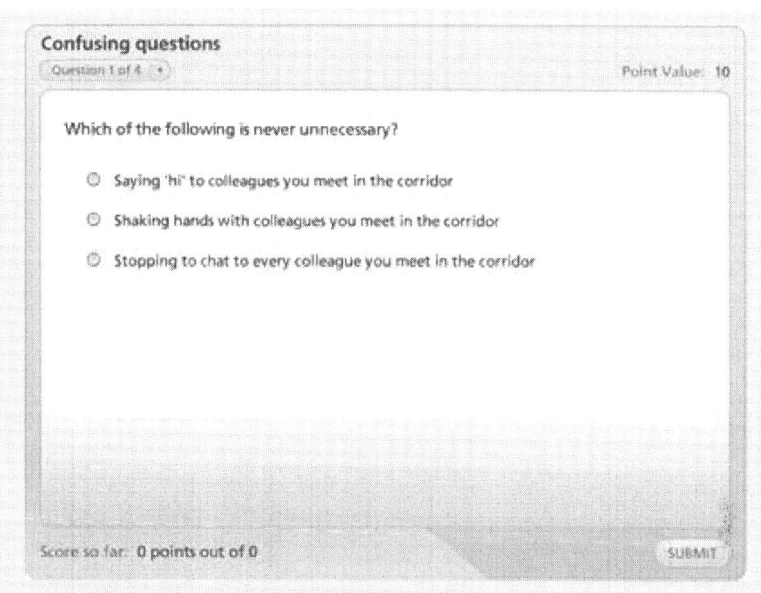

Creating quizzes

Confusing questions
Question 1 of 4
Point Value: 10

Which of the following is never unnecessary?

○ Saying 'hi' to colleagues you meet in the corridor

○ Shaking hands with colleagues you meet in the corridor

○ Stopping to chat to every colleague you meet in the corridor

Score so far: 0 points out of 0   SUBMIT

A double negative is a big no-no!

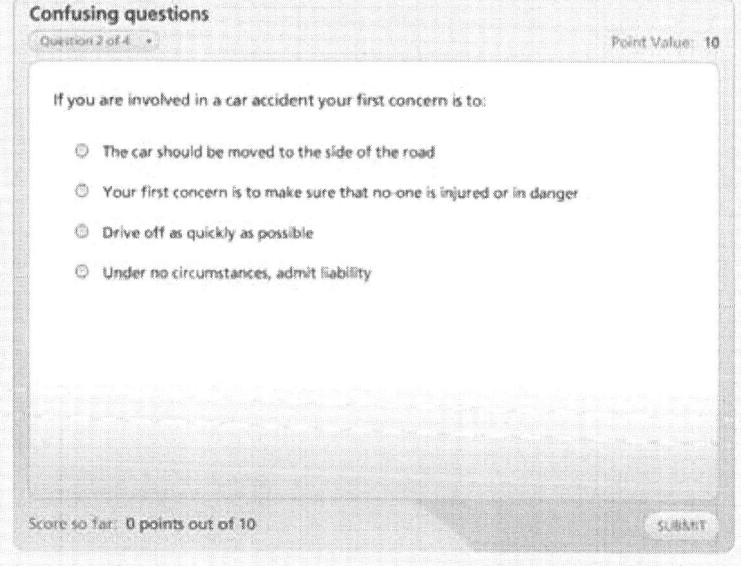

Confusing questions
Question 2 of 4
Point Value: 10

If you are involved in a car accident your first concern is to:

○ The car should be moved to the side of the road

○ Your first concern is to make sure that no-one is injured or in danger

○ Drive off as quickly as possible

○ Under no circumstances, admit liability

Score so far: 0 points out of 10   SUBMIT

There is no grammatical consistency in the way the options are expressed

DIGITAL LEARNING CONTENT

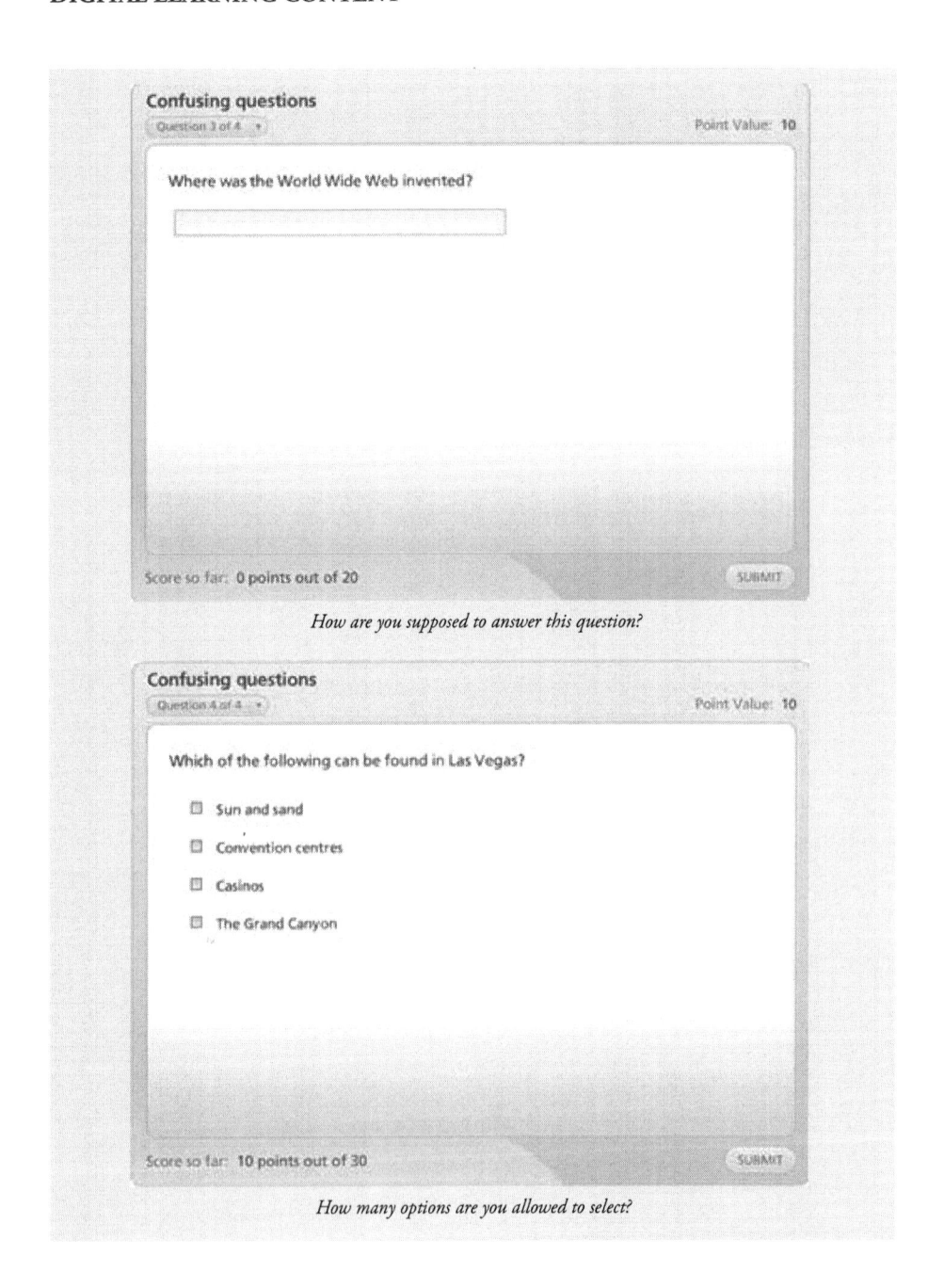

Confusing questions

Question 3 of 4

Point Value: 10

Where was the World Wide Web invented?

Score so far: 0 points out of 20

SUBMIT

How are you supposed to answer this question?

Confusing questions

Question 4 of 4

Point Value: 10

Which of the following can be found in Las Vegas?

☐ Sun and sand
☐ Convention centres
☐ Casinos
☐ The Grand Canyon

Score so far: 10 points out of 30

SUBMIT

How many options are you allowed to select?

Creating quizzes

then you must be prepared to accept both "Geneva" and "Genève".

The problem with the question below left is that it is not clear whether you are looking for a single response or multiple responses. Experienced computer users will recognise that the use of check boxes implies you can pick any number of options, but that won't be obvious to everyone. Better to say "You can choose more than one option."

Chances are you won't see your own obvious answers and confusing questions. You have no option really but to have your quiz questions tested by typical learners. Believe me, you will learn lots from what they have to tell you.

Quizzes as games

Quiz games are still quizzes, in that they can be used assist and assess learning, but they employ gaming techniques to increase learner engagement. We all know how compulsive games can be, so it takes little in the way of imagination to appreciate how much they can add to what would otherwise be a very dry process of drill and practice.

To demonstrate a wide variety of quiz game techniques, we've taken examples from a quiz-making package called Quizit, which unfortunately is no longer available. Similar results could be achieved by those with coding skills, using Adobe Flash Professional or HTML 5, or by using a number of off-the-shelf quiz game tools.

The first example, *Ident*, shown above right, is based on a classic 'picture board.'

Players try to identify as many as possible of the six pictured people, objects or places.

Players select a number then have to type in the name of the pictured object that is then revealed.

Quotient, shown below, is a variant of a multiple choice quiz. Players get rewarded for how close they can get to the right answer. The rather irreverent feedback is delivered randomly from a pool, depending on the accuracy of the answer.

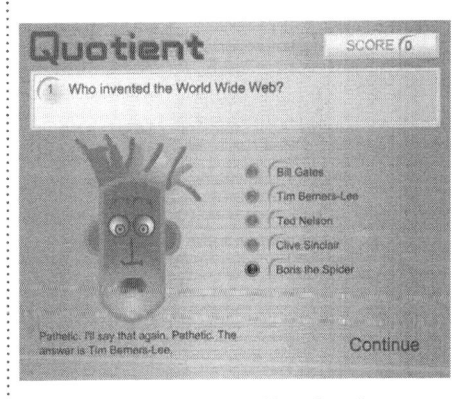

Players try to get as close as possible to the right answers for each question. Each option is graded as to how right or wrong it is and scored accordingly.

www.onlignment.com

195

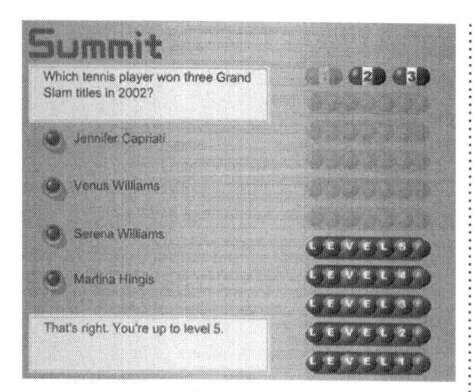

DIGITAL LEARNING CONTENT

Players aim to get to the highest level that they can

Levels are a classic gaming feature. In the game *Sumit*, above, as the player moves up the levels, the questions get correspondingly more difficult.

Players aim to get to the highest level that they can (10 being the highest). They have three 'lives', which allow them to have another go when they make a mistake.

In *Guess*, shown below, players attempt to guess the identity of a person, object, place or event from the clues provided. The more

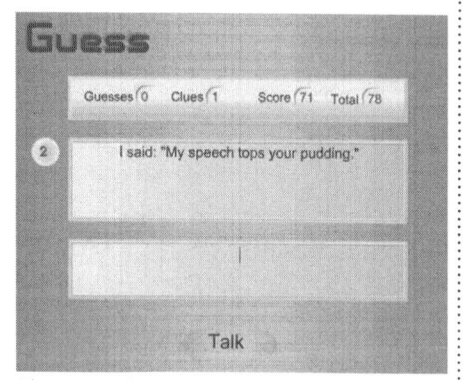

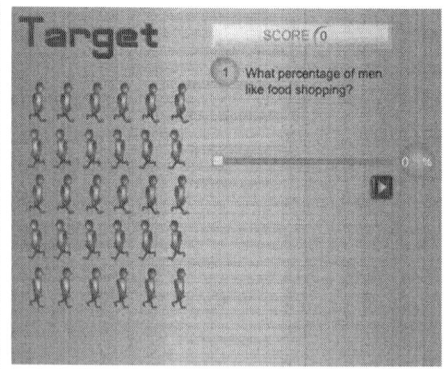

Players use a slider to make estimates

time they take, guesses they make or clues they ask for, the lower their score.

This game is unusual in that it works entirely as a 'conversation' between questioner and player. All input is by natural text. Time pressures add to the level of engagement.

The game *Target*, above, works with a slider, which the player uses to make estimates about the characteristics of a particular target group. They nearer they

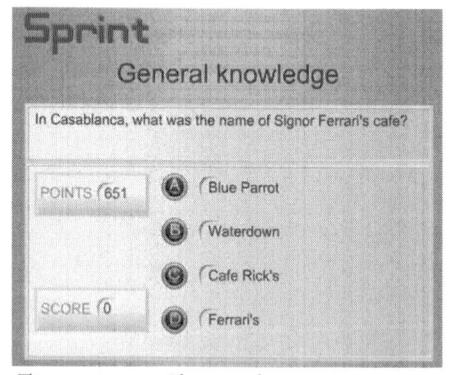

This game works as a conversation between questioner and player

This game is a race. Players can have as many attempts at each question as they like but this loses them time.

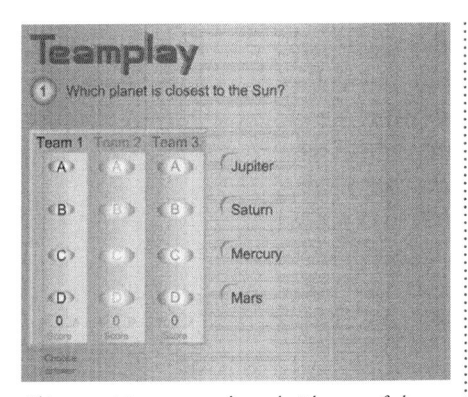

Creating quizzes

This competitive game can be used with teams of players in a classroom.

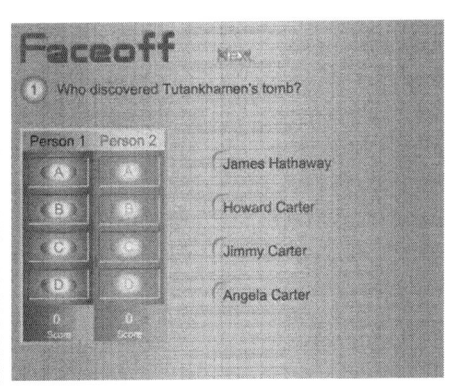

Here two players can compete with each other around the same computer

get to the actual percentages, the higher their score.

In *Sprint*, below and left, players answer a series of questions as fast as they can. They can have as many attempts as they like at each question, but the time lost reduces their score accordingly.

In *Teamplay*, above, three teams or three individual players each answer a series of questions, to see who can answer the most correctly.

Faceoff, above right, pits two players sitting round the same computer against each other.

Making your quizzes robust

We finish off this guide by looking at the steps you can take to make your quizzes robust and reliable.

Being thorough

Assuming your quiz is being used to test knowledge, then you need to take some care to ensure that it performs this function effectively. Prepare at least one quiz question for each of your knowledge objectives. You cannot be sure that a learner has achieved mastery if you test only a sub-set of your objectives. To be absolutely sure the learner has not simply got lucky by guessing answers, you may well prepare more than question for each objective.

Don't write questions to test skills, unless you are absolutely sure quiz questions are capable of assessing these effectively, which will be rarely.

As we discussed earlier, you need to select a question format that's appropriate to the type of knowledge you are testing. For example, if you need to test recall of a technical term, use a text input question and not a multiple choice, which only tests recognition of the term. Don't be tempted to select different formats simply to increase variety – that's not your purpose here.

www.onlignment.com 197

DIGITAL LEARNING CONTENT

Hopefully all that deep thinking is to come up with the right answer, not just to make a good guess

If your objective is that a learner is able to come up with a response quickly, then add time limits to your questions.

Discouraging guessing

Some people reckon they can pass any multiple-choice quiz by guessing the right answers. Your job is to prove them wrong. Earlier we looked at techniques you can use to make life difficult for the chancer – no give-away distractors, no obvious right answers. A simple improvement would be to prepare at least four options for each multi-choice question, and even better five. That does make it even harder to write the questions, but then there really is no pain, no gain when it comes to question writing.

Another technique you could try is to include a 'don't know' or 'not sure' option for each question. This would score no points. Then penalise wrong answers with negative scores. This ups the stakes for the learner who wants to guess the right answers.

Discouraging cheating

The greater the reward for passing an assessment, the more tempting it becomes to cheat. Really high-stakes assessments are beyond the scope of this chapter, but you should be aware of the difficulties in authenticating whether the person answering the questions really is who they say they are. All sorts of complex and expensive technologies are available to authenticate remote users, including finger-printing and retina scanning, but the only way you can be really sure that the learner is who they say they are and is getting no help from a third-party or some reference source is to have them attend a testing centre which has an invigilator present. Most quizzes are not that serious, so there's no point getting carried away with the security!

A more routine way to avoid cheating is to randomise the order in which the questions are presented and the order in which options are displayed within the

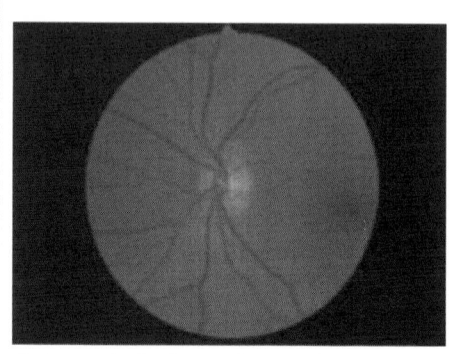

Sophisticated technologies such as retinal scanning can be used to authenticate learners, but are only really necessary for very high stakes assessments

Creating quizzes

Timing
- Open the quiz — 26 September 2011
- Close the quiz — 26 September 2011
- Time limit (minutes) — 0 ☐ Enable
- Time delay between first and second attempt — None
- Time delay between later attempts — None

Display
- Questions per page — Unlimited
- Shuffle questions — No
- Shuffle within questions — Yes

Attempts
- Attempts allowed — Unlimited
- Each attempt builds on the last — No
- Adaptive mode — Yes

Grades
- Grading method — Highest grade
- Apply penalties — Yes
- Decimal digits in grades — 2

Every quiz tool will provide you with different configuration options. This shows some of the options available in the Moodle quiz module, including the ability to set time limits and shuffle questions and options.

questions themselves. That way, no-one can simply write down the question and option numbers and pass them on to others. A step further is to create a bank of questions from which the system selects the questions to display. This means that every learner

DIGITAL LEARNING CONTENT

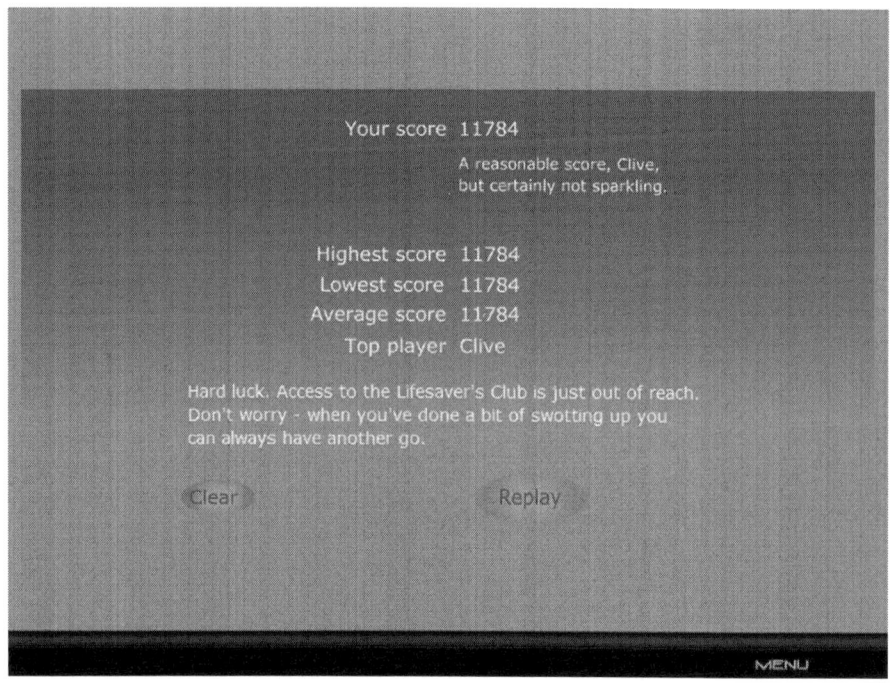

At the finish of this quiz, the user is presented with some light-hearted feedback and a summary of their scores to date. No feedback is presented on the questions, so the user can repeat the quiz as many times as they want.

will receive a different set of questions. Yes, this is a lot more work, but the chances of successful cheating will be much reduced.

Providing feedback

Assuming you are using a quiz as a form of assessment, then if you tell the learner whether they have got each question right or wrong, you are making it easy for them to pass the quiz on a second attempt, without necessarily curing any misunderstandings they may have had. To avoid this problem, you could create a completely different quiz for second attempts, or have the system draw another set of questions from a bank, as described above.

At the end of the quiz, inform learners whether or not they have passed. If your software allows it, let them know how they performed against each of the topics addressed by the quiz. Pass or fail, provide advice to learners on what they should do next.

If the quiz is being used in a *formative* manner (to help the learner progress towards the learning objectives), rather than *summative* (to assess mastery), then it is vitally important that you provide helpful feedback for every question. Ideally this should be provided for each option of each question, rather than just for correct and incorrect answers. The purpose of this feedback is to correct errors and misunderstandings and to reinforce key learning points.

Scoring fairly

Another consideration is how you score correct answers. Most authoring tools will allow you to specify the number of points you award to each correct answer. In a simple multiple-choice question, this is straightforward enough – you either allocate the same number of points to each question or award more points for particularly difficult questions.

The problem comes with questions that ask for multiple responses. Your first consideration is whether these questions should score higher than MCQs because they are actually asking the learner for a series of decisions, not just one.

Another issue is how you apportion the points across the various options. Let's say there are five alternative options, three of which are correct. Ideally, each correct option will score 20% of the available points. But the learner should also be rewarded for not choosing incorrect options, so each option not chosen should also score 20% of the total.

Whether you can achieve this with your software is another matter!

17
Creating reference information

17
Creating reference information

Strictly speaking, reference information isn't learning content at all, because its purpose is on-demand performance support, not learning. In a performance support context, there is no requirement for the information that is being referenced to be learned, i.e. to be stored in long-term memory. The information is required only to answer a current question or solve a current problem and, as such, it will be processed only in working memory.

Because working memory is so limited (current thinking is that humans can hold only 3-5 items of information in their conscious working memory at any one time), it is vital that reference information is extremely clear, simple and concise, minimising the risk of cognitive overload.

Reference information is playing an ever bigger part in our lives. There's so much we could know and it's changing so regularly that it really is pointless trying to remember it all – we couldn't do it if we tried. True, it is still as important as ever that we understand the key concepts, principles and rules that underpin our work, as well as the skills to apply these on a day-to-day basis, but the rest we can draw down as and when it's needed.

As a learning designer you may be wondering what reference information has to do with you, but you can play a key role. When you design a learning solution, you have to decide what's *course* and what's *resource*, and in many cases you will share materials between the two. And, as an expert in communication, you are better placed than many to do a good job of putting together reference materials that are clear, concise and usable.

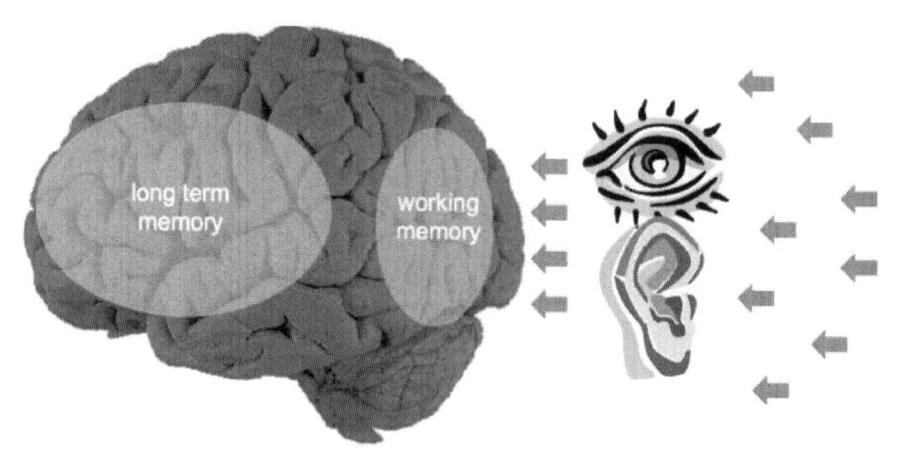

Reference information need go no further than working memory

Media elements

Reference information can utilise any media element, but tends to centre on text. There are good reasons for this. Text is fast to load, it can be quickly skimmed, it can be easily cross-referenced with links and can be copied and pasted with ease. The key with reference information is to get users in, get them to what they want and get them out again as quickly as possible. Text – supported where appropriate by photos, illustrations, charts and diagrams – performs these functions really well.

There are exceptions of course. Some tasks are best explained visually, using video or screencasts with accompanying narration. As long as these are kept short and sweet, they can do the job. As we have dealt with both of these formats in previous chapters, we won't be covering them here.

Interactive capability

Because the purpose of reference materials is just-in-time support and not learning, interactions which encourage users to explore ideas or which assess learning are not relevant. Apart from anything else, they would drastically slow up the user in getting in and getting to the required information. On the other hand, as we shall see later on in this chapter, navigational interactivity is critical to good reference materials, whether that's through search, indexes, tables of contents or cross-references. Some more advanced performance support materials may also allow users to configure the information

Assuming it is formatted properly for reference use, text does an excellent job of getting the user to the information they require

they want to receive (think of something like a weather or stock price app on a mobile device) or will ask users a series of questions to help them trouble-shoot a problem or narrow down a decision.

Applications

Reference materials fit classically within the exploration learning strategy. As such they are designed not to be 'pushed' at the user but 'pulled' as required. In the context of a blended learning solution, they supplement courses with easily accessible resources. Whereas historically some 80% of a learning designer's effort might have been put into the courses and only 20% into providing on-demand resources, we can

DIGITAL LEARNING CONTENT

expect that ratio to reverse in coming years. People no longer expect to have to store loads of information in their heads; they do expect to be able to access it online.

Formats

Reference information can be presented in a number of formats:

Embedded in a software application: One of the most common requirements for on-demand help is to explain how to use a particular software application, or how to enter appropriate data into that application. An advantage of embedding the help within the application itself is that the information presented can be context-sensitive, i.e. directly relevant to the activity that the user is currently undertaking.

In a native document format: Much reference information is stored in a native document format such as Microsoft Word. While tools like Word have very sophisticated editing capabilities, they are not best suited to online use. Native files are slow to open and depend on the user having a copy of the application with which they were created. More importantly, it becomes clumsy to link from document to document and it is all too easy for different versions of the document to be available at the same time.

As a PDF file: PDF is versatile in that a wide range of applications can save in this format. It also overcomes the need for users to have copies of Word, PowerPoint or whatever other applications were used to

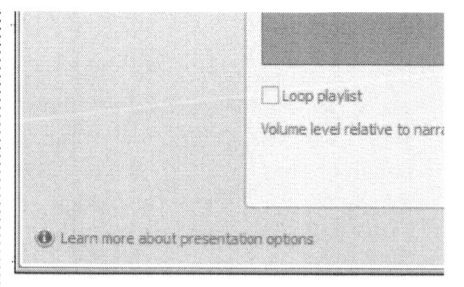

Embedded help can be context-sensitive, taking you directly to the information relating to your current task

create the materials. PDFs are particularly suitable when users need to be able to access information without an online connection or when they want to print materials out. In all other circumstances, HTML wins out.

In HTML: HTML is the format of the web and, as such, is standard across all computing devices. Web pages are ideal for displaying reference information because they download quickly, can be accessed from any device, and can be kept up-to-date centrally. They can also be easily cross-referenced using hyperlinks.

As a mobile app: As any smart phone or tablet user can attest, apps are the quickest and easiest way possible to access information. They are particularly suited to situations in which a body of content or an up-to-date information source needs to be accessed very regularly.

They score over mobile web browsers which access simple HTML pages online because the way the information is displayed can be designed specifically for the mobile device in question.

Creating reference information

The application itself is stored locally which speeds up access, and less volatile information can be stored on the device itself, making the information accessible even when there is no internet connection.

So how do I get started?

Assuming you have researched fully what information is needed by whom and in what circumstances, your next job is to choose the format in which the information will be presented. This format will dictate the tools you'll need:

Embedded information: Here your best route is to liaise with the developers to see what's possible and what help creation tools are available.

Native document format: This is simple enough – just use Word, PowerPoint or whatever to create your materials and then publish in the version most widely available to your users.

PDF: It used to be you had to purchase special Adobe Acrobat software to create PDFs, but now you'll find that many of the applications you're already using can save directly to PDF format.

HTML: The tools you use here will depend on the infrastructure your organisation already has in place for distributing information. You probably already have a content management system for your intranet and that's a good place to start looking. If not, and you're focusing particularly on providing information to support software users, you may want to purchase a system that's specially designed for creating online help materials.

Whatever the case, you do not want to be hand crafting HTML pages. Those days are long over. Creating web pages should be no more complicated than filling in a form.

Mobile app: Although some easy-to-use tools are coming available, developing an app is still a specialised and highly technical process. For now, it is probably best to liaise with your own IT team or engage an external contractor.

Let's move on to how best to design your reference information:

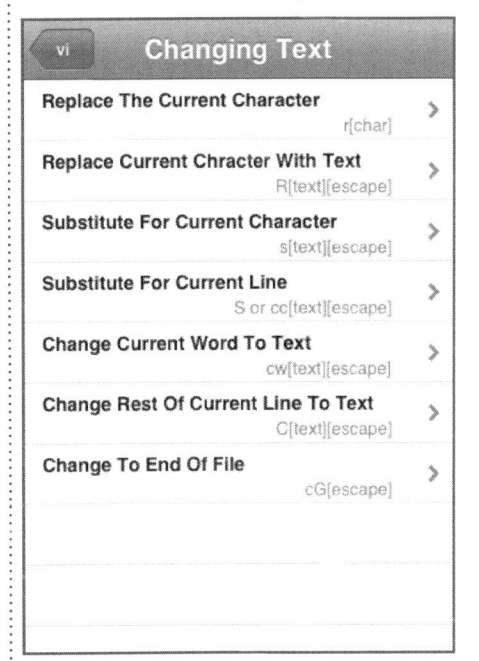

vi	Changing Text
Replace The Current Character	>
	r[char]
Replace Current Chracter With Text	>
	R[text][escape]
Substitute For Current Character	>
	s[text][escape]
Substitute For Current Line	>
	S or cc[text][escape]
Change Current Word To Text	>
	cw[text][escape]
Change Rest Of Current Line To Text	>
	C[text][escape]
Change To End Of File	>
	cG[escape]

Reference apps for mobile devices are ideal for information you need to access regularly

www.onlignment.com

DIGITAL LEARNING CONTENT

General design guidelines

Reference information is different from other learning content because its purpose is to meet a short term need, not to have some long-term effect on the user. It does not need to engage the user, because you can assume that anyone who has made the decision to consult reference material is already engaged. It does not seek to stimulate thought or discussion. It does not need to assess the degree to which learning has taken place, because learning is not its purpose. You should have one simple aim in designing your materials: getting the user to the information they need as quickly and simply as possible and then presenting that information in such a way that it can be used immediately.

Here are some general tips that you can apply to any type of online reference material:

Provide structured information, not prose: What works in a book, a report or a magazine does not work for reference. Very few people will read your material from beginning to end, if they read it at all. They will jump around and skim at lightening speed until they find what they are looking for. Long paragraphs of text are very hard to skim, so focus instead on using tables, lists and diagrams. If you must use prose, keep paragraphs and sentences short and focus on one point at a time. Use plenty of clear, descriptive headings. Leave out the anecdotes and witticisms.

Be consistent: It is much easier to navigate information that is presented consistently. Choose a format for each type of information and use this every time. Adopt a typographical standard and apply this universally. Never vary your means for navigation. What should stand out should

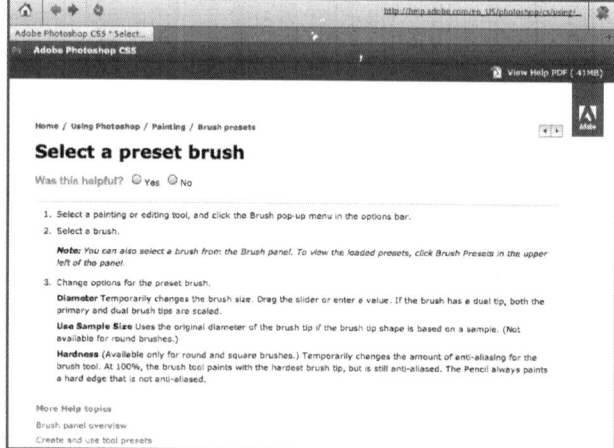

Unstructured prose is fine if you're relaxing reading a novel but is no good if you're hunting down information. Contrast the extract on the right from Adobe Community Help.

208 www.onlignment.com

be important information such as rules and warnings. The only way you will achieve this is against a uniform backdrop.

Ditch the numbering system: It is debatable whether elaborate numbering systems ever helped anyone to navigate a print document, but they are completely unnecessary and unhelpful online. Online information is accessed using search boxes and links. Numbers only get in the way.

Presenting factual information

Factual information, such as names, dates, email addresses, spellings and codes, is best structured into databases or tables, and sequenced alphabetically, numerically or chronologically.

As software becomes more intelligent, we will have less need for these tables; we should expect frequently-used data to be suggested to us automatically, based on our historical usage pattern and the particular context. But there will always be exceptions and we do not only need factual information when we using a software application.

Presenting concepts

According to Ruth Clark, a concept is a category of objects or ideas that is usually designated by a single word. Essentially when we refer to concepts, we are talking about the terminology which helps us to find our way around a particular knowledge domain. Without a common understanding of this terminology, we cannot communicate with our peers.

What you want to do	What you press
Bold	[Ctrl][B]
Change case	[Shift][F3]
Center Align	[Ctrl][E]
Copy	[Ctrl][C]
Cut	[Ctrl][X]
Delete a word	[Ctrl][Backspace]
Find and replace	[Ctrl][F]
Go to page, section, line, etc.	[Ctrl][G]
Go to the beginning of the document	[Ctrl][Home]
Go to the end of the document	[Ctrl][End]
Insert a hyperlink	[Ctrl][K]
Italicize	[Ctrl][I]
Left Align	[Ctrl][L]
New Document	[Ctrl][N]
Open	[Ctrl][O]
Open the thesaurus	[Shift][F7]
Paste	[Ctrl][V]
Print	[Ctrl][P]
Repeat your last action	[F4] or [Ctrl][Y]
Save	[Ctrl][S]
Select all	[Ctrl][A]
Select to the beginning of the document	[Ctrl][Shift][Home]
Select to the end of the document	[Ctrl][Shift][End]
Spell check	[F7]
Undo	[Ctrl][Z]

This alphabetical table of keyboard shortcuts from Techicious makes it easy to reference factual information

An example of a concept is the hashtag used by Twitter. To understand this term we need a definition, one that makes clear what a hash tag is and what relevance it has. We could do with some examples and some non-examples; for example, #devlearn is a hashtag to be used when referring to the DevLearn conference, but @devlearn is a Twitter username.

Some concepts are less abstract and benefit from a non-verbal approach. So don't just list the characteristics of different species of bird; show what they look like and what they sound like.

Sometimes we need to explain a concept in conjunction with a procedure, because

DIGITAL LEARNING CONTENT

```
Definitions of key e-learning terms

                        [Search]  [_____]  ☑ Search full text
                                   [Add a new entry]
              Browse by alphabet | Browse by category | Browse by date | Browse by Author
                              Browse the glossary using this index
                          Special | A | B | C | D | E | F | G | H | I | J | K | L | M | N | O
                                   P | Q | R | S | T | U | V | W | X | Y | Z | ALL
                                                       A

AAC Audio:
AAC (Advanced Audio Coding) is an audio compression format, designed as a successor to MP3 audio. AAC is best known
as the format used for audio on the Apple iPod.
                                                                                                      X 🗑

Actionscript:
Actionscript is a programming language (very similar in format to Javascript), which is an integral part of Adobe Flash.
                                                                                                      X 🗑

ADDIE Model:
The ADDIE model is a process for instructional design: Analysis > Design > Development > Implementation > Evaluation.
Most of the current instructional design models are spin-offs or variations of the ADDIE model; others include the Dick and
Carey model and Kemp model. One commonly accepted improvement to ADDIE is the use of rapid prototyping. This is the
idea of receiving continual or formative feedback while instructional materials are being created.
                                                                                                      X 🗑

AICC:
AICC is short for Aviation Industry CBT Committee, one of the earliest standards for passing student progress data between
elearning content and a learning management system (LMS). AICC is now largely subsumed within the SCORM standard.
                                                                                                      X 🗑

Alpha testing:
Alpha testing is the first major test of a piece of software once it has been completed. The purpose of alpha testing is to
identify any major bugs, before release to users for beta testing.
                                                                                                      X 🗑
```

This Moodle glossary provides easy access to definitions of e-learning terms

the procedure only makes sense when the concept is clear. More typically, when we have many concepts to explain we are better off building a dictionary or glossary.

Presenting procedures

A procedure is a series of rules for carrying out a routine task in a logical sequence. Some procedures are essentially linear: we carry out the same steps each time. Others are conditional: at each step we need to progress differently depending on the particular situation.

Linear procedures can be laid out in a simple tabular form, with tips and warnings at each step where appropriate. If you are presenting a software procedure, use screen shots at each step, but only if these are really needed to make the procedure clear. Remember that these will need revising regularly as the software is updated.

Creating reference information

Conditional tasks can be hard to explain in tabular form, so you might like instead to create a flow chart. These too can become complex and unwieldy, in which case an interactive tool might be more appropriate. Each step can be presented in turn, with conditional links depending on the decision made at each point.

Presenting processes

A process is a description of how something works. Processes typically involve a number of stages, with the output of one stage being the input to the next.

Some processes, such as the water cycle, are cyclical. Others, such as a disciplinary process, continue until some goal or end point is reached.

When users understand a process, they get the bigger picture; they understand how what they do impacts on others.

Processes can be presented in a tabular fashion, but they will often benefit from a process flow diagram of some sort.

Presenting structures

Some information is essentially structural in nature; it describes the 'parts of' things, like the bones in the body, the towns in a region, the elements in a software interface, the roles in an organisation chart, the events in a timeline.

Unsurprisingly, this information is best presented visually, with each part clearly labelled. You can also configure each element as a link to further information.

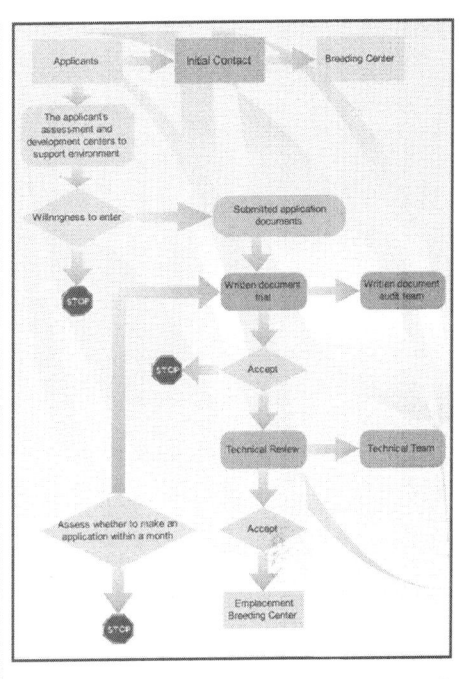

This flowchart from Edraw Soft provides an overview of a business process

Problem-solving and decision making

Sometimes it is not just information that a user needs, but help in troubleshooting a problem or making a decision.

One of the most common ways of addressing the former is with an FAQ, a list of frequently-asked questions, but for more complex problems, such as a network fault, an interactive troubleshooting tool is likely to be much more useful.

Decision aids could be structured as a simple comparison table, listing the pros and cons of each option, or more helpfully

www.onlignment.com

DIGITAL LEARNING CONTENT

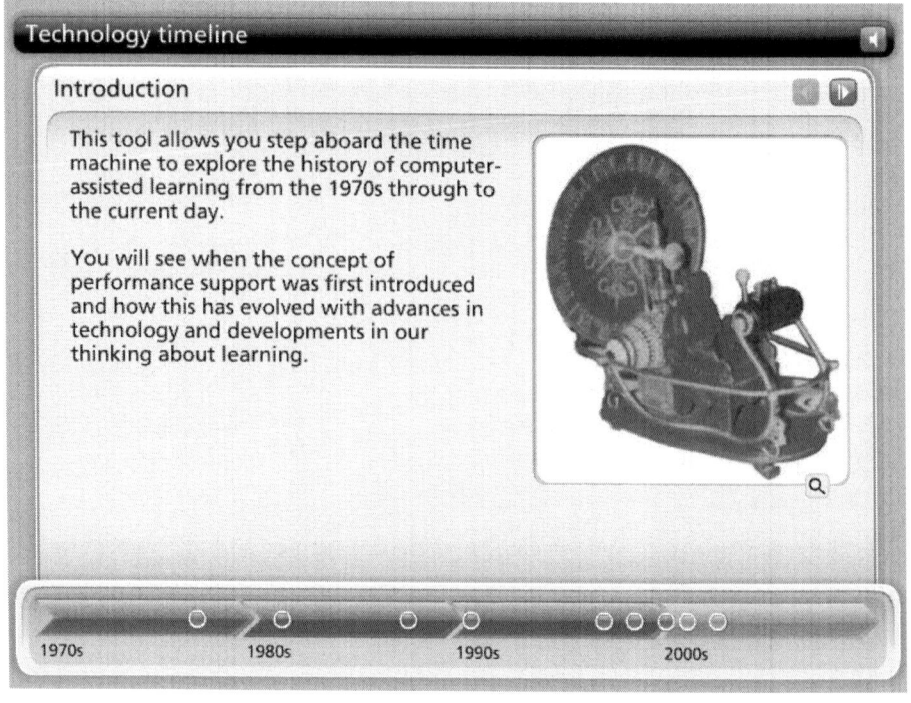

This interactive timeline, produced using Articulate's Engage tool, provides a way for users to explore the history of learning technology

as an 'if ... then' list, which recommends a different option for each potential circumstance. A more interactive tool might ask a series of questions in order to narrow down a suggestion to a single alternative.

Let's move on look at the various ways you can provide access to your information:

Tables of contents

Tables of contents (TOCs) are usually associated with print publications but still have a valid role to play in digital media. Whereas searching can be a rather hit and miss affair, a TOC provides an organised and orderly gateway to a body of information. Every situation is different, but there are some general rules that will help you in preparing a TOC:

Organise the table in a way that makes sense to your user, not what is easiest for you. Think of all the situations in which a user might come to your information and how they would expect to drill down to find what they want. Ask whether the

Creating reference information

> **What can we help you with?**
>
> [   ] [Search Help]
>
> Example: "search box" or "clear history"
>
> **Learn more about using Google Chrome**
>
> | Get started | How to |
> |---|---|
> | Install Google Chrome | Bookmark your favorite pages |
> | New to Google Chrome? | Manage your tabs and windows |
> | Frequently asked questions | Search the web |
> | Using the address bar (omnibox) | Manage your personal settings |
> | Importing or exporting bookmarks | Manage language and display settings |
> | More... | Chrome Web Store |

Google provides access to its Chrome help library though a table of contents, but also – as you would expect – through a search box

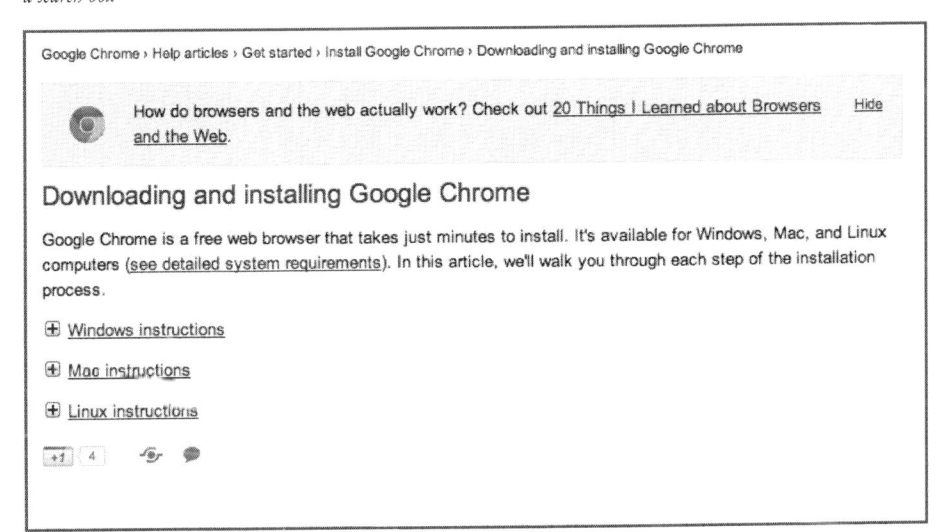

> Google Chrome › Help articles › Get started › Install Google Chrome › Downloading and installing Google Chrome
>
> How do browsers and the web actually work? Check out 20 Things I Learned about Browsers and the Web.   Hide
>
> **Downloading and installing Google Chrome**
>
> Google Chrome is a free web browser that takes just minutes to install. It's available for Windows, Mac, and Linux computers (see detailed system requirements). In this article, we'll walk you through each step of the installation process.
>
> ⊞ Windows instructions
>
> ⊞ Mac instructions
>
> ⊞ Linux instructions

The length of this menu is kept to a minimum by the use of collapsible menus. The user chooses which menu is appropriate to their operating system. Notice how Google draw your attention to a popular favourite – '20 things I learned about browsers and the web'.

www.onlignment.com   213

DIGITAL LEARNING CONTENT

information be organised in task order, by category, chronologically or alphabetically?

Keep menus to a reasonable length while keeping the loading of new menu pages to a minimum. This might sound an impossible compromise to make, but there are all sorts of ways of hiding and revealing lower-level menu items using the sorts of tree menus you find in your computer's file manager.

Draw your user's attention to the most commonly sought after items of information. You could even have a top ten list.

Search

Search used to be considered a rather unfriendly way for users to access information, but search technologies and users skills in searching have come on in

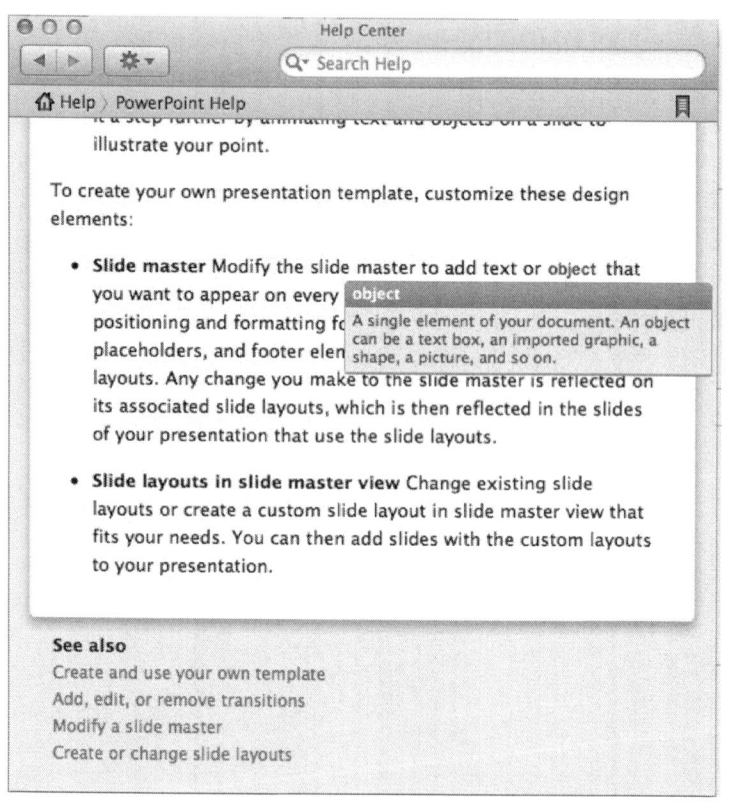

This entry in the PowerPoint help system is supplemented by links to related items. Notice also how the word 'object' is a link which calls up a glossary entry

Creating reference information

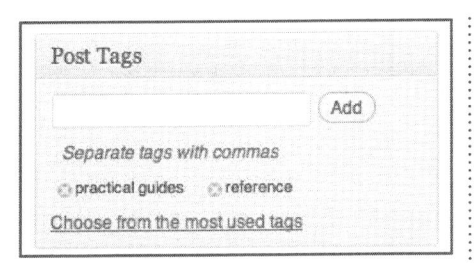

This box is used to add tags to postings on the Onlignment blog

leaps and bounds. The advantage from a user's perspective of using search over a TOC is that it shortcuts all that drilling down through menus. A search facility is now expected and should definitely be provided if at all possible.

Search can be improved by tagging, the process whereby descriptive labels are applied to content. Tagging can be applied on a top-down basis, by content authors, or bottom-up, when users supply their own labels.

Making suggestions

Another way to get users to information that they could find useful is to provide them with intelligent suggestions. An easy and obvious way to do this is to provide 'Related items' links at the bottom of each piece of information.

You could go a little further by building up a profile of each user and then suggesting links that you know from their past usage history would be relevant to them – something like what Amazon do with their 'People who bought this title also bought …' suggestions.

Peer recommendations are always the best, so you may also want to provide a facility to let users recommend items of content to their colleagues, perhaps by emailing them a web address or through some social networking tool.

Unless you have a great deal of programming expertise at your disposal, chances are you'll be limited in the way you can provide access to information by the tools already available to you. Where you do have choices, use them wisely. Listen to your users and let them tell you what they find useful and what's just dressing.

18

What does exemplary digital learning content look like?

18

What does exemplary learning content look like?

When used effectively, digital learning resources have the power to engage and stimulate learners and to contribute greatly to learning achievement. It is not possible to specify exactly what makes a 'good quality' learning resource, because so much depends on the type of the resource (tutorial, simulation, game, podcast, screencast, video, presentation, text document, etc.), the purpose of the resource, the way in which the resource is used and the characteristics of the particular users.

As ever quality is an issue of 'fitness for purpose.' Sometimes the simplest of content does the job perfectly; at other times a highly-sophisticated resource is required to satisfy the need.

Given these provisos, we hope this checklist will both support learning professionals in evaluating existing resources and guide content developers in the design of future resources.

Does the resource meet an identified need?

A good digital learning resource should clearly relate to an identified learning need whether within a curriculum/programme of learning activities or within a user population.

Does the resource:

- allow the user to easily establish which curriculum or learning outcome it is intended to support?
- provide content that is relevant, accurate and appropriate for the outcome it is intended to support?
- provide evidence that it is authoritative, i.e. is it endorsed by a relevant authority?

Is the resource accessible and inclusive?

Resources should be able to meet the needs of all the learners within the intended target population.

Does the resource:

- support learners with differing levels of need?
- enable access by those with visual, auditory and other disabilities?
- avoid bias and stereotyping?

Is the resource (and the material within it) easy to locate and navigate?

Resources should be able to meet the needs of all the users within the intended target population.

Is the resource:

- tagged with descriptive metadata to make it easy to find in searches?
- capable of being linked to from other online resources?

What does exemplary content look like?

- searchable, so relevant elements of the resource can be easily located?
- organised and indexed in a clear and consistent fashion?
- designed in such a way that it is easy and intuitive to navigate?

Does the resource provide valuable guidance and information for learners, managers and L&D staff?

If users are to make effective use of digital learning resources, they require clear and accurate information.

Does the guidance:

- explain clearly how the resource is intended to be used, e.g. for self-directed learning, as just-in-time reference information, as the focus for a group activity?
- explain in plain English how the resource is licenced and what the implications are for copying and adaptation?
- indicate the format that the resource takes (tutorial, simulation, video, audio, text, etc.)?
- indicate how much time it would normally take to complete the resource?
- make clear on what devices (computers, mobile phones, tablets, etc.) the resource will run and what technical specification is required?

Does it provide adequate flexibility and support for those who design, deliver and support learning interventions?

Although some content is designed to be used by the user alone, in many cases trainers, facilitators, managers and others need to provide support to individual learners, to use content as a stimulus for group activity, to integrate content within blended solutions or to use resources in the classroom. The most valuable resources are those that can be re-used in a wide variety of contexts.

Is the resource:

- constructed in a modular fashion, so modules can be easily omitted, substituted or supplemented, to meet the needs of different learners?
- constructed, where appropriate, in bite-sized chunks?
- modifiable to meet the needs of different learners and different work contexts?
- supported by notes that help the trainer, tutor or manager to use the resource within a wide variety of situations?

Does it engage learners?

A good quality digital learning resource will engage the learner throughout and provide a memorable and challenging learning experience.

www.onlignment.com

DIGITAL LEARNING CONTENT

Does the resource:

- engage the learner with material that is directly relevant to their experience and current concerns?

- encourage the learner to participate and contribute to the experience rather than passively observe or progress?

- avoid the use of irrelevant or insufficiently challenging interaction?

- support or promote collaboration with others, either as part of the resource or subsequent to use of the resource?

- make use of story-telling to engage the learner and encourage retention?

- look and feel professional enough to be credible, without wasting money on excessively high production values?

- make effective and engaging use of imagery (graphics, animation, video, 3D models, etc.) to clarify and illuminate important elements of the content?

- make effective and engaging use of speech as an alternative verbal channel to on-screen text?

- keep reading from the screen to a minimum?

- avoid competing media elements, e.g. duplicating on-screen text and narration, simultaneous use of video and other imagery?

Does it enable effective learning?

A good quality digital learning resource will be effective in helping lasting learning to take place. Some resources will aim to provide a complete learning experience; in other cases, the resource will work alongside other elements in a blended solution. The strategies for learning will differ according to the nature of the desired outcomes, so not all of the elements listed below will be needed in all cases.

Does the resource:

- employ a strategy for learning which is appropriate to the desired learning outcome?

- avoid overloading the learner with excessive new information, without adequate opportunity for reflection and consolidation?

- make clear what is must-know, should-know and nice-to-know?

- provide plenty of relevant examples of any new concepts, principles, rules, etc.?

- provide sufficient opportunities for the learner to consolidate must-know information?

- illustrate effective performance using demonstrations and worked examples?

- provide sufficient opportunities for the learner to practise using new skills in realistic situations?

- allow the learner to experiment with new principles and processes, learning from both successes and failures?

- support the learner in reflecting on their own performance?
- respond to the progress different learners might make with activities and exercises?
- point the learner to activities and resources which will enable them to continue their learning?

Does it track progression and achievement?

Unless a resource is entirely passive (such as a podcast or video), the resource should incorporate mechanisms that assist the learner and others in tracking progress in terms of what has been completed or learned.

Does the resource:

- have an interface that clearly indicates progress along the learning pathway in terms of completion and/or learning?
- provide timely and personalised feedback to learners on their performance, including suggestions for ways that they could improve their performance?
- provide opportunities for self- or peer assessment or reflection?
- exchange tracking data with learning management systems and other platforms, using specifications and standards such as SCORM and AICC?
- make it easy for learners to bookmark their place and return to it at a later time or date?

Is it distinctive and innovative?

Some products are innovative in the way they are designed and in the technology they use. Others encourage innovative use in learning and teaching. While it is not necessary for resources to be distinctive and innovative to be effective, exemplary materials will have these characteristics.

Does the resource:

- provide functionality or experience that is new and distinctive to the user?
- harness technology to tackle a topic or skill in a way that improves upon traditional approaches?
- inspire learners to be creative and imaginative?
- provide a learning experience that does not rely upon traditional methods of information uptake or assessment?
- take advantage of recent advances in the use of technology?

This checklist has been adapted by Clive Shepherd from a document originally produced by Becta. This version is particularly directed at those looking to develop or purchase digital learning content for the workplace. It is reproduced courtesy of Towards Maturity – www.towardsmaturity.org.